AF830570

DRAFT INTERNATIONAL COVENANT ON ENVIRONMENT AND DEVELOPMENT

Second Edition: Updated Text

DRAFT INTERNATIONAL COVENANT ON ENVIRONMENT AND DEVELOPMENT

Second Edition: Updated Text

Commission on Environmental Law of
IUCN - The World Conservation Union
in cooperation with the
International Council of Environmental Law

Environmental Policy and Law Paper No. 31 Rev.

IUCN - The World Conservation Union
2000

Published by: IUCN, Gland, Switzerland and Cambridge, UK

IUCN Commission on Environmental Law
Godesberger Allee 108-112, D-53175 Bonn, Germany

International Council of Environmental Law (ICEL)
Godesberger Allee 108-112, D-53175 Bonn, Germany

IUCN
The World Conservation Union

ICEL

First published 1995
Second edition 2000

Citation: IUCN Commission on Environmental Law (2000). *Draft International Covenant on Environment and Development. Second edition: Updated Text.* Prepared in cooperation with the International Council of Environmental Law. IUCN, Gland and Cambridge. xxviii + 194 pp.

ISBN: 2-8317-0524-X 2nd edition
2-8317-0288-7 1st edition

Cover design by: IUCN Environmental Law Centre

Layout by: Barbara Weiner, Desktop Publications Co-ordinator

Printed by: Daemisch Mohr, Siegburg

Available from: IUCN Publications Services Unit
219c Huntingdon Road, Cambridge, CB3 0DL, UK
or
IUCN Environmental Law Centre
Godesberger Allee 108-112, D-53175 Bonn, Germany
or
International Council of Environmental Law (ICEL)
Godesberger Allee 108-112, D-53175 Bonn, Germany

TABLE OF CONTENTS

FOREWORD
to the second edition

In 1995 the Draft Covenant on Environment and Development was launched at the United Nations' Congress on Public International Law. Professor Edith Brown-Weiss discussed on this occasion the need for such a framework treaty bridging the sectors of environment and development.

Since that time, internationally and regionally several new international agreements have been concluded, on topics as varied as straddling and migratory fish stocks, desertification, and public participation in decision-making. State practice has continued, albeit incrementally, to seek to integrate environment and development. In light of these new developments in public international law, the Commission on Environmental Law of the International Union for the Conservation of Nature and Natural Resources (IUCN) and the International Council of Environmental Law (ICEL), as the two sponsors of the draft Covenant, undertook a review of the text, with a view to reflecting these developments.

We made a general call for comments on the draft of the text and were gratified to receive many useful comments from around the world. We also made an inventory of all new treaties negotiated since 1994,[1] and requested a small team of legal experts to consider comments received as well as the impact of new agreements on the Draft Covenant and to modify its text as appropriate. We have also consulted with the drafters of the "Earth Charter" to ensure consistency among the principles set forth in both texts.

Convinced that the need for an umbrella agreement was increasing more than ever in order to knit together the principles reflected in the sectoral treaties impacting upon environment and development, IUCN and ICEL convened a meeting of the small law experts team on 20-22 May 1999. One of the contributors in the preparation of the initial draft, Ambassador Ramon Piriz-Ballon of Uruguay, assumed the chairmanship of this meeting which was convened in the Treaty Signature Room at United Nations Headquarters in New York. More than one participant noted that the venue was a good omen, encouraging hard work, hot debate and a critical appraisal of needed updates. In the course of the meeting, differences were resolved harmoniously and the consensus is reflected in the following amended text.

The list of all who contributed to this revision is too lengthy for inclusion here, but we have included them in the list of contributors. Particular thanks go to Professor Dinah Shelton, who as rapporteur for the meeting has collected all decisions and proposals made and has amended, edited and perfected the commentary on the Draft Covenant.

---

[1] Footnote to list major treaties adopted since 1994

We are constantly asked about the future of this Draft Covenant. Our response has been consistent since this project began. To secure negotiation internationally of a legally binding agreement requires a broad consensus of States. While all States profess a strong desire to promote sustainable development, many as yet struggle internally to integrate the legal requirements of environmentally sustainable development. We are well aware that the codification of international law for sustainable development will take time. A consensus is growing, favouring a framework agreement like that of the Draft Covenant. Many nations are considering or have chosen to adopt a comparable framework law to integrate their sectoral laws within the nation. It is evident to us that consolidation of international norms in such a Draft Covenant would facilitate their integration and implementation nationally, and the consensus in favour of this view is growing.

In the meantime, we are greatly encouraged that in international negotiations diplomats indicate that they are using the Draft Covenant as a checklist to ensure consistency among the treaty obligations for sustainable development and to coordinate their positions with respect to new negotiations. At the same time, we have learned that legislators as well as the responsible ministers and civil servants in many states are using the Draft Covenant as an authoritative reference as well as a useful checklist for national legislation designed to foster sustainable development.

We have, accordingly, resolved to continue the promotion of an integrated umbrella agreement and be patient until there is sufficient support to go forward. We fully comprehend that, in the course of international negotiations, the content of the draft provisions will change. This is to be expected. However, if the expectations of the nations that participated in the 1992 UN Conference on Environment and Development are to be realised, a framework agreement not unlike that set forth in the Draft Covenant will greatly facilitate the process leading to sustainable development.

Wolfgang E. Burhenne, Executive Governor
International Council of Environmental Law

Nicholas A. Robinson, Chairman
IUCN Commission on Environmental Law

FOREWORD

The Charter of the United Nations governs relations between States. The Universal Declaration of Human Rights pertains to relations between the State and the individual. The time has come to devise a covenant regulating relations between humankind and nature.

UN Secretary-General's 1990 Report

1992 was a historical watershed, with the convening of the world's largest ever international conference, the UN Conference on Environment and Development (UNCED), attended by representatives of 178 States, including many heads of State and government. UNCED's action plan, Agenda 21, identifies concrete steps to integrate environment and development. UNCED further endorsed roles of environmental law in guiding all nations toward this integration.[1]

The law is an essential component for setting and implementing global, regional, and national policy on environment and development. UNCED emphasized the need to integrate "environment and development issues at national, sub-regional, regional and international levels,"[2] including: (a) elaborating the "balance between environmental and developmental concerns;" (b) clarifying the relationships between the various existing treaties; and (c) ensuring national participation in both developing and implementing these legal measures, with particular focus on developing countries.[3]

IUCN's Commission on Environmental Law (CEL), in cooperation with the International Council of Environmental Law (ICEL) and with the assistance of UNEP's Environmental Law and Institutions Programme Activity Centre (ELI/PAC), has responded to UNCED's recommendations by elaborating a *Draft International Covenant on Environment and Development.*

Why do nations need a Covenant on environment and development? While there already exists a wide body of international law on this subject, it has, like national law, of necessity developed incrementally, largely in a piecemeal and *ad hoc* manner. Most international agreements are sector-specific in nature, concluded at different times at uneven stages of international knowledge and concern. They also vary regionally, so that norms applicable to some parts of the world do not apply elsewhere, or are global in scope but not yet universally ratified.

---

1 See N. A. Robinson, P. Hassan and F. Burhenne-Guilmin (eds.), 1992-94. AGENDA 21 & THE UNCED PROCEEDINGS, Volumes I-VI, Oceana Publications, New York.

2 Paragraph 38.7 of Agenda 21.

3 Paragraph 39.1 of Agenda 21.

The reasons why a Draft Covenant is necessary are evident:

- to provide the legal framework to support the further integration of the various aspects of environment and development;
- to create an agreed single set of fundamental principles like a "code of conduct", as used in many civil law, socialist, and theocratic traditions, which may guide States, intergovernmental organizations, and individuals;
- to consolidate into a single juridical framework the vast body of widely accepted, but disparate principles, of "soft law" on environment and development (many of which are now declaratory of customary international law);
- to facilitate institutional and other linkages to be made between existing treaties and their implementation;
- to reinforce the consensus on basic legal norms, both internationally, where not all States are party to all environmental treaties, even though the principles embodied in them are universally subscribed to, and nationally, where administrative jurisdiction is often fragmented among diverse agencies and the legislation still has gaps;
- to fill in gaps in international law, by placing in a global context principles which only appear in certain places and by adding matters which are of fundamental importance but which are not in any universal treaty;
- to help level the playing field for international trade by minimizing the likelihood of non-tariff barriers based on vastly differing environmental and developmental policies;
- to save on scarce resources and diplomatic time by consolidating in one single instrument norms, which thereafter can be incorporated by reference into future agreements, thereby eliminating unnecessary reformulation and repetition, unless such reformulation is considered necessary; and
- to lay out a common basis upon which future lawmaking efforts might be developed.

Agenda 21 elaborated the "vital aspects" of treaty-making in Chapter 39. There is a need to identify and agree on "universal principles," to "set priorities for future lawmaking at the global, regional and sub- regional level," to ensure that "trade policy measures for environmental purposes do not emerge as a disguised restriction on international trade," and to identify ways to minimize or resolve conflicts between "environmental and social/economic agreements or instruments."[4]

---

[4] Paragraph 39.3 of Agenda 21.

The integration of socio-economic development with the maintenance of renewable natural resources such as fish, soils, forests, fresh drinking water is critical. As pollution levels mount, especially in cities in developing States, maintenance of public health requires their abatement. There must be an increase in the transfer of technology from the "North" to the "South." As we learn more about the natural world, we also learn how to better protect and manage it; nature reserves and parks are of ever more importance and ever innovative biodiversity conservation techniques are being constantly introduced, but many endangered and other species are still being devastated at an alarming rate. All of these problems are linked to each other and need to be dealt with globally and locally.

This will be difficult to achieve without an international legal instrument of general scope, addressing the whole field of environment and development. The Stockholm Declaration on the Human Environment (1972), the World Charter for Nature (1982), and the Rio Declaration on Environment and Development (1992) contain important widely accepted principles in this regard, but most of these principles cannot be implemented directly. They announce objectives of the international community and in some cases provide directives to achieve them. However, none of them state a general international obligation on all States to protect the whole of the environment, comparable to Article 192 of the Law of the Sea Convention.

The progression of legal principles from recommendatory "soft" to legally clear "hard" is well known in international law. For example, the 1948 Universal Declaration of Human Rights, a "soft-law" instrument was the precursor to the two 1966 UN Covenants on Human Rights. Those treaties elaborated in legally-binding form the principles enunciated in "soft -law" form in the 1948 Universal Declaration of Human Rights. For this reason, the proposed text on environment and development should be called a "Covenant", as well as to signal the special importance of such a treaty. Also, the UN Secretary-General in 1990 proposed the same sequence (see above). Accordingly, with the Stockholm Declaration, the World Charter for Nature, and later the Rio Declaration behind them, the consensus within the IUCN Commission on Environmental Law was that a general framework treaty on the environment was the next step.

Once the World Charter for Nature was adopted and solemnly proclaimed by the UN General Assembly in 1982,[5] the CEL Working Group which had draft that instrument in 1975 perceived the necessity of exploring whether the World Charter for Nature should be followed by a "hard law" instrument. This idea was also taken up by the World Commission on Environment and Development ("Bruntland Commission"), which was established in 1983 along with an associated Experts Group on Environmental Law. The Experts Group recommended that the United Nations prepare a new and legally binding universal Convention on environmental protection and sustainable devel-

---

[5] For a detailed account of the development of the World Charter for Nature, see W. Burhenne and W. Irwin (1986). THE WORLD CHARTER FOR NATURE (2nd edn). Erich Schmidt Verlag, Berlin.

opment.[6] The World Commission itself in 1986 recommended the preparation of a Universal Declaration and a Convention on environmental protection and sustainable development.[7] Then, in 1988, expressly taking into account the many "soft-law" instruments already existing, the IUCN General Assembly in San Jose, Costa Rica, expressed its formal support for CEL to continue what it had by then already begun, in preparing elements for an international convention on environmental protection and sustainable development.[8]

Subsequently, a new formal CEL Working Group was established, which met in Bonn in November 1989 under the chairmanship of Dr. Wolfgang E. Burhenne. The composition of this group included leading experts from all regions of the globe, including governmental lawyers, judges, academics and private practitioners, all acting in their personal capacities. Many had been active participants in the 1972 Stockholm Conference, the CEL Working Group on the World Charter for Nature, and the Bruntland Commission's Experts Group on Environmental Law. A document entitled "Draft Covenant on Environmental Conservation and Sustainable Use of Natural Resources", containing 88 provisions, was the basis of discussion at that meeting. Many comments and suggestions were made, which were incorporated into the next draft.

The second meeting took place in March 1991, under the chairmanship of Dr. Parvez Hassan, who in 1990 had become the Chair of CEL. At this meeting, the concerns of developing countries were especially focused on, and Articles were elaborated concerning the transboundary movement of hazardous waste, as well as the environmental degradation caused by transnational corporations. The CEL Working Group then sought UNCED PrepComm input. On the request of Iceland and other States, the then current version of the Draft Covenant was translated by the UN into its six official languages and distributed to PrepComm Working Group III as a background document.[9]

The third meeting occurred in the aftermath of UNCED, where a concerted effort was made to incorporate the results of that event into the draft Covenant. Furthermore, the CEL Working Group

---

6 Proposal 1 states,

It is recommended that a new and legally-binding universal Convention be prepared under United Nations auspices.

(a) The Convention should consolidate existing and establish new legal principles, and set out the associated rights and responsibilities of States individually and collectively for securing environmental protection and sustainable development to the year 2000 and beyond.

(b) The Convention should also include effective measures for protecting those rights and for fulfilling those responsibilities.

...

7 See World Commission on Environment and Development (1987). OUR COMMON FUTURE, Oxford University Press, Oxford, at p. 333.

8 For a detailed account of the drafting history, see P. Hassan (1993), *The IUCN Draft International Covenant on Environment and Development: Background and Prospects*, in A. Kiss and F. Burhenne-Guilmin (eds), A LAW FOR THE ENVIRONMENT: ESSAYS IN HONOUR OF WOLFGANG E. BURHENNE, EPLP Special Issue, IUCN, Gland and Cambridge, at pp. 43, et. seq.

9 It was reproduced as UN Doc. A/CONF/151/PC/WG.III/4.

decided to expand its membership to include experts who had been significant contributors to the UNCED process.

A small Drafting Committee met in April, 1993, to continue the work of integrating the ideas of UNCED into the draft Covenant. The text was recast to include a Part on Fundamental Principles addressing, *inter alia*, the right to development, eradication of poverty, demographic policies, wasteful consumption patterns, and international financing mechanisms. The final title of the document became the *Draft International Covenant on Environment and Development.*

The fourth meeting of the full, and now expanded, Working Group took place in Bonn in September 1993. Because of the important moral element of the Draft Covenant, leading members of the IUCN Ethics Working Group were invited to attend. Further, in view of the importance of biological diversity, George Rabb, the Chair of the IUCN Species Survival Commission also attended and contributed actively. The proposals of the Drafting Committee were, on the whole, well received. But as expected, North-South issues emerged in the same manner before the Covenant Working Group as they had done in other international fora such as UNCED. However, it was a measure of the commitment of the participants to reaching amicable and acceptable solutions that the discussions and inputs were not governed or dictated by geographic backgrounds or regional perceptions. The participants brought a deep understanding for the concerns of the developing countries and this was essential to the resolution of complex issues.

The Drafting Committee met again in December of that year, as well as in April 1994, to incorporate all the comments of the full Working Group into the text. In addition, the Draft Covenant was the subject of a two day workshop at the IUCN General Assembly in Buenos Aires in January 1994, where it received a favourable response and helpful comments were made. The final meeting on the Draft Covenant took place in September 1994 in New York, when a small group of specialists on international liability examined and reformulated those provisions dealing with this complex legal subject.

In addition to being reviewed in Buenos Aires, ideas and support for the Draft Covenant were received from discussions at meetings in Washington D.C., USA, in 1993, of the American Society of International Law[10] and of the Southeast Asian Programme in Ocean Law, Policy, and Management (SEAPOL) in Bangkok, Thailand, in 1994. It was also discussed earlier this year at meetings at UNEP and IUCN in Nairobi, Kenya, and at the Asia Law Conference on Social Development, in Hyderabad, India, convened by the International Jurists Organization (Asia).

This document is divided into two sections. The first is the Draft International Covenant on Environment and Development. The second is a commentary which explains and provides the legal derivations for each of the provisions of the Draft Covenant.

---

10 See P. Hassan, *Towards and International Covenant on Environment and Development*, ASIL Proc, pp. 513-522 (1993).

The Draft Covenant contains a Preamble and 72 Articles arranged topically in eleven Parts:

The Preamble articulates the scientific realities underlying the Covenant, as well as relevant social, economic and ethical rationales. It also mentions the main legal premise for the Covenant.

Part I states the objective of the Covenant in a single Article.

Part II contains the most widely accepted and established concepts and principles of international environmental law, as they have been proclaimed by numerous international texts. The remaining parts of the Covenant are founded on these "Fundamental Principles".

Part III creates the broad framework of the obligations of Parties in respect of the environment, towards each other, the international community collectively, and all persons individually. It integrates environment and development and couples rights with duties. The provisions in this Part are applicable to all subsequent sections of the Covenant, in particular to the specific obligations of Parts IV, V and VI.

Part IV provides the specific obligations of Parties respecting the conservation of the biosphere and its various components, including cultural and natural heritage.

Part V concerns substances, technologies and activities that produce adverse effects on the environment. It articulates the duties of Parties to prevent, control and mitigate harm to the environment caused by such substances, technologies and activities.

Part VI sets forth the obligations of the Parties regarding broad structural issues and aspects of international relations that impact on both environmental protection and sustainable development: demography, armed conflict, patterns of international trade and resource utilization.

Part VII contains and develops the traditional rules concerning problems of transboundary pollution and shared natural resources.

Part VIII seeks to develop the national and international procedures necessary to assess, monitor and control environmental impacts. It establishes duties to share environmental information and technology, provide international financing, and foster public awareness through training and education.

Part IX deals with the legal consequences of environmental harm, especially responsibility, liability and the provision of remedies.

Part X places the Draft Covenant in the broader context of international law, by speaking to potential conflicts with existing treaties and concurrent jurisdiction. It also provides for dispute avoidance and settlement mechanisms.

Part XI creates the formal mechanisms available to change the Covenant, details the means to adhere to it, its entry into force and other procedural matters.

The Draft Covenant aims to be a document which could form the basis for intergovernmental negotiations. As co-chairs of this joint project by ICEL and IUCN-CEL, we should observe that none of us in the Drafting Group were so arrogant as to think that we could predict what States would be willing to accept, or to think we drafted the perfect document. We fully expect that the negotiators will do so! The Working Group did wish to provide a solid foundation from which intergovernmental discussions could proceed.

But we must say that we have not been as "progressive" as we might have liked to be, always bearing in mind that the Draft Covenant should first and foremost be realistic. As such, the Draft Covenant contains essentially three types of provisions:

(a) those which consolidate existing principles of international law, including those "soft-law" principles which were considered ripe for "hardening";
(b) those which contain very modest progressive developments; and
(c) those which are further progressive than in (b) which we felt were absolutely necessary.

In presenting this Draft Covenant on Environment and Development to the United Nations in 1995 on the occasion of its fiftieth anniversary, it is hoped that this will become a negotiating document for a global treaty on environmental conservation and sustainable development. To a very large extent, accomplishing the integrated goals of sustainable development is the UN's foremost challenge in the next 50 years.

This rather extensive introduction to the Draft Covenant was deliberate. It was meant to highlight the extraordinary reach and scope of this effort. CEL's objective is not only to restate or codify existing environmental law, but to assist the evolution of "soft-law" into binding law. CEL has tried to be practical and realistic: it always has been mindful of the limitations inherent in the intergovernmental negotiating process and determined to produce a draft which has a reasonable chance of being accepted by States. But this is not to say that we have been timid. We have innovated where we found the progressive development of international law to be essential to achieving the success of UNCED's objectives. Whether we have struck the right balance is for the future intergovernmental process to judge.

Lastly, it remains for us to thank those who have helped make the Draft Covenant a reality. Many people contributed to this project, too many to count, but the most important contributors are listed at page xix. Several of the contributors have been associated with prestigious and important legal bodies, such as the Legal Experts Group of the Bruntland Commission, the International Law Commission, UN Member delegations to UNCED and the UN's Commission on Sustainable Development, and the Institut de Droit International. UNEP should be singled out for special mention in encouraging and contributing senior members of its legal staff to actively participate in the Working Group on a regular basis. We would also like to acknowledge the role of Professor Nicholas A.

Robinson, who as vice-chair of the Working Group provided valuable support. In saying this, however, we stress that all who contributed to this process did so in their personal capacity and the text of the Draft Covenant does not necessarily reflect unanimous agreement.

As to the Commentary, a number of members of the Working Group provided valuable input. Particular thanks are due to Alexandre Kiss and Dinah Shelton for their inputs, especially in reviewing, editing and perfecting the final text. In addition, we are grateful to Richard G. Tarasofsky, of the IUCN Environmental Law Centre, for coordinating the work on the Commentary.

We also thank the Government of the Netherlands and the International Council of Environmental Law for providing the means to support our work. And finally, we are indebted to the staff of the IUCN Environmental Law Centre, who worked so long and hard to support our effort. CEL and ICEL are committed to cooperating with all interested in the further evolution of this process.

Dr. Wolfgang E. Burhenne
Executive-Governor
International Council of
Environmental Law

Dr. Parvez Hassan
Chair
IUCN Commission on
Environmental Law

Bonn (Germany) and Lahore (Pakistan)
March, 1995

CONTRIBUTORS

The following persons have contributed to the development of the Draft Covenant and the Commentary,* either by participating in a meeting of the Working Group** or by submitting written comments:

Dr. Andronico Adede (Kenya) - Deputy Director, UN Office of Legal Affairs, Codification Division
Francis Auburn (Australia) - Associate Law Professor, University of Western Australia
Julio Barboza (Argentina) - Ambassador; President of International Law Commission
Richard A. Baer, Jr. (United States) - Professor, Department of Natural Resources, Cornell University
Dr. John Allan Beesley (Canada) - O.C., Q.C., Former External Affairs Legal Advisor; UNCLOS Drafting Committee Chairman; Member of the International Law Commission; Ambassador for Marine Conservation
Mohammed Abdelwahab-Beckeshi (Algeria) - Professor, Law Faculty, Université d'Oran
R.J. Berry (United Kingdom) - Professor, Department of Biology, University of London; Member of the IUCN Ethics Working Group
Bernhard Willem Boer (Australia) - Professor of Law, University of Sydney; Co-Director of the Australian Center for Environmental Law
Dr. Michael Bothe (Germany) - Professor of Law, University of Frankfurt/Main
Wen Boping (China) - Professor of Law, Senior Research Fellow, Chinese Academy of Social Sciences
Alan E. Boyle (United Kingdom) - Professor of International Law, University of Edinburgh
Dr. Wolfgang E. Burhenne (Germany) - Secretary General, Inter-Parliamentary Working Centre; Former Chair of IUCN Commission on Environmental Law; Executive Governor, International Council of Environmental Law
Claire Burden (United Kingdom) - The Royal Society
Thomas Busha (United Kingdom) - Former Senior Counsel of the International Maritime Organization
Lynton Caldwell (United States) - Professor Emeritus of Political Science and Professor of Public and Environmental Affairs, University of Indiana
J. Baird Callicott (United States) - Professor, University of Wisconsin-Stevens Point
Dr. Luis Camacho (Costa Rica) - Professor, University of Costa Rica; Member of the IUCN Ethics Working Group
Arthur Campeau (Canada) - Former Ambassador for the Environment and Sustainable Development
Guillermo Cano (Argentina) - Professor; Ambassador (rtd); Former Chairman Latin-American Law Association; Member, UN Committee on Natural Resources
Lorne Clark (Canada) - Legal Counsel, International Aviation Transportation Association; Ambassador (rtd); Former Chairman UNEP Environmental Group
Donna Craig (Australia) - Lecturer, Macquarie University School of Law; Member of IUCN Inter-Commission Task Force on Indigenous People; Vice-Chair of IUCN Commission on Environmental Law
Dr. Clarence Dias (India) - President, International Centre for Law in Development
Dr. Strachan Donnelley (United States) - Director of Education, Associate for Environmental Ethics, The Hastings Center
Dr. O.P. Dwivedi (Canada) - Professor of Political Studies, University of Guelph
Martin Edwards (Canada) - Professor of Physics, Royal Military College; Former Member of IUCN Council
J. Ronald Engel *(United States)* - Professor, Meadville Theological School; Chair of the IUCN Ethics Work Group
Jens Evensen (Norway) - Judge, International Court of Justice; Center of International Studies
Richard Falk (United States) - Professor, Princeton University
Dr. Mohiuddin Farooque (Bangladesh) - Secretary General, Bangladesh Environmental Lawyers Association

---

* All persons contributed in their personal capacities and the contents of the text do not necessarily reflect the views of every contributor; titles of contributors are those provided at the time of the last contribution to the Draft Covenant.

** All persons whose names appear in italics participated in at least one meeting of the *ad hoc* Working Group.

Vinio Floris (United States) - Member of International Ethics Association
Malcolm Forster (United Kingdom) - Head of Environment Group, Freshfields Solicitors; Former Vice-Chair of IUCN-Commission on Environmental Law
Dr. Yutaka Furuta (Japan) - Professor, Suzukia Junior College
Arnoldo José Gabaldon (Venezuela) - Member of Parliament, Former Environment Minister
William Gibson (United States) - Staff Associate, ECO-Justice Project and Network
David Given (United Kingdom) - David Given & Associates
Dr. Lothar Gündling (Germany) - International Environmental Law Consultant; Former Project Coordinator at IUCN Environmental Law Centre
Dr. Parvez Hassan (Pakistan) - Senior Partner, Hassan & Hassan (Advocates); Former Chair of IUCN Commission on Environmental Law
Dr. Martin Holdgate (United Kingdom) - Former Director-General of IUCN
Sophie Jakowska (Dominican Republic) - Member of IUCN Commission on Education
Dr. C.M. Jariwala (India) - Professor of Law, Hindu University Law School
Yolanda Kakabadse (Ecuador) - Executive President, Fundación Futuro Latinoamericano; Member, Board of Directors, WWF; President, WWF Planning Commission
Maurice Kamto (Cameroun) - Professor, Centre d'Etudes de Recherches et de Documentation en Droit International
Bankary Kante (Senegal) - Directeur de l'Environnement
Alexandre Kiss (France) - Directeur de Recherche, Centre National de Recherche Scientifique; Vice-Chair of IUCN Commission on Environmental Law
Cyrille de Klemm (France) - Legal Consultant to IUCN
Veit Koester (Denmark) - Head of Ecological Division, Ministry of Environment and Energy
Dr. Palitha T. B. Kohona (Australia) - Chief, Treaty Office, Office of Legal Affairs, United Nations Secretariat
Dr. Oleg Kolbasov (Russia) - Deputy Minister, Ministry of the Ecology & Natural Resources; Vice-Chair of IUCN Commission on Environmental Law
Dr. Johan Lammers (Netherlands) - Legal Adviser, Ministry of Foreign Affairs
Winfried Lang (Austria) - Ambassador, Head of the Austrian Permanent Mission to the UN-Geneva
Dr. Richard Laster (Israel) - Attorney, Laster & Gouldman Law Office
Roy S. Lee (China) - Principal Officer, Office of Legal Affairs, UN-New York
Enrique Leff (Mexico) - Coordinator for Environmental Training, UNEP Office for Latin America and the Caribbean
Dr. Galo Leoro (Ecuador) - Minister of Foreign Relations
Song Li (China) - Interim Secretariat for the Convention on Biological Diversity
Dr. Gerhard Loibl (Austria) - Professor, University of Vienna; Director, International Affairs, Federal Ministry for Environment, Youth and Family Affairs
Irene Lin Heng Lye (Singapore) - Associate Professor, National University of Singapore
David Lyons (United States) - Professor of Law and Philosophy, Cornell University
Dr. Mateo J. Magariños de Mello (Uruguay) - Consultor Juridico Internacional y en derecho ambiental Asociacion Uruguay de Derecho Ambiental
Daniel Magraw (United States) - Associate General Counsel for International Activities, United States Environmental Protection Agency
Ajai Malhotra (India) - Director, Ministry of External Affairs
Dr. Stephen McCaffrey (United States) - Professor, University of the Pacific, McGeorge School of Law; Former Member of International Law Commission
Richard J. McNeil (United States) - Professor, New York State College of Agriculture and Life Sciences, Cornell University; Member of IUCN Ethics Working Group
Natasha Minsker (United States) - Department of Natural Resources, Cornell University
Robert Munro (Canada) - Policy Advisor on Sustainable Development and Policy Planning
Dr. David A. Munro (Canada) - Naivasha Consultants
Dr. Charles Odidi-Okidi (Kenya) - Dean, School of Environmental Studies, Moi University Eldoret; Vice-Chair of the IUCN Commission on Environmental Law
C.K. Omari (Tanzania) - Professor of Sociology, University of Dar es Salaam

Dr. Marc Pallemaerts (Belgium) - Lecturer in International Environmental Law, Vrije Universiteit Brussel & Université Libre de Bruxelles
Efraín Perez (Ecuador) - Executive Director, ESTADE (Estudios de Estructura y Administración del Estado); Vice-Chair of IUCN Commission on Environmental Law
Adrian Phillips (United Kingdom) - Chairman of IUCN Commission on National Parks and Protected Areas
Ramiro Piriz-Ballon (Uruguay) - Ambassador, Permanent Mission of Uruguay to UN-New York
Diana Ponce-Nava (Mexico) - Legal Consultant, UNEP
Dimitra Popescu (Rumania) - Institute for Legal Research
Amedeo Postiglione (Italy) - Magistrate, Italian Supreme Court
Mere Pulea (Vanuatu) - Professor, University of the South Pacific
George Rabb (United States) - Chairman of the IUCN Species Survival Commission
Dr. Alfred Rest (Germany) - Professor of Law, University of Cologne
Nicholas Robinson (United States) - Professor of Law, Pace University; Chair of IUCN Commission on Environmental Law
Stephen Rockefeller (United States) - Professor, Middlebury College
Per Rydén (Sweden) - Assistant Director General-Conservation Policy a.i. of IUCN
Peter Sand (Germany) - Former Legal Advisor Environmental Affairs, World Bank; Former Legal Advisor for UNCED
Philippe Sands (United Kingdom) - Barrister, Lecturer and Legal Director of the Foundation for International Environmental Law and Development (FIELD), University of London
Dr. Mokul Sanwal (India) - Senior Policy Advisor UNEP; Formerly at the Ministry of Environment and Forests of India
Gunnar Schram (Iceland) - Professor of International Law, University of Iceland; Head of Iceland´s Prepatory Committee for UNCED
Finn Seyersted (Norway) - Professor of International Law, University of Oslo
Dinah Shelton (United States) - Professor of Law, University of Notre Dame Law School
Henri Smets (Belgium) - OECD Environmental Division
Douglas Sturm (United States) - Professor of Religion, Bucknell University
M.S. Swaminathan (India) - Chairman, M.S. Swaminathan Research Foundation
Dr. Alberto Szekely (Mexico) - Ambassador, Member of the International Law Commission
Patrick Széll (United Kingdom) - Head, International Environmental Law Division, Department of Environment
Alexandre Timoshenko *(Russia)* - Senior Programme Officer, UNEP; Institute of State and Law; Russian Academy of Sciences
***Amado Tolentino**, Jr.* (Philippines) - Attorney; Vice-Chair of IUCN Commission on Environmental Law
Robert Traer (United Kingdom) - General Secretary, International Association for Religious Freedom
Bjornar S. Utheim (Norway) - Ambassador, Royal Ministry of Foreign Affairs
Dr. Gabriela Verhoeven-Cueva (Ecuador) - Consultant and Researcher, ESTADE (Estudios de Estructura y Administración del Estado)
Dr. Franz Vranitzky (Austria) - Chancellor of Austria
Budislav Vukas (Croatia) - Professor, University of Zagreb
Arthur Westing (United States) - Westing Associates in Environment, Security and Education
Dr. Antonio Andaluz Westreicher (Peru) - Executive Director, PROTERRA; Former Vice-Chair of IUCN Commission on Environmental Law
John Williams (United States) - Former Director of IUCN Social Policy Service
Nicholas Yost (United States) - Attorney, Sonnenschein Nath & Rosenthal
Chen Zhengkang (China) - Professor, Peking University Law School

Secretariat – IUCN Environmental Law Centre

Françoise Burhenne-Guilmin - Head of the Environmental Law Centre (until July 1999)
Charles Di Leva - Director, Environmental Law Programme (1999 onwards)

Ekaterina A. Michos-Ederer - Rapporteur (until 1990)
Susan Casey-Lefkowitz - Rapporteur (1990-1993)
Richard G. Tarasofsky - Rapporteur (1993-1995); Coordinator and Special Rapporteur of the Covenant Commentary[***]
Ann-Mari Brockman - Research Assistant (1995)

[***] At different times, research assistance for the Commentary was provided by Ansley Samson, Edward Helgeson, and Dorothy McLean.

TABLE OF ABBREVIATIONS

AJIL	American Journal of International Law
ASIL	American Society of International Law
ACP-EEC	Africa Caribbean Pacific – European Economic Community
ASEAN	Association of Southeast Asian Nations
Burhenne	International Environmental Law Multilateral Treaties
CCD	Conference of the Committee of Disarmament
CFCs	Chloroflurocarbons
CFR	Consolidated Federal Regulations (USA)
CITES	Convention on the International Trade in Endangered Species (1973)
CMLR	Common Market Law Report
EC	European Communities
ECE	Economic Conference for Europe
ECE CRTD	Economic Conference for Europe Convention on Civil Liability for Damage Caused during Carriage of Dangerous Goods by Road, Rail and Inland Navigation Vessels (1989)
ECHR	European Court for Human Rights
ECJ	European Court of Justice
ECOSOC	UN Economic and Social Council
EEC	European Economic Community
EEZ	Exclusive Economic Zone
EIA	Environmental Impact Assessment
EMEP	Protocol on a Programme for Monitoring and Evaluation of the Long-Range Transmission of Air Pollutants in Europe
EMuT	International Environmental Law – Multilateral Treaties
ENMOD	Convention on the Prohibition of Military or Other Use of Environmental Modification Techniques
EPL	Environmental Policy and Law
ESoL	International Environmental Soft Law
ETS	European Treaty Series
FAO	UN Food and Agriculture Organization
GAOR	UN General Assembly Official Records
GATT	General Agreement on Tariffs and Trade
GYIL	German Yearbook of International Law
HRC	UN Human Rights Committee
IAEA	International Atomic Energy Agency
ICAO	International Civil Aviation Organization
ICEL	International Council of Environmental Law
ICES	International Council in the Exploration of the Sea
ICJ	International Court of Justice
ICRC	International Committee of the Red Cross
ICSU	International Council of Scientific Unions
ILA	International Law Association
ILC	International Law Commission (United Nations)

ILM	International Legal Materials
ILO	International Labour Organization
ILR	International Law Reports
IMCO	International Maritime Consultative Organization
IMO	International Maritime Organization
IPE/SD	International Protection of the Environment/Conservation in Sustainable Development
IUCN	World Conservation Union
IWC	International Whaling Commission
Kiss	Kiss Treaty Series
LDC	London Dumping Convention
LRTAP	Convention on Long-Range Transboundary Air Pollution
MARPOL	International Convention on the Prevention of Pollution from Ships
NEPA	National Environmental Protection Act
NGO	Non-Governmental Organization
NYIL	Netherlands Yearbook of International Law
OASTS	Organization of American States Treaty Series
OAU	Organization of African Unity
OECD	Organization for Economic Co-operation and Development
OILPOL	International Convention for the Prevention of Pollution of the Sea by Oil
OJ	Official Journal of the European Communities
PCIJ	Permanent Court of International Justice
REIO	Regional Economic Integration Organization
SOLAS	International Convention for Safety of Life at Sea
TIAS	United States Treaties and Other International Acts Series
TRIPS	Agreement on Trade-Related Aspects of Intellectual Property Rights
UKTS	United Kingdom Treaty Series
UN	United Nations
UNCED	United Nations Conference on Environment and Development
UNCLOS	United Nations Convention on the Law of the Sea
UNDP	United Nations Development Programme
UNECE	United Nations Economic Commission for Europe
UNEP	United Nations Environment Program
UNGA	United Nations General Assembly Resolution
UNRIAA	United Nations Reports of International Arbitral Awards
UNTS	United Nations Treaty Series
USC	United States Code
UST	United States Treaty Series
USTS	United States Treaty Series
VOC	Volatile Organic Compounds
WCED	World Commission on Environment and Development
WHO	World Health Organization
WTO	World Trade Organization
WWF	World Wide Fund for Nature

SUBJECT INDEX

DRAFT INTERNATIONAL COVENANT ON ENVIRONMENT AND DEVELOPMENT

PREAMBLE

The Parties to this Covenant:

Recognizing the unity of the biosphere, a unique and indivisible ecosystem, and the interdependence of all its components;

Conscious that humanity is a part of nature and that all life depends on the functioning of natural systems which ensure the supply of energy and nutrients;

Convinced that living in harmony with nature is a prerequisite for sustainable development, because civilization is rooted in nature, which shapes human culture and inspires artistic and scientific achievement;

Sharing the belief that humanity stands at a decisive point in history, which calls for a global partnership to achieve sustainable development;

Mindful of the increasing degradation of the global environment and deterioration and depletion of natural resources, owing to excessive consumption, rising population pressures, pollution, poverty, and armed conflict;

Recognizing the need to integrate environmental and developmental policies and laws in order to fulfil basic human needs, improve the quality of life, and ensure a more secure future for all;

Aware that the respect for human rights and fundamental freedoms contributes to sustainable development;

Conscious that the right to development must be fulfilled so as to meet the developmental and environmental needs of present and future generations in a sustainable and equitable manner;

Recognizing that inter-generational and intragenerational responsibility, as well as solidarity and cooperation among the peoples of the Earth, are necessary to overcome the obstacles to sustainable development;

Acknowledging that addressing the particular situation and needs of developing countries, especially those of the least developed and of the most environmentally vulnerable, is a high priority, and that developed countries bear a special responsibility in the pursuit of sustainable development;

Affirming the essential duty of all to respect and preserve the environment;

Considering that the existing and future international and national policies and laws on environment and development need an integrated legal framework to provide individuals, States, and other entities, with ecological and ethical guidance, as recommended by the United Nations Conference on Environment and Development assembled in Rio de Janeiro in June 1992;

AGREE as follows:

I. OBJECTIVE

ARTICLE 1

OBJECTIVE

The objective of this Covenant is to achieve environmental conservation and sustainable development by establishing integrated rights and obligations.

II. FUNDAMENTAL PRINCIPLES

In their actions to achieve the objective of this Covenant and to implement its provisions, the Parties shall co-operate in a spirit of global partnership and shall be guided, *inter alia*, by the following fundamental principles:

ARTICLE 2

RESPECT FOR ALL LIFE FORMS

Nature as a whole warrants respect. The integrity of the Earth's ecological systems shall be maintained and restored. Every form of life is unique and is to be safeguarded independent of its value to humanity.

ARTICLE 3

COMMON CONCERN OF HUMANITY

The global environment is a common concern of humanity.

ARTICLE 4

INTERDEPENDENT VALUES

Peace, development, environmental protection and respect for human rights and fundamental freedoms are interdependent.

ARTICLE 5

INTERGENERATIONAL EQUITY

The freedom of action of each generation in regard to the environment is qualified by the needs of future generations.

ARTICLE 6

PREVENTION

Protection of the environment is best achieved by preventing environmental harm rather than by attempting to remedy or compensate for such harm.

ARTICLE 7

PRECAUTION

Lack of scientific certainty is no reason to postpone action to avoid potentially serious or irreversible harm to the environment.

ARTICLE 8

RIGHT TO DEVELOPMENT

The exercise of the right to development entails the obligation to meet the developmental and environmental needs of humanity in a sustainable and equitable manner.

ARTICLE 9

ERADICATION OF POVERTY

The eradication of poverty, which in particular necessitates a global partnership, is an indispensable requirement for sustainable development.

ARTICLE 10

CONSUMPTION PATTERNS AND DEMOGRAPHIC POLICIES

The elimination of unsustainable patterns of consumption and production and the promotion of appropriate demographic policies are necessary to enhance the quality of life for all humanity and reduce disparities in standards of living.

III. GENERAL OBLIGATIONS

ARTICLE 11

STATES

1. States have, in accordance with the Charter of the United Nations and the principles of international law, the sovereign right to utilize their resources to meet their environmental and sustainable developmental needs, and the obligations:
   (a) to protect and preserve the environment within the limits of their national jurisdiction; and

(b) to ensure that activities within their jurisdiction or control do not cause potential or actual harm to the environment of other States or of areas beyond the limits of national jurisdiction.

2. States have, in accordance with the Charter of the United Nations and principles of international law, the right to protect the environment under their jurisdiction from significant harm caused by activities outside their national jurisdiction. If such harm has occurred, they are entitled to appropriate remedies.

3. Parties shall take all appropriate measures to avoid wasteful use of natural resources and, in particular, to ensure the sustainable use of renewable resources.

4. Parties shall provide the public, including non-governmental organizations, local communities and indigenous peoples, with appropriate opportunities to participate during decision-making processes relating to the environment.

5. Parties who are members of international organizations undertake to pursue within such organizations policies that are consistent with the provisions of this Covenant.

6. Parties shall apply the principle that the costs of preventing, controlling and reducing potential or actual harm to the environment are to be borne by the originator.

ARTICLE 12

PERSONS

1. Parties undertake to achieve progressively the full realization of the right of everyone to an environment and a level of development adequate for their health, well-being and dignity.

2. All persons have a duty to protect and preserve the environment.

3. All persons, without being required to prove an interest, have the right to seek, receive, and disseminate information in respect to the environment, subject only to such restrictions as may be provided by law and are necessary for respect for the rights of others, for the protection of national security or for the protection of the environment.

4. All concerned persons have the right to participate effectively during decision-making processes at the local, national and international levels regarding activities, measures, plans, programs and policies that may have a significant effect on the environment.

5. All persons have a right of effective access to administrative and judicial procedures, including for redress and remedies, to enforce their rights in respect to the environment, under national and international law.

6. Parties shall respect and ensure the rights and the fulfillment of the duties recognized in this Article and shall devote special attention to the satisfaction of basic human needs, in particular the provision of potable water.

7. Parties shall develop or improve mechanisms to facilitate the involvement of indigenous peoples and local communities in environmental decision-making at all levels and shall take measures to enable them to pursue sustainable traditional practices.

ARTICLE 13

INTEGRATING ENVIRONMENT AND DEVELOPMENT

1. Parties shall pursue sustainable development policies aimed at the eradication of poverty, the general improvement of economic, social and cultural conditions, the conservation of biological diversity, and the maintenance of essential ecological processes and life-support systems.

2. Parties shall ensure that environmental conservation is treated as an integral part of the planning and implementation of activities at all stages and at all levels, giving full and equal consideration to environmental, economic, social and cultural factors. To this end, Parties shall

   (a) conduct regular national reviews of environmental and developmental policies and plans;

   (b) enact effective laws and regulations which use, where appropriate, economic instruments; and

   (c) establish or strengthen institutional structures and procedures to fully integrate environmental and developmental issues in all spheres of decision-making.

ARTICLE 14

TRANSFER OR TRANSFORMATION OF ENVIRONMENTAL HARM

Parties shall not transfer, directly or indirectly, harm or hazards from one area to another or transform one type of environmental harm to another.

ARTICLE 15

EMERGENCIES

1. Each Party shall, without delay and by the most expeditious means available, notify potentially affected States and competent international organizations of any emergency originating within its jurisdiction or control, or of which it has knowledge, that it may cause harm to the environment.

2. A Party within whose jurisdiction or control an emergency originates shall immediately take all practicable measures necessitated by the circumstances, in cooperation with potentially affected States, and where appropriate, competent international organizations, to prevent, mitigate and eliminate harmful effects of the emergency.

3. Parties shall develop joint contingency plans for responding to emergencies, in cooperation, where appropriate, with other States and competent international organizations.

IV. OBLIGATIONS RELATING TO NATURAL SYSTEMS AND RESOURCES

ARTICLE 16

STRATOSPHERIC OZONE

Parties shall take all appropriate measures to prevent the depletion of stratospheric ozone. To that end, Parties shall restrict human activities which modify or are likely to modify the stratospheric ozone layer in ways that adversely affect human health and the environment.

ARTICLE 17

GLOBAL CLIMATE

Parties shall take all appropriate measures to achieve the stabilization of concentrations of greenhouse gases in the atmosphere at a level that prevents dangerous anthropogenic interference with the climate system. Such a level should be achieved within a time frame sufficient to allow ecosystems to adapt naturally to climate change, to ensure that food production, essential ecological processes, and biological diversity are not threatened, and to enable economic development to proceed in a sustainable manner.

ARTICLE 18

SOIL

Parties shall take all appropriate measures to ensure the conservation and where necessary the regeneration of soils for all living systems by taking effective measures to prevent soil erosion, to combat desertification, to safeguard the processes of organic decomposition and to promote the continuing fertility of soils.

ARTICLE 19

WATER

Parties shall take all appropriate measures to maintain and restore the quality of water, including atmospheric, marine, ground and surface fresh water, to meet basic human needs and as an essential component of aquatic systems. Parties also shall take all appropriate measures, in particular through conservation and management of water resources, to ensure the availability of a sufficient quantity of water to satisfy basic human needs and to maintain aquatic systems.

ARTICLE 20

NATURAL SYSTEMS

1. Parties shall take appropriate measures to conserve and, where necessary and possible, restore natural systems which support life on Earth in all its diversity, including biological

diversity, and to maintain and restore the ecological functions of these systems as an essential basis for sustainable development, including *inter alia,*

(a) forests as natural means to control erosion and floods, and for their role in the climate system;

(b) freshwater wetlands and floodplains as recharge areas for groundwaters, floodwater buffers, filters and oxidizing areas for contaminants;

(c) marine ecosystems, in particular coastal ecosystems including barrier islands, estuaries, mangroves, sea grass beds, coral reefs and mudflats as natural defenses against coastal erosion and essential habitats for the support of fisheries.

2. Parties shall, within their jurisdiction, manage natural systems as single ecological units. In particular they shall,

(a) manage aquatic systems as entire units covering the full extent of the catchment area, and

(b) manage coastal systems as entire units covering both aquatic and terrestrial components.

ARTICLE 21

BIOLOGICAL DIVERSITY

1. Parties shall take all appropriate measures to conserve biological diversity, including species diversity, genetic diversity within species, and ecosystem diversity, especially through in situ conservation. To this end, Parties shall:

(a) integrate conservation of biological diversity into their physical planning systems,

(b) establish a system of protected areas, where appropriate with buffer zones and interconnected corridors, and

(c) prohibit the taking or destruction of endangered species, protect their habitats, and develop recovery plans for such species.

2. States shall regulate or manage biological resources with a view to ensuring their conservation, sustainable use, and where necessary and possible, restoration. To this end, Parties shall:

(a) develop and implement conservation and management plans for harvested biological resources;

(b) prevent a decrease in the size of harvested populations below the level necessary to ensure stable recruitment;

(c) safeguard and restore habitats essential to the continued existence of the species or populations concerned;

(d) preserve and restore ecological relationships between harvested and dependant or associated species or populations; and

(e) prevent or minimize incidental taking of non-target species and prohibit indiscriminate means of taking.

ARTICLE 22

CULTURAL AND NATURAL HERITAGE

Parties shall take all appropriate measures to conserve or rehabilitate cultural and natural monuments, and areas, including Antarctica, of outstanding scientific, cultural, spiritual, or aesthetic significance and to prevent all deliberate measures and acts which might harm or threaten such monuments or areas.

V. OBLIGATIONS RELATING TO PROCESSES AND ACTIVITIES

ARTICLE 23

PREVENTION OF HARM

Parties shall identify and evaluate substances, technologies, processes and categories of activities which have or are likely to have significant adverse effects on the environment. They shall systematically survey, regulate or manage them with a view to preventing any significant environmental harm.

ARTICLE 24

POLLUTION

Parties shall take, individually or jointly, all appropriate measures to prevent, reduce, control, and eliminate to the fullest extent possible, detrimental changes in the environment, in particular from radioactive, toxic, and other hazardous substances. For this purpose, they shall use the best practicable means at their disposal and shall endeavor to harmonize their policies.

ARTICLE 25

WASTE

1. Parties shall ensure that the generation of waste is reduced to a minimum, particularly through the use of non-waste technology.

2. Waste shall be reused, recovered, and recycled to the fullest extent possible.

3. Waste which cannot be reused, recovered, or recycled, shall be disposed of in an environmentally sound manner, to the fullest extent possible in the source Party.

4. Under no circumstances shall there be any export of waste where the exporting Party has reason to believe that it will not be managed in an environmentally sound manner or to a place where waste import has been banned. If a transboundary movement cannot be completed in compliance with these requirements, the exporting Party shall ensure that such waste is taken back if alternative environmentally sound arrangements cannot be made.

ARTICLE 26

INTRODUCTION OF ALIEN OR MODIFIED ORGANISMS

1. Parties shall prohibit the intentional introduction into the environment of alien or modified organisms which are likely to have adverse effects on other organisms or the environment. They shall also take the appropriate measures to prevent accidental introduction or escape of such organisms.

2. Parties shall regulate and manage the risks associated with the development, use and release of modified organisms resulting from biotechnologies which are likely to have adverse effects on other organisms or the environment.

3. Parties shall take all appropriate measures to control and, to the extent possible, eradicate introduced alien or modified organisms when such organisms have or are likely to have a significant adverse effect on other organisms or the environment.

VI. OBLIGATIONS RELATING TO GLOBAL ISSUES

ARTICLE 27

ERADICATION OF POVERTY

Parties, with the assistance of and in cooperation with other States and international organizations as appropriate, shall seek to take measures which will, directly or indirectly, contribute to the eradication of poverty, including measures to:

(a) enable all individuals to achieve sustainable livelihoods;

(b) promote food security and, where appropriate, food self-sufficiency in the context of sustainable agriculture;

(c) rehabilitate degraded resources, to the extent practicable, and promote sustainable use of resources for basic human needs;

(d) provide potable water and sanitation; and

(e) provide education.

ARTICLE 28

CONSUMPTION AND PRODUCTION PATTERNS

Parties shall seek to develop strategies to eliminate unsustainable patterns of consumption and production. Such strategies shall be designed, in particular, to meet the basic needs of the poor and to reduce use of non–renewable resources in the production process. To this end, Parties shall:

(a) collect and disseminate information on consumption patterns and develop or improve methodologies for analysis;

(b) ensure that all raw materials and energy are conserved and used as efficiently as possible in all products and processes;

(c) require reusing and recycling of used materials to the fullest extent possible;

(d) promote product designs that increase reuse and recycling and as far as possible eliminate waste; and

(e) facilitate the role and participation of consumer organizations in promoting more sustainable consumption patterns.

(f) ensure that sufficient product information is made available to the public in a manner that enables consumers to make informed environmental choices.

ARTICLE 29

DEMOGRAPHIC POLICIES

Parties shall develop or strengthen demographic policies in order to achieve sustainable development. To this end, Parties shall:

(a) conduct studies to estimate the size of the human population their environment is capable of supporting and develop programs relating to population growth at corresponding levels;

(b) cooperate to alleviate the stress on natural support systems caused by major population flows;

(c) cooperate as requested to provide a necessary infrastructure on a priority basis for areas with rapid population growth; and

(d) provide to their populations full information on the options concerning family planning.

ARTICLE 30

TRADE AND ENVIRONMENT

1. Parties shall co-operate to establish and maintain an international economic system that equitably meets the developmental and environmental needs of present and future generations. To this end, Parties shall endeavor to ensure that:

   (a) trade does not lead to the wasteful use of natural resources nor interfere with their conservation or sustainable use;

   (b) trade measures addressing transboundary or global environmental problems are based, as far as possible, on international consensus;

   (c) trade measures for environmental purposes do not constitute a means of arbitrary or unjustifiable discrimination or a disguised restriction on international trade;

   (d) unilateral trade measures by importing Parties in response to activities which are harmful or potentially harmful to the environment outside the jurisdiction of such Parties are avoided as far as possible or occur only after consultation with affected States and are implemented in a transparent manner; and

   (e) prices of commodities and raw materials reflect the full direct and indirect social and environmental costs of their extraction, production, transport, marketing, and, where appropriate, ultimate disposal.

2. As regards biological resources, products and derivatives, Parties shall endeavor to ensure that:

   (a) trade is based on management plans for the sustainable harvesting of such resources and does not endanger any species or ecosystem; and

   (b) Parties, whose biological resources cannot be exported due to prohibitions imposed by a multilateral environmental agreement, shall receive appropriate compensation for losses suffered due to non-compliance by any other party to that agreement.

ARTICLE 31

ECONOMIC ACTIVITIES OF FOREIGN ORIGIN

1. Parties shall require, from all economic entities and in regard to activities of foreign origin conducted within their jurisdiction, information on:

   (a) potential or actual harm to the environment resulting from their activities;

   (b) the relevant environmental legal requirements and standards applicable in the State of origin;

   (c) the techniques in use in the State of origin to comply with such requirements and standards; and

(d) reasonably available data and information concerning the state-of-the-art techniques to prevent environmental harm.

2. The Party of origin shall, upon request of the host Party,

(a) provide it with all relevant information on applicable environmental requirements and standards within the limits of its jurisdiction; and

(b) enter into consultations with the host Party to enable the host Party to take appropriate measures regarding such activities.

3. The Party of origin shall ensure that, in the absence of equally strict or higher environmental standards in the host Party or express agreement by the host Party to the contrary, it shall cause its nationals to apply the relevant standards of the Party of origin.

ARTICLE 32

MILITARY AND HOSTILE ACTIVITIES

1. Parties shall protect the environment during periods of armed conflict. In particular, Parties shall:

(a) observe, outside areas of armed conflict, all national and international environmental rules by which they are bound in times of peace;

(b) take care to protect the environment against avoidable harm in areas of armed conflict;

(c) not employ or threaten to employ methods or means of warfare which are intended or may be expected to cause widespread, long–term, or severe harm to the environment and ensure that such means and methods of warfare are not developed, produced, tested, or transferred; and

(d) not use the destruction or modification of the environment as a means of warfare or reprisal.

2. Parties shall cooperate to further develop and implement rules and measures to protect the environment during international armed conflict and establish rules and measures to protect the environment during non-international armed conflict.

3. All Parties involved in armed conflicts shall take the necessary measures to protect natural and cultural sites of special interest, in particular sites designated for protection under applicable national laws and international treaties, as well as potentially dangerous installations, from being subject to attack as a result of armed conflict, insurgency, terrorism, or sabotage. Military personnel shall be instructed as to the existence and location of such sites and installations.

4. Parties shall take measures to ensure that persons are held responsible for the deliberate and intentional use of means or methods of warfare which cause widespread, long–term, or severe harm to the environment.

5. Parties shall ensure that military personnel, aircraft, vessels and other equipment and installations are not exempted in times of peace from rules, standards, and measures for environmental protection.

VII. TRANSBOUNDARY ISSUES

ARTICLE 33

TRANSBOUNDARY ENVIRONMENTAL EFFECTS

Parties shall take appropriate measures to prevent transboundary environmental harm. When a proposed activity may generate such harm, Parties shall:

(a) ensure that an environmental impact assessment is undertaken, as provided in Article 37;

(b) give prior and timely notification, along with relevant information, to potentially affected States, and consult in good faith with those States at an early stage; and

(c) grant potentially affected persons in other States access to, as well as due process in, administrative and judicial proceedings, without discrimination on the basis of residence or nationality.

ARTICLE 33 BIS

PRIOR INFORMED CONSENT

Prior to the export of domestically prohibited hazardous substances and of hazardous waste, Parties shall require the prior informed consent of importing and, where appropriate, transit States.

ARTICLE 34

TRANSBOUNDARY NATURAL RESOURCES

Parties shall co-operate in the conservation, management and restoration of natural resources which occur in areas under the jurisdiction of more than one State, or fully or partly in areas beyond the limits of national jurisdiction. To this end,

(a) Parties sharing the same natural system shall manage that system as a single ecological unit notwithstanding national boundaries. They shall co-operate on the basis of equity and reciprocity, in particular through bilateral and multilateral agreements, in order to develop harmonized policies and strategies covering the entire system and the ecosystems it contains. With regard to aquatic systems, such agreements shall cover the entire catchment area, including the adjoining marine environment.

(b) Parties sharing the same species or population, whether migratory or not, shall treat such species or population as a single biological unit. They shall cooperate, in particular through bilateral and multilateral agreements, in order to maintain the species or population concerned in a favorable conservation status. In the case of a harvested species or population, all the Parties that are range states of that species or population shall cooperate in the development and implementation of a joint management plan to ensure the sustainable use of that resource and the equitable sharing of the benefits deriving from that use.

VIII. IMPLEMENTATION AND COOPERATION

ARTICLE 35

NATIONAL ACTION PLANS

Parties shall establish action plans, with targets and time-tables, and update them as necessary, to meet the objective of this Covenant.

ARTICLE 36

PHYSICAL PLANNING

1. Parties shall establish and implement integrated physical planning systems, including provisions for infrastructure and town and country planning, with a view to integrating conservation of the environment, including biological diversity, into social and economic development.

2. In such planning, Parties shall take into account natural systems, in particular drainage basins, coastal areas and their adjacent waters, and any other areas constituting identifiable ecological units.

3. Parties shall take into account the natural characteristics and ecological constraints of areas when allocating them for agricultural, grazing, forestry, or other use.

ARTICLE 37

ENVIRONMENTAL IMPACT ASSESSMENT

1. Parties shall establish or strengthen environmental impact assessment procedures to ensure that all activities which are likely to have a significant adverse effect on the environment are evaluated before approval.

2. The assessment shall include evaluation of:

   (a) cumulative, long-term, indirect, long-distance, and transboundary effects,

   (b) the possible alternative actions, including not conducting the proposed activity, and

   (c) measures to avert or minimize the potential adverse effects.

3. Parties shall designate appropriate national authorities to ensure that environmental impact assessments are effective and conducted under procedures accessible to concerned States, international organizations, persons and non-governmental organizations. Parties shall also ensure that the authority deciding on approval takes into consideration all observations made during the environmental impact assessment process and makes its final decision public.

4. Parties shall conduct periodic reviews both to determine whether activities approved by them are carried out in compliance with the conditions set out in the approval and to evaluate the effectiveness of the prescribed mitigation measures. The results of such reviews shall be made public.

5. Parties shall take appropriate measures to ensure that before they adopt policies, programs, and plans that are likely to have a significant adverse effect on the environment, the environmental consequences of such actions are duly taken into account.

ARTICLE 38

ENVIRONMENTAL STANDARDS AND CONTROLS

1. Parties shall co-operate to formulate, develop, and strengthen international rules, standards and recommended practices on issues of common concern for the protection and preservation of the environment and sustainable use of natural resources, taking into account the need for flexible means of implementation based on their respective capabilities.

2. Parties shall adopt, strengthen and implement specific national standards, including emission, quality, product, and process standards, designed to prevent or abate harm to the environment or to restore or enhance environmental quality.

ARTICLE 39

MONITORING OF ENVIRONMENTAL QUALITY

1. Parties shall conduct scientific research and establish, strengthen, and implement scientific monitoring programs for the collection of environmental data and information to determine, *inter alia*,

   (a) the condition of all components of the environment, including changes in the status of natural resources; and

   (b) the effects, especially the cumulative or synergistic effects, of particular substances, activities, or combinations thereof on the environment.

2. To this end and as appropriate, Parties shall co-operate with each other and with competent international organizations.

ARTICLE 40

SCIENTIFIC AND TECHNICAL COOPERATION

1. Parties shall promote scientific and technical cooperation in the field of environmental conservation and sustainable use of natural resources, in particular with developing countries. In promoting such cooperation, special attention should be given to the development and strengthening of national capacities, through the development of human resources, legislation and institutions.

2. Parties shall:

   (a) cooperate to establish comparable or standardized research techniques, harmonize international methods to measure environmental parameters, and promote widespread and effective participation of all States in establishing such international methodologies;

   (b) exchange, on a regular basis, appropriate scientific, technical and legal data, information and experience, in particular concerning the status of biological resources; and

   (c) inform each other on their environmental conservation measures and endeavor to coordinate such measures.

ARTICLE 41

DEVELOPMENT AND TRANSFER OF TECHNOLOGY

Parties shall encourage and strengthen cooperation for the development and use, as well as access to and transfer of, environmentally sound technologies on mutually agreed terms, with a view to accelerating the transition to sustainable development, in particular by establishing joint research programs and joint ventures.

ARTICLE 42

SHARING BENEFITS OF BIOTECHNOLOGY

Parties shall provide for the fair and equitable sharing of benefits arising out of biotechnologies based upon genetic resources with States providing access to such genetic resources on mutually agreed terms.

ARTICLE 43

INFORMATION AND KNOWLEDGE

1. Parties shall facilitate the exchange of publicly available information relevant to the conservation and sustainable use of natural resources, taking into account the special needs of developing countries.

2. Parties shall require that access to indigenous knowledge be subject to the prior informed consent of the concerned communities and to specific regulations recognizing their rights to, and the appropriate economic value of, such knowledge.

ARTICLE 44

EDUCATION, TRAINING AND PUBLIC AWARENESS

1. Parties shall disseminate environmental knowledge by providing to their public and, in particular, to indigenous peoples and local communities, information, educational materials, and opportunities for environmental training and education.

2. Parties shall co-operate with each other, and where appropriate with competent international and national organizations, to promote environmental education, training, capacity-building, and public awareness.

ARTICLE 45

NATIONAL FINANCIAL RESOURCES

1. Parties undertake to provide, in accordance with their capabilities, financial support and incentives for those national activities aimed at achieving the objectives of this Covenant.

2. Parties shall pursue innovative ways of generating new public and private financial resources for sustainable development, including the use of economic instruments, regulatory fees and taxes, and reallocation of resources at present committed to military purposes.

ARTICLE 46

INTERNATIONAL FINANCIAL RESOURCES

1. Parties shall co-operate in establishing, maintaining, and strengthening ways and means of providing new and additional financial resources, particularly to developing countries for:

   (a) environmentally sound development programs and projects;

   (b) measures directed towards solving major environmental problems of global concern, and for the implementation measures of this Covenant where they would entail special or abnormal burdens, owing, in particular, to the lack of sufficient financial resources, expertise or technical capacity; and

   (c) making available, under favorable conditions, the transfer of environmentally sound technologies.

2. Parties, taking into account their respective capabilities and specific national and regional developmental priorities, objectives and circumstances, shall endeavor to augment their aid programs to reach the United Nations General Assembly target of 0.7% of Gross National Product for Official Development Assistance or such other agreed figure as may be established.

3. Parties shall consider ways and means of providing relief to debtor developing countries, including by way of cancellations, rescheduling or conversion of debts to investments, provided that such relief is limited to enable the debtor developing countries to further their sustainable development.

4. A Party that provides financial resources to a State for activities that may result in a significant adverse impact on the environment shall, in cooperation with the recipient State, ensure that an environmental impact is conducted. The resources provided shall include those necessary for the recipient State to carry out such assessment.

IX. RESPONSIBILITY AND LIABILITY

ARTICLE 47

STATE RESPONSIBILITY

Each State Party is responsible under international law for the breach of its obligations under this Covenant or of other rules of international law concerning the environment.

ARTICLE 48

STATE LIABILITY

Each State Party is liable for significant harm to the environment of other States or of areas beyond the limits of national jurisdiction, as well as for injury to persons resulting therefrom, caused by acts or omissions of its organs or by activities under its jurisdiction or control.

ARTICLE 49

CESSATION, RESTITUTION AND COMPENSATION

1. Each State Party shall cease activities causing significant harm to the environment and shall, as far as practicable, re-establish the situation that would have existed if the harm had not occurred. Where that is not possible, the State Party of the origin of the harm shall provide compensation or other remedy for the harm. In particular, Parties shall co-operate to develop and improve means to remedy the harm, including measures for rehabilitation, restoration or reinstatement of habitats of particular conservation concern.

2. Where a State Party suffers such harm caused in part by its own negligence or that of persons under its jurisdiction or control, the extent of any redress or the level of any compensation due may be reduced to the extent that the harm is caused by negligence of that Party or persons under its jurisdiction or control.

ARTICLE 50

CONSEQUENCES OF FAILURE TO PREVENT HARM

Each State Party may be held responsible for significant harm to the environment resulting from its failure to carry out the obligations of prevention contained in this Covenant, in respect to its activities or those of its nationals.

ARTICLE 51

EXEMPTIONS

The State Party of origin of the harm shall not be responsible or liable if the harm,

(a) is directly due to an act of armed conflict or a hostile activity where the requirements under Article 32 of this Covenant are met, except an armed conflict initiated by the State Party of origin in violation of international law;

(b) is directly due to a natural phenomenon of an exceptional and inevitable character; or

(c) is caused wholly by an act or omission of a third party.

ARTICLE 52

CIVIL REMEDIES

1. Parties shall ensure the availability of effective civil remedies that provide for cessation of harmful activities as well as for compensation to victims of environmental harm irrespective of the nationality or the domicile of the victims.

2. Parties that do not provide such remedies shall ensure that compensation is paid for the damage caused by their acts or omissions or by activities of persons under their jurisdiction or control.

3. In cases of significant environmental harm, if an effective remedy is not provided in accordance with paragraph 1, the State Party of nationality of the victim shall espouse the victim's claim by presenting it to the State Party of origin of the harm. The State Party of origin shall not require the exhaustion of local remedies as a pre-condition for presentation of such claim.

ARTICLE 52 BIS

OFFENSES

1. Parties shall establish, as appropriate, criminal or administrative offenses for violations of environmental law or for activities that cause or are likely to cause serious harm to the environment.

2. Parties shall establish sanctions for such offenses that take into account the seriousness of the offenses and may include fines, confiscation, suspension or cancellation of permits or other benefits, imprisonment, and the obligation to reinstate the environment.

ARTICLE 53

RECOURSE UNDER DOMESTIC LAW AND NON-DISCRIMINATION

1. Each State Party of origin shall ensure that any person in another State Party who is adversely affected by transboundary environmental harm has the right of access to administrative and judicial procedures equal to that afforded nationals or residents of the State Party of origin in cases of domestic environmental harm.

2. Each State Party shall ensure that adversely affected persons have a right of recourse for violations of environmental regulations by that Party or any person or entity associated with that Party.

ARTICLE 54

IMMUNITY FROM JURISDICTION

Parties may not claim sovereign immunity in respect of proceedings instituted under this Covenant.

ARTICLE 55

ENVIRONMENTAL HARM IN AREAS BEYOND NATIONAL JURISDICTION

The provisions of Articles 47 to 54 may be invoked by any affected person for harm to the environment of areas beyond national jurisdiction.

X. APPLICATION AND COMPLIANCE

ARTICLE 56

OTHER TREATIES

Parties shall endeavor to become and remain party to treaties relating to the subject matter of this Covenant and shall implement them.

ARTICLE 57

MORE STRINGENT MEASURES

1. The provisions of this Covenant shall not affect the right of Parties individually or jointly to adopt and implement more stringent measures than those required under this Covenant.

2. The provisions of this Covenant shall not prejudice any stricter obligation which Parties have entered into or may enter into under existing or future treaties.

ARTICLE 58

AREAS BEYOND THE LIMITS OF NATIONAL JURISDICTION

In areas beyond the limits of national jurisdiction, Parties shall observe the provisions of the present Covenant to the full extent of their competence.

ARTICLE 59

RELATIONS WITH NON-PARTIES

Parties shall encourage non-Parties to act in a manner that is consistent with the objective of this Covenant.

ARTICLE 60

REPORTING

1. Parties undertake to submit periodic reports on the measures they have adopted, progress made, and difficulties encountered in implementing their obligations under this Covenant.

2. All reports shall be submitted to the Secretary-General of the United Nations.

ARTICLE 61

COMPLIANCE AND DISPUTE AVOIDANCE

In the framework of environmental treaties to which they are party or by other means, Parties shall maintain or promote the establishment of procedures and institutional mechanisms, including enquiry and fact-finding, to assist and encourage States to comply fully with their obligations and to avoid environmental disputes. Such procedures and mechanisms should improve and strengthen reporting requirements, and be simple, transparent, and non-confrontational.

ARTICLE 62

SETTLEMENT OF DISPUTES

1. Parties shall settle disputes concerning the interpretation or application of this Covenant by peaceful means, such as by negotiation, enquiry, mediation, conciliation, arbitration, judicial settlement, resort to regional agencies or arrangements, or by any other peaceful means of their own choice.

2. If parties to a dispute do not reach agreement on a solution or on a dispute settlement arrangement within one year following the notification by one party to another that a dispute

exists, the dispute shall, at the request of one of the parties, be submitted to either an arbitral tribunal, including the Permanent Court of Arbitration, or to judicial settlement, including by the International Court of Justice and the International Tribunal for the Law of the Sea as appropriate.

ARTICLE 63

REVIEW CONFERENCE

After the entry into force of this Covenant, the Secretary General of the United Nations shall convene every five years a conference of Parties to it in order to review its implementation. The United Nations, its specialized agencies and the International Atomic Energy Agency, as well as any State or regional economic integration organization not party to this Covenant may be represented at the Review Conference as observers. The International Union for Conservation of Nature and Natural Resources and the International Council of Scientific Unions may also be represented as observers. Any non-governmental organization accredited to the UN Economic and Social Council and qualified in matters covered by this Covenant, may be represented at a session of the Review Conference as an observer in accordance with the rules of procedure the Review Conference may adopt.

XI. FINAL CLAUSES

ARTICLE 64

AMENDMENT

1. Any Party may propose amendments to this Covenant. The text of any such proposed amendment shall be submitted to the Secretary-General of the United Nations who shall transmit it, within six months, to all the Parties.

2. At the request of one-third of the Parties, the Secretary-General of the United Nations shall call a special conference to consider the proposed amendment. The Parties shall make every effort to reach agreement on any proposed amendment by consensus. If all efforts at reaching a consensus have been exhausted, and no agreement reached, the amendment shall as a last resort be adopted by a two-thirds majority vote of the Parties to this Covenant who are present and voting at the special conference. The adopted amendment shall be communicated by the Secretary-General of the United Nations, who shall circulate it to all Parties for ratification, acceptance or approval. For purposes of this Article present and voting means Parties present and casting an affirmative or negative vote.

3. Instruments of ratification, acceptance or approval in respect of an amendment shall be deposited with the Secretary-General of the United Nations. An amendment shall enter into force for those States accepting it on the ninetieth day after the date of receipt by the Secretary-General of the United Nations of an instrument of ratification, acceptance or approval by at least two-thirds of the Parties. An amendment shall enter into force for any other Party on the ninetieth day following the date on which that Party deposits its instrument of ratification, acceptance or approval of the said amendment with the Secretary-General of the United Nations.

ARTICLE 65

SIGNATURE

1. This Covenant shall be open for signature at ________________ by all States and any regional economic integration organization from _____________ until _______________.

2. For purposes of this Covenant, regional economic integration organization means an organization constituted by sovereign States of a given region, to which its member States have transferred competence in respect of matters governed by this Covenant and which has been duly authorized, in accordance with its internal procedures, to sign, ratify, accept, approve or accede to it.

ARTICLE 66

RATIFICATION, ACCEPTANCE OR APPROVAL

1. This Covenant shall be subject to ratification, acceptance or approval by States and by regional economic integration organizations. Instruments of ratification, acceptance, or approval, shall be deposited with the Secretary-General of the United Nations.

2. Any regional economic integration organization which becomes party to this Covenant without any of its member States being party shall be bound by all the obligations under this Covenant. In the case of such organizations, one or more of whose member States is party to this Covenant, the organization and its member States shall decide on their respective responsibilities for the performance of their obligations under this Covenant. In such cases, the organization and the member States shall not be entitled to exercise rights under this Covenant concurrently.

3. In their instruments of ratification, acceptance or approval, regional economic integration organizations shall declare the extent of their competence with respect to the matters governed by this Covenant. These organizations shall also inform the Depositary of any relevant modification in the extent of their competence.

ARTICLE 67

ACCESSION

1. This Covenant shall be open for accession by States and by regional economic integration organizations from the date on which this Covenant is closed for signature. The instruments of accession shall be deposited with the Secretary-General of the United Nations.

2. In their instruments of accession, regional economic integration organizations shall declare the extent of their competence with respect to the matters governed by this Covenant. These organizations shall also inform the Secretary-General of the United Nations of any relevant modification in the extent of their competence.

ARTICLE 68

ENTRY INTO FORCE

1. This Covenant shall enter into force on the ninetieth day after the deposit of the twenty-first instrument of ratification, acceptance, approval, or accession.

2. For each State or regional economic integration organization that ratifies, accepts, or approves, this Covenant or accedes thereto after the deposit of the twenty-first instrument of ratification, acceptance, approval, or accession, this Covenant shall enter into force on the ninetieth day after the date of deposit by such State or regional economic integration organization of its instrument of ratification, acceptance, approval, or accession.

3. For the purposes of paragraph 1 above, any instrument deposited by a regional economic integration organization shall not be counted as additional to those deposited by member States of such organization.

ARTICLE 69

RESERVATIONS

No reservations may be made to this Covenant.

ARTICLE 70

WITHDRAWALS

1. At any time after two years from the date on which this Covenant has entered into force for a Party, that Party may withdraw from this Covenant by giving written notification to the Secretary-General of the United Nations.

2. Any such withdrawal shall take place upon expiry of one year after the date of its receipt by the Secretary-General of the United Nations, or on such later date as may be specified in the notification of the withdrawal.

ARTICLE 71

DEPOSITARY

1. The Secretary-General of the United Nations shall be the Depositary of this Covenant.

2. In addition to his functions as Depositary, the Secretary-General shall:

   (a) establish a schedule for the submission, consideration, and dissemination of the periodic reports submitted under Article 60;

(b) report to all Parties, as well as to competent international organizations, on issues of a general nature that have arisen with respect to the implementation of this Covenant; and

(c) convene necessary conferences of Parties in accordance with this Covenant.

ARTICLE 72

AUTHENTIC TEXTS

The Arabic, Chinese, English, French, Russian and Spanish texts of this Covenant are equally authentic.

IN WITNESS WHEREOF the undersigned, being duly authorized to that effect, have signed this Covenant.

COMMENTARY ON THE DRAFT INTERNATIONAL COVENANT ON ENVIRONMENT AND DEVELOPMENT*

PREAMBLE

The Parties to this Covenant:

Article 65 (Signature) and 66 (Ratification, Acceptance or Approval) of the Covenant open it for signature and adherence by all States and regional economic integration organizations. The latter are defined in Paragraph 2 of Article 65 (see Commentary thereto). Throughout the Draft Covenant the term "Parties" is used to designate those adhering to this instrument. In some provisions the term "States" is used for one of two reasons. First, where the Covenant is restating customary international law on fundamental issues, it extends beyond Parties (e.g., Article 11(1) (States)). Second, the term "State" is used where the objective of the Covenant can only be met by extending certain rights or benefits to States that are not Parties (e.g., Articles 11 (2) (States), 15(1) (Emergencies) and Article 30(2,b) (Trade and Environment)). In a few cases, where the rights or duties only pertain to Parties who are States, as distinct from regional economic integration organizations, the term "State Parties" is used (see especially Part IX (Responsibility and Liability)).

***Recognizing* the unity of the biosphere, a unique and indivisible ecosystem, and the interdependence of all its components;**

This clause recognizes the uniqueness of the Earth's biosphere and stresses the interdependence of its various components. The unhindered interaction of these components is the basis for the continued existence and well-being of the biosphere.[1] Each form of life is unique in itself and interacts both as a discrete part and an integral component of the natural systems which form the biosphere upon which mankind depends.

***Conscious* that humanity is a part of nature and that all life depends on the functioning of natural systems which ensure the supply of energy and nutrients;**

This statement has its origin in the World Charter for Nature.[2] It contains two ideas. First, human beings cannot be separated from nature whatever the degree of scientific and technological progress humans manage to achieve: there is a unity with and dependence on nature. Second, all

---

* Editorial Notes: (1) each provision of the Draft Covenant is reproduced and then followed by the commentary on that provision; (2) several document names have been abbreviated in the Commentary – full titles appear in the Table of Authorties on page 169 *et seq.*

1 The clause is supported by The World Charter for Nature (1982) (preambular paragraphs). See also, the Convention on Biological Diversity (1992) and Agenda 21 (1992) (particularly Chapter 15 (Conservation of Biological Diversity)).

2 See also the more recent Rio Declaration (1992). These instruments drew upon earlier expressions of similar ideas in the Stockholm Declaration (1972), and the Covenant on Economic, Social and Cultural Rights (1966).

life, including human, requires the energy and nutrients that nature supplies. These basic needs can be ensured only if the functions of all components of nature, as they interrelate, are not disrupted.

***Convinced* that living in harmony with nature is a prerequisite for sustainable development, because civilization is rooted in nature, which shapes human culture and inspires artistic and scientific achievement;**

Throughout history, the peoples of Earth have adapted themselves to the various ecosystems in which they live. To a considerable extent, all civilizations spring from and are shaped by the quality of their surrounding natural elements; indeed, the histories of different peoples are inseparable from the natural conditions in which they have lived for millennia. Nature also inspires human culture. Art, literature and science cannot be understood, or even imagined, without acknowledging the influence of nature and its components. Thus, cultural diversity, like biological diversity, emerges from the various ecosystems.[3] Human beings must continue to respect this diversity, because no society will achieve sustainable development unless it adapts to and builds upon its surrounding natural systems.

***Sharing* the belief that humanity stands at a decisive point in history, which calls for a global partnership to achieve sustainable development;**

Humanity stands at a decisive point in history because the growing degradation of the world's environment, detailed in the following paragraph, could produce irreversible destruction. It therefore is incumbent upon mankind to recognize fully the urgency of maintaining the stability and quality of nature to ensure the continued functioning of the biosphere. The need to maintain and improve the conditions of life, including the conservation of biological diversity, is a common thread binding together humanity. Progress in communications and the ability to perceive the biosphere as a whole, along with science and technology capable of addressing global problems, increase the responsibility and capacity to act. This fundamental common interest leads to the new concept in international law of a global partnership. The "partnership" idea is based upon the existing fundamental obligation of co-operation as between States,[4] as well as with and between individuals, implying greater interdependence and joint responsibility for the well-being of all.[5]

---

3 See Preamble to the World Charter for Nature (1982) which asserts that "Civilization is rooted in nature, which has shaped human culture and influenced all artistic and scientific achievement, and living in harmony with nature gives man the best opportunities for the development of his creativity, and for rest and recreation."

4 Article 1(3) of the UN Charter (1945); Article 1 of the Declaration of Principles of International Law (1970) (Principle of Co-operation).

5 This proposition is supported by Part XII of UNCLOS (1982), especially Articles 194(1), 197, 202, 205; Article 1 of the UN Charter (1945) and by Agenda 21 (1992), particularly Chapters 1 (Preamble), 34 (Transfer of environmentally sound technology, cooperation and capacity-building), 35 (Science for sustainable development), and 37 (National mechanisms and international cooperation for capacity-building in developing countries).

Mindful **of the increasing degradation of the global environment and deterioration and depletion of natural resources, owing to excessive consumption, rising population pressures, pollution, poverty, and armed conflict;**

This clause distinguishes the two categories of environmental problems addressed by the Draft Covenant and refers to their major underlying causes. The first problem is increasing degradation of the global environment or biosphere, the only known place where human and other forms of life are possible. The second problem is the deterioration and depletion of natural resources, renewable and non-renewable, on which our continued existence depends. These problems already have led to the conclusion of numerous treaties and other international instruments. Responding to these problems is a fundamental motivation for the Draft Covenant. The second part of this clause points to some of the major causes of environmental and resource depletion problems. All of the causes have been mentioned in earlier international documents[6] and, whether they affect the environment and natural resources directly or indirectly, are addressed in substantive provisions of the Draft Covenant.

Recognizing **the need to integrate environmental and developmental policies and laws in order to fulfil basic human needs, improve the quality of life, and ensure a more secure future for all;**

This clause emphasizes that neither environmental protection nor long-term economic development can be achieved independently of each other. In contrast to a common misunderstanding, the two fields are interdependent and mutually reinforcing. This is the true meaning of the term "sustainable development".[7]

The second part of this clause makes clear that human beings will benefit from the integration of environment and development in the ways indicated. "Quality of life" implies more than just the satisfaction of human needs, incorporating also non-material attributes. Achievement of both forms part of the obligations of States contained in the Universal Declaration of Human Rights and the Covenant on Economic, Social and Cultural Rights (1966).[8]

---

6 See e.g., Covenant on Economic, Social and Cultural Rights (1966); Covenant on Civil and Political Rights (1966); ENMOD Convention (1976); LRTAP Convention (1979). See also Principle 24 of the Rio Declaration (1992); Stockholm Declaration (1972); World Charter for Nature (1982); Universal Declaration of Human Rights (1948); Declaration on Social Progress and Development (1969); and Agenda 21 (1992): Chapter 3 (Combatting Poverty), Chapter 4 (Changing consumption patterns), Chapter 5 (Demographic dynamics and sustainability), and Chapter 7 (Promoting sustainable human settlement development).

7 World Conservation Strategy (1980), WCED Brundtland Report (1987), Caring for the Earth (1991).

8 Universal Declaration of Human Rights (1948); Covenant on Economic, Social and Cultural Rights (1966).

The reference to a more secure future indicates that environmental deterioration and problems of development, such as economic dislocation and poverty can affect international peace and security in the sense of the UN Charter.[9]

Aware **that the respect for human rights and fundamental freedoms contributes to sustainable development;**

The reference in this clause to sustainable development is based on the conception developed in the prior clause and adds a third interdependent element. It reflects the understanding that just as environmental protection and economic development are interdependent, both can be achieved only if human rights and fundamental freedoms are respected. Such respect is required by customary international law and numerous international instruments.[10] Neither environmental protection, nor economic development can justify denial of such rights and freedoms. On the contrary, respect for human rights enhances progress towards sustainable development.

Conscious **that the right to development must be fulfilled so as to meet the developmental and environmental needs of present and future generations in a sustainable and equitable manner;**

The reference to the "right to development" derives from the Rio Declaration.[11] It stresses that the right to development means a right to sustainable development. This is confirmed by the reference to future generations and to sustainability. At the same time, the needs of present and future generations, as well as equity, recall the prior clauses concerned with human rights and indicate those who hold the right to development. See also Articles 5 and 8 herein.

Recognizing **that inter-generational and intra-generational responsibility, as well as solidarity and cooperation among the peoples of the Earth, are necessary to overcome the obstacles to sustainable development;**

The peoples of the current generation must work with each other (intra-generational equity), taking into account the interests of future generations (inter-generational equity). The use of the term "responsibility" includes a moral obligation that each person has towards others. Solidarity and co-operation have long been recognized as duties of States. The reference here indicates that for achieving sustainable development these duties must extend to peoples as well. Education and long-term planning may be necessary aspects of the duties of the present generation.

---

9 See Article 1 of the UN Charter (1945).

10 E.g., Article 55(c) of the UN Charter (1945), and generally Covenant on Economic, Social and Cultural Rights (1966), Covenant on Civil and Political Rights (1966), European Human Rights Convention (1950), American Convention on Human Rights (1969), African Charter on Human Rights (1981). See also the Universal Declaration of Human Rights (1948).

11 Principle 3.

Acknowledging **that addressing the particular situation and needs of developing countries, especially those of the least developed and of the most environmentally vulnerable, is a high priority, and that developed countries bear a special responsibility in the pursuit of sustainable development;**

This clause is a restatement of the conclusions of UNCED contained in the Declaration adopted at that conference.[12] Developing countries have special needs relative to their individual situations which must be taken into account and given special priority. Because of their greater capability and the greater proportion of environmental stress that they cause, developed countries share a responsibility to assist developing countries and especially the least developed ones to progress towards the goal of sustainable development. The concept of common but differentiated responsibilities, which was affirmed at the Rio Conference, is one of the foundations of this clause.

Affirming **the essential duty of all to respect and preserve the environment;**

This clause is comprehensive in a double sense. First, it addresses all actors: international organizations, States, the business community, associations and individuals. Second, the object of protection is the totality of the environment. In carrying out the duty, all actors must abstain from harm to the environment ("respect") and take affirmative action ("preserve") to protect and, where necessary, rehabilitate it. Finally, the term "duty" carries a legal obligation and not only a moral one.

Considering **that the existing and future international and national policies and laws on environment and development need an integrated legal framework to provide individuals, States, and other entities, with ecological and ethical guidance, as recommended by the United Nations Conference on Environment and Development assembled in Rio de Janeiro in June 1992;**

The last clause describes the motivations in law for the Draft Covenant. It reflects the basic need for an integrated legal framework, comparable to those existing in other fields of international law, such as the law of the sea and the international protection of human rights. In addition to legal norms, it provides ecological and ethical guidance to all actors. Finally, the reference to "future" international and national laws and policies indicates the recognition that environmental protection is inherently dynamic and, as conditions change, must evolve on the basis of a permanent framework. The Draft Covenant is intended to supply the necessary framework.

---

[12] Principle 6 of the Rio Declaration (1992).

PART I. OBJECTIVE

ARTICLE 1

OBJECTIVE

The objective of this Covenant is to achieve environmental conservation and sustainable development by establishing integrated rights and obligations.

The stated objective of the Covenant emphasizes the indivisibility of "environmental conservation" and "sustainable development", as articulated in the documents adopted at UNCED. The use of the singular – "objective" rather than "objectives" – reinforces the indivisibility of the two concepts. This provision alludes to the need for a comprehensive approach as it calls for integrating rights and obligations. The third point to be noted is the use of the term "establishing". This reflects the Draft Covenant's dual aspects of codification and progressive development.

PART II. FUNDAMENTAL PRINCIPLES

In their actions to achieve the objective of this Covenant and to implement its provisions, the Parties shall co-operate in a spirit of global partnership and shall be guided, *inter alia*, by the following fundamental principles:

The Fundamental Principles express the underlying legal norms in a declaratory form and constitute the basis for all the obligations contained in the Draft Covenant. They reflect international consensus, contained in legal texts adopted since the founding of the United Nations. The objective of the Draft Covenant cannot be met without respect for these principles. The chapeau to this Part indicates that this list of Fundamental Principles is not intended to be exhaustive.

ARTICLE 2

RESPECT FOR ALL LIFE FORMS

Nature as a whole warrants respect. The integrity of the Earth's ecological systems shall be maintained and restored. Every form of life is unique and is to be safeguarded independent of its value to humanity.

The World Charter for Nature (1982) proclaims that every form of life is unique and warrants respect regardless of its material worth to man.[13] The implicit recognition of intrinsic value re-

---

[13] Preamble.

flected in that instrument is made explicit in the first preambular paragraph of the Convention on Biological Diversity (1992).

The provision focuses on nature as a whole because of the interrelationship of all its components. The phrase "every form of life" reflects the concept of biological diversity.[14] It does not focus on the protection of individual members of a class.

The phrase "independent of its value to humanity" is a reaction to former utilitarian approaches which limited legal protection to forms of life perceived to be immediately useful to economic interests, ignoring the functions of different species in ecosystems and even their future or potential usefulness.

ARTICLE 3

COMMON CONCERN OF HUMANITY

The global environment is a common concern of humanity.

Article 3 states the basis upon which the international community at all levels can and must take joint and separate action to protect the environment. It is based on the scientific reality that harm to the environment resulting from human activities (e.g., depletion of the stratospheric ozone layer, climate modification, and the erosion of biological diversity) adversely affects all humanity. World-wide cooperation to take concerted action is necessary to avoid environmental disaster. This implies acceptance of both the right and the duty of the international community as a whole to have concern for the global environment.

"Common concern" does not connote specific rules and obligations, but establishes the general basis for the international community to act. "Common concern" must be distinguished from doctrines of *res communis* and "common heritage of mankind", both of which provide an inadequate legal basis for protecting the global environment although they might entail some conservation elements. *Res communis* is the customary international law regime applicable to areas beyond national jurisdiction: in particular, to the high seas and outer space, and grants States freedom of use, including access to resources, so long as there is due regard for the interests of other states.[15] As such, *res communis* can, especially with regard to living resources, risk creating a "tragedy of the commons". In contrast, "common heritage" also permits access, but the international agreements which have applied it, notably UNCLOS, established international management regimes to

---

14 The Convention on Biological Diversity (1992) defines the term "biological diversity" as:

> ... the variability among living organisms from all sources including, *inter alia*, terrestrial, marine and other aquatic ecosystems and the ecological complexes of which they are part; this includes diversity within species, between species and of ecosystems.

15 See e.g., Pacific Fur Seals Arbitration, (1898) and the High Seas Convention (1958).

ensure that resources are conserved, exploitation is for the benefit of all, and the proceeds of the exploitation are distributed in an equitable fashion, including to States which do not actually participate in the exploitation.[16] It must be recalled that "common concern" was developed specifically to be a less comprehensive concept than "common heritage".

The conclusion that the global environment is a matter of "common concern" implies that it can no longer be considered as solely within the domestic jurisdiction of states due to its global importance and consequences for all.[17] It also expresses a shift from classical treaty-making notions of reciprocity and material advantage, to action in the long-term interests of humanity.

The concept of "common concern" is not new and has been applied in other fields. It forms the basis for international laws relating to human rights, humanitarian relief and international labour relations. Those obligations are now recognized as obligations *erga omnes*, owed by all States to the entire international community.[18]

The inter-dependence of the world's ecosystems and the severity of current environmental problems call for global solutions to most environmental problems, thereby justifying designation of the global environment as a matter of "common concern".[19] However, it is only recently that environmental protection has been seen in this way. The concept can be found in many multilateral environmental treaties[20] and the term itself appears in texts concerning global climate change[21] and

---

16 To date, "common heritage" has only been applied in treaty law in relation to the moon and the deep-seabed. The UNESCO Convention for the Protection of World Cultural and Natural Heritage uses the similar term "world heritage of mankind as a whole."

17 As such, Article 2(7) of the UN Charter (1945) would not apply (analogy can be drawn here to human rights matters, where Article 2(7) has not prevented the UN from being active when deemed appropriate).

18 These obligations have been recognized by the International Court of Justice – see *Reservations to the Convention on the Prevention and Punishment of the Crime of Genocide case, Barcelona Traction, (Second Phase), Legal Consequences for States of the Continual Presence of South Africa in Namibia (Southwest Africa) case.*

19 This view is reflected in UNGA Res olution 44/228 on convening UNCED and is implicit in Article 192 of UNCLOS (1982) and Principles 2 and 7 of the Rio Declaration (1992).

20 E.g., The Ramsar Convention (1971) and the World Heritage Convention (1972) are each premised on the notion that some sites within national jurisdiction are matters of international scrutiny; the Preamble to the Whaling Convention (1946) speaks of the interest of nations of the world in safeguarding whale stocks; the Preamble to the London Convention (1972) indicates that the marine environment and the living organisms supported by it are of vital importance to humanity; the Preamble to the Vienna Convention on the Ozone Layer (1985) calls for international cooperation and action to protect the ozone layer from human modification; and the Preamble to the African Convention (1968) recognizes that soil, water, flora and fauna resources are a capital of vital importance to mankind.

21 Preamble to the Climate Change Convention (1992); UNGA Resolutions 43/53 (1988), 44/207 (1989), 45/212 (1990), and 46/169 (1991).

the conservation of biological diversity.[22] The Draft Covenant is the first international treaty to declare the global environment as such a "common concern."[23]

In its application to the environment, "common concern" contains both spatial and temporal elements. The spatial element is the need to consider the earth as a whole and the state of the biosphere in its entirety because of the interdependence of all its elements within states and the global commons. This aspect calls for equitable burden sharing among states in the efforts to resolve global environmental problems and the acceptance of "common but differentiated responsibilities."[24] The temporal element is the recognition that the consequences of environmental degradation are often long-term and that duties to protect the environment are owed to future generations (see Article 4 (Interdependent Values)).

This provision is directed at all actors, including non-governmental organizations and individuals, reflecting the view prevalent in the Rio Declaration that non-state actors have an important role to play in the attainment of sustainable development.[25] The same approach can be seen in Article 11(3) (States) and Article 12(4) (Persons).

ARTICLE 4

INTERDEPENDENT VALUES

Peace, development, environmental protection and respect for human rights and fundamental freedoms are interdependent.

Article 4 brings together various international precedents, recognizing that all four of the subjects mentioned form an indivisible whole.

At the first United Nations Conference on Human Rights, held in Teheran in 1968, the international community proclaimed the interdependence of peace and human rights.[26] The General

---

22 Preamble to the Convention on Biological Diversity (1992).

23 See also the Langkawi Declaration on the Environment (1990), where the Heads of Government of the Commonwealth declared that "the current threat to the environment is a common concern of all mankind"; Beijing Ministerial Declaration on Environment and Development (1991) which deems environmental protection and sustainable development "as a matter of common concern to humankind".

24 This concept is reflected in Principle 7 of the Rio Declaration (1992) and in Article 3(1) of the Climate Change Convention (1992). See also Articles 24 and 25 of the Straddling Stocks Agreement, recognizing the special requirements of developing states.

25 See e.g., Principles 10, 20, 21, 22, and 27.

26 Proclamation of Teheran (1968). The text also recognizes that economic disparities separating developed and developing countries constitute an obstacle to effective respect for human rights and that

Assembly later declared the interdependence of peace, development and human rights in resolution 37/199 of 18 December 1982. Most recently, the 1993 Vienna Declaration on Human Rights affirmed that efforts by the United Nations to ensure respect for and implementation of human rights contribute to the establishment of conditions conducive to peace, security and economic and social development.[27] It also declared that democracy, development and respect for human rights and fundamental freedoms are interdependent and mutually reinforcing.[28]

Principle 1 of the Stockholm Declaration underlined the link between human rights and environmental protection, affirming that "Man has the fundamental right to freedom, equality and adequate conditions of life, in an environment of a quality that permits a life of dignity and well-being ..." The Rio Declaration similarly states that human beings "are entitled to a healthy and productive life in harmony with nature."[29] It also asserts that peace, development and environmental protection are interdependent and indivisible.[30] The Preamble to the Aarhus Convention (1998) underlines the link, recognizing that "adequate protection of the environment is essential to human well-being and the enjoyment of basic human rights, including the right to life itself."

Development and environmental protection depend upon respect for human rights, in particular rights of information, political participation, and due process (see Article 12 (Persons), Article 43 (Information and Knowledge), and Article 44 (Education, Training and Public Awareness)). In turn, full and effective exercise of human rights cannot be achieved without development and a sound environment because some of the most fundamental rights, e.g., the rights to life and health,[31] are jeopardized when basic needs, such as sufficient food and water, cannot be provided.[32] Of course, as the Vienna Declaration emphasizes, development facilitates the enjoyment of human

---

effective implementation of human rights supposes rational social and economic development (paragraphs 12 and 13). These statements echo Article 28 of the Universal Declaration of Human Rights (1948) which provides that everyone is entitled to a social and international order in which the rights and freedoms set forth in the Declaration can be fully realized.

27 Paragraph 6 of the Declaration and Program of Action of Vienna (1993).

28 Paragraph 8.

29 Principle 1.

30 Principle 25 of the Rio Declaration (1992).

31 The right to life is contained in all global and regional human rights instruments, e.g., Article 3 of the Universal Declaration of Human Rights ((1948) and Article 6 of the Covenant on Civil and Political Rights (1966). The right to health and well-being is expressed in, *inter alia*, Article 25 of the Universal Declaration of Human Rights (1948) and Article 12 of the Covenant on Economic, Social and Cultural Rights (1966). Paragraph 5 of the Vienna Declaration (1993) strongly underlines that all human rights are "universal, indivisible and interdependent and interrelated".

32 The Vienna Declaration recognizes that illicit movements of substances and toxic and hazardous wastes can constitute a grave danger to the rights of each person to life and health (See Paragraph 11). See also UNGA Resolution 45/94 (1990) on the Need to Ensure a Healthy Environment for the Well-Being of Individuals.

rights, but lack of development cannot be invoked to justify limitations on internationally recognized human rights.[33]

Finally, armed conflicts are inherently destructive of the environment and of human rights,[34] and thus hamper or even preclude development. To achieve the objective of the Draft Covenant, Parties must recognize the indivisibility of and need to fully apply international rules for the protection of human rights, prevention and limitation of armed conflicts, protection of the environment and achievement of development.

ARTICLE 5

INTERGENERATIONAL EQUITY

The freedom of action of each generation in regard to the environment is qualified by the needs of future generations.

Article 5, closely related to the principles of Article 6 (Prevention) and Article 7 (Precaution), is an essential foundation of all international law relating to environmental protection and to the concept of sustainable development. It holds that each generation owes a duty to future ones to avoid impairing their abilities to fulfil their basic needs.[35] Although it is difficult to predict with precision the aspirations of future generations, the basic human needs and values expressed in the two 1966 United Nations Covenants on Human Rights must be taken as the minimum requirements.[36] Clearly, these are predicated on an adequate environment. This entails the conservation of all natural resources and the sustainable use of those which are harvested, both within national jurisdictions and in areas beyond. Article 5 should be read in conjunction with Article 8 (Right to Development) and Article 9 (Eradication of Poverty), which express principles of intra-generational equity.

---

33 Paragraph 10 of the Vienna Declaration.

34 See e.g., Paragraph 29 of the Vienna Declaration.

35 See, *inter alia*, Goa Guidelines (1988), which identify as the principle's central premise that "the right of each generation to benefit from and develop this natural and cultural heritage is inseparably coupled with the obligation to use this heritage in such a manner that it can be passed on to future generations in no worse condition than it was received from past generations."

36 Note too that the Vienna Declaration (1993) provides that the right to development should be realized in a manner that equitably satisfies the needs of present and future generations (paragraph 11). The Goa Guidelines (1988), suggest specific measures to ensure such inter-generational rights and obligations, including: (a) representation by States of the interests of future generations; (b) designation of ombudsmen or commissioners for protecting the interests of future generations; (c) conservation assessments giving particular attention to long-term consequences.

Part I of the World Charter for Nature provides some guidance on the meaning of inter-generational equity: not compromising genetic viability on earth; maintaining populations of all life forms at least at levels sufficient for their survival; applying conservation principles to all areas on Earth, with special protection for unique and representative areas and endangered species; utilizing natural resources (when used) so as to ensure optimal sustainable productivity; and safeguarding nature from degradation due to military activities.[37]

Numerous international instruments affirm this basic principle.[38] Indeed, the Whaling Convention (1946) reveals that the concept has early antecedents.[39] Some national constitutions[40] also contain direct references to inter-generational equity or it is implied from provisions guaranteeing a right to a safe and healthy environment.[41]

ARTICLE 6

PREVENTION

Protection of the environment is best achieved by preventing environmental harm rather than by attempting to remedy or compensate for such harm.

Article 6 expresses a principle fundamental to environmental protection, the preventive approach, which is applicable to all actors wherever the consequences of their actions may be felt. It restates an ecological fact that preventive efforts are always preferable to remedial actions that may

---

37 See Principles 1 - 6.

38 See e.g., Article 1 of the Aarhus Convention on Information, Participation and Remedies, states that its objective is "protection of the right of every person of present and future generations to live in an environment adequate to his or her health and well-being." Article 2 of the Convention on Biological Diversity (1992), which defines "sustainable use" as use, *inter alia*, which maintains the potential of biological diversity to "meet the needs and aspirations of present and future generations"; Article 3(1) of the Climate Change Convention (1992), which calls on its parties to "protect the climate system for the benefit of present and future generations." See also Preambles to CITES (1973); Barcelona Convention (1976); Apia Convention on South Pacific Nature (1976); ENMOD Convention (1976); Kuwait Regional Convention (1978); Convention on Migratory Species (1980); Berne Convention on European Wildlife (1979); Wider Caribbean Marine Environment Convention (1983); ASEAN Agreement (1985); and ECE Industrial Accidents Convention (1992). See also Principles 1 and 2 of the Stockholm Declaration (1972) and Principle 3 of the Rio Declaration (1992).

39 See Preamble.

40 See e.g., the Constitutions of Brazil (Article 23), India (Part IV, Article 48-A and Part IVA, Article 51A), Islamic Republic of Iran (Chapter IV, Article 50), Namibia (Chapter II, Article 95), Papua New Guinea (Chapter IV)

41 See Minors Oposa case (1993), where the petitioners challenging the grant of timber licenses in the Philippines were accorded *locus standi* to proceed with their claim on behalf of future generations.

be attempted after harm has occurred.[42] Not only is harm irreversible in many cases, but *ex post facto* action is usually more expensive and less effective than preventive measures. Experience reveals that preventive measures are most efficient when aimed at the sources of environmental harm, particularly those causing pollution, rather than at the end-of-the-pipe. This is especially true of diffuse and cumulative sources.

The preventive approach requires each Party to exercise "due diligence," i.e., to act reasonably and in good faith and to regulate public and private activities subject to its jurisdiction or control that are potentially harmful to any part of the environment.[43] The principle does not include a minimum threshold of harm, because the obligation is one of conduct (due diligence), not of result. Thus, the principle does not impose an absolute duty to prevent all harm, making the state a guarantor, but rather an obligation on each State to minimize detrimental consequences of permissible activities through regulation.[44] Of course, in certain circumstances, the principle of prevention will require the State to prohibit activities that could cause serious harm to the environment.[45] While this principle has been reiterated in many international instruments,[46] the more common application has been to create minimum standards[47] or require employment of the "best available

---

[42] See e.g., EC Environmental Action Programme (1973). Note that this principle does not negate obligations to take remedial action once harm has occurred. See Article 27 of the UN Watercourses Convention (1997) and Covenant Articles 23 and 33. See the requirement of Article 4(2)b of the Basel Convention (1989) that each Party shall ensure adequate disposal facilities exist within the State for environmentally sound management of hazardous and other wastes; Principle 12(a) of the World Charter for Nature (1982); Strategic Element 2(i) of the European Charter on Environment and Health (1989); and Paragraph 3(f) of UNGA Resolution 42/186 (1987) on Environment Perspective to the Year 2000 and Beyond.

[43] In the Alabama case (1872), due diligence was defined to mean "a diligence proportioned to the magnitude of the subject and to the dignity and strength of the power which is exercising it".

[44] See Article 6 of the Danube Convention (1994) which indicates that preventive measures should take into account long-term needs. States Parties shall "[p]revent the pollution of ground-water resources, especially those in a long-term perspective reserved for drinking water supply, in particular caused by nitrates, plant protection agents and pesticides as well as other hazardous substances." Article 6(b).

[45] The duty to prohibit certain hazardous activities is clear, but the threshold of likely harm required to trigger such an obligation is not. Some legal instruments or decisions refer to "serious consequence" (*Trail Smelter*), others to "significant", "appreciable" or "measurable" harm. In general, prohibited activities are specifically designated by international or national law. *Cf.* Article 3(1)(d) of the ECE Transboundary Watercourses Convention (1992), which requires as part of the duty of prevention that Parties impose stricter requirements, "even leading to prohibition in individual cases, where the quality of the receiving water or the ecosystem so requires." See also Article 48 of the Draft Covenant.

[46] E.g., Article 130(r)(2) of the EC Treaty (1957) as amended, and Article 35 of the Lomé IV Convention (1989).

[47] See e.g., Annexes 1-5 of the MARPOL Convention (1973), Articles 210-211 of UNCLOS (1982); Articles IV, VI and VII and Annexes I-III of the London Convention (1972).

technology."[48] Environmental impact assessments (see Article 37 (Environmental Impact Assessment)) are widely used by States to identify potential threats to the environment so that preventive action can be taken.[49] The principle of prevention also is given effect through licensing and other intensive regulation of human activities, including the imposition of penalties in the event of breach of the duty to prevent harm (see Article 50 (Consequences of Failure to Prevent Harm)).[50]

The duty to prevent harm at the transboundary level has deep roots in customary international law and indeed it finds expression in nearly every provision of the Draft Covenant. It is inherent in the *Trail Smelter* arbitral decision and finds related support in the statement of the International Court of Justice in the *Corfu Channel* case that every state has a duty "not to allow knowingly its territory to be used for acts contrary to the rights of other states."[51] The principle is restated in numerous international instruments (see Article 11(1)(b) (States))[52] and is the basis of most national environmental legislation (see Article 11(1)(a)).

ARTICLE 7

PRECAUTION

Lack of scientific certainty is no reason to postpone action to avoid potentially serious or irreversible harm to the environment.

Article 7, affirming the precautionary approach, derives from the principle of prevention (Article 6 (Prevention)) but is designed to apply where there is evidence that an activity might cause harm to the environment, but full scientific certainty is lacking. The primary distinction between the two provisions is the standard of proof required before preventive action is to be undertaken to avoid environmental harm. In international law, the traditional obligation to prevent transboundary harm is triggered after "convincing evidence" exists that such harm will occur.[53] There is, as such,

---

48 See e.g., Article 2(3)(a)(i) of North-East Atlantic Convention (1992); Article 6 of the LRTAP Convention (1979); Article 194(1) of UNCLOS (1982); Annex 1 of the Danube Convention (1994). See also Principle 11 of the World Charter for Nature (1982).

49 See also Article 2(1) of the Espoo Convention (1991); and generally see the National Environmental Policy Act (USA).

50 See generally, Toxic Substances Control Act (USA); Law on the Environment (Egypt); General Law on the Environment (Honduras), and Decree 179 of 2 February 1993 (Cuba).

51 See also *Lac Lanoux* arbitration.

52 Principle 21 of Stockholm Declaration (1972); Principle 2 of Rio Declaration (1992); Article 194 of UNCLOS (1982); Article 3 of the Convention on Biological Diversity (1992). Even at Stockholm, several States declared that Principle 21 accorded with existing international law. UNGA Resolution 2996 (XXVII) (1972) asserts that Principle 21 lays down "the basic rules governing the matter".

53 E.g., *Trail Smelter* Arbitration.

a focus on foreseeability or likelihood of harm based on knowledge or ability to know. In contrast, the precautionary approach calls for action even when there is scientific uncertainty about the precise degree of risk or the magnitude of potentially significant or irreversible environmental harm. It is based on the assumption that scientific knowledge about the environment is still developing and new activities or substances may be found to be harmful only after irreversible or catastrophic damage occurs. Thus, to avoid environmental harm it is better to err on the side of caution. As envisaged by the Bergen Ministerial Declaration on Sustainable Development (16 May 1990), "Environmental measures must anticipate, prevent and attack the causes of environmental degradation."[54]

By focusing on the risk of harm, the precautionary approach seeks to prevent harm that may be serious or irremediable. Once such a risk is identified, action will vary according to the severity of the risk and may require temporary or permanent restrictions. Thus, dumping of wastes at sea has, in some circumstances, been considered particularly hazardous, to the point that the burden of proof has shifted entirely onto the proponent of the activity to demonstrate that harm will not occur.[55]

International instruments widely refer to and reiterate the precautionary principle.[56] In addition, the precautionary principle is an unexpressed rationale underlying other instruments.[57] Various regulatory techniques are encompassed by it: e.g., environmental quality standards, regulation or prohibition of hazardous substances, use of the best available technology, integrated environmental regulation, and comprehensive EIAs. It is also clear that the precautionary principle is greatly strengthened if there is full public participation in decisions that affect the environment, so that all known and possible risks can be evaluated before action (see Article 12(3) (Persons)).

Article 6 of the Straddling Stocks Agreement (1995) details some of the means that may be required. In applying the precautionary approach widely to conservation, management and exploi-

---

54 Paragraph 7 (15 May 1990).

55 See e.g., London Convention (1972); IMO London Dumping Consultative Meeting Resolution on Dumping of Radioactive Wastes on suspending disposal of low-level radioactive waste at sea, annex 4 (1985), (by agreement of the Contracting Parties, this has since been superseded by a moratorium agreed on 12 November 1993); Oslo Commission's Prior Justification Procedure for dumping in the North Sea (see OSCOM Decision 89/1 on the Reduction and Cessation of Dumping Industrial Wastes at Sea (1989)).

56 See e.g., Article 3(3) of the Climate Change Convention (1992); Preamble to the Convention on Biological Diversity (1992); Article 2(2)(a) of the North-East Atlantic Convention (1992); Article 4(3)(f) of the Bamako Convention (1991); Article 130(r)(2) of the EC Treaty (1957) as amended; Article 2(5)(a) of the ECE Transboundary Watercourses Convention (1992); Article 3(2) of the Baltic Sea Convention (1992); and Article 2(4) of the Danube Convention (1994); Article 5(c) Straddling Stocks Agreement. See also Principle 15 of the Rio Declaration (1992) and UNEP Governing Council Decision 15/27 (1989).

57 E.g., Vienna Convention on the Ozone Layer (1985) and its Montreal Protocol (1987).

tation of straddling fish stocks and highly migratory fish stocks in order to protect the living marine resources and preserve the marine environment, States Parties "shall be more cautious when information is uncertain, unreliable or inadequate. The absence of adequate scientific information shall not be used as a reason for postponing or failing to take conservation and management measures." In operational terms, they shall obtain and share the best scientific information and improve techniques for dealing with risk and uncertainty; apply guidelines; take into account uncertainties, *inter alia*, on size and productivity of stocks; develop data collection and research programs to assess impact of fishing; and enhance monitoring. For new or exploratory fisheries, they must adopt cautious conservation and management measures.

ARTICLE 8

RIGHT TO DEVELOPMENT

The exercise of the right to development entails the obligation to meet the developmental and environmental needs of humanity in a sustainable and equitable manner.

Article 8 sets forth the fundamental principle that the right to development necessitates environmental protection and global equity.

It symbiotically joins environment with development, a theme affirmed at UNCED. It is generally recognized that long-term development prospects are severely and increasingly limited when the environment becomes degraded; hence the concept of sustainable development, implying a fusion of these two imperatives.[58] Although international consensus has not crystallized over the precise content of the right to development, full consensus may emerge over time.[59]

The direct precedent for Article 8 is found in Principle 3 of the Rio Declaration and in recent global treaties which integrate development and environmental conservation.[60] In the Draft Cov-

[58] The roots of this notion can be traced to the Stockholm Declaration (1972) and to the WCED Brundtland Report (1987).

[59] The Draft Covenant would be the first global treaty to refer to the right to development, although it has been recognized in regional treaty law (see e.g., Article 22 of the African Charter on Human and People's Rights (1981) and in soft-law (e.g. UNGA Resolution 41/128 (1986)). Without prejudice to further evolution of this right, it might be helpful to consider the right to development as an entitlement to the preconditions necessary to exercising the rights under the Covenant on Economic and Social Rights (1966) and as being dependant for its own fulfilment on the implementation of the general international law of human rights.

[60] See e.g., Climate Change Convention (1992) and Convention on Biological Diversity (1992). See also Principle 2 of the Rio Declaration.

enant, this provision is directly related to Article 3 (Common Concern of Humanity), Article 4 (Interdependent Values) and Article 5 (Inter-generational Equity), and is given operational details *inter alia* in Article 13 (Integrating Environment and Development).

The reference to "humanity" in Article 8 is based on recognition that human beings are the central subject of development.[61] As such, this Fundamental Principle applies not only in relation to each Parties' own citizens, but in a way that takes account of the needs of all persons. In this sense, it creates a notion of "intra-generational" equity. The implementation of this right in a "sustainable and equitable manner" connotes a balance, so that "sustainable" brings environmental concepts into the development process, while "equitable" inserts developmental matters into international environmental protection efforts. Equity will be achieved through implementation of the international economic order foreseen, *inter alia*, in Article 30(1) (Trade and Environment) and through transfers of resources to developing countries to build their capacities. Both are essential to effecting global solutions to modern environmental and economic challenges.

ARTICLE 9

ERADICATION OF POVERTY

The eradication of poverty, which in particular necessitates a global partnership, is an indispensable requirement for sustainable development.

Article 9 expresses a truism, that a certain level of economic well-being is a precondition of sustainable development. Conservation and sustainable use are impossible where dire poverty precludes fulfillment of basic needs, because overriding priority is given to the elimination of poverty and because, even if the will to conserve exists, capacity to do so is lacking.[62] This principle thus affirms the fundamental link between environmental protection and economic development.[63] It also emphasizes that minimum economic levels cannot be achieved globally without efforts by the entire international community.

---

61 See, Vienna Declaration (1993) and the UN Declaration on the Right to Development (1986), which states that "the right to development is an inalienable human right by virtue of which every human person and all peoples are entitled to participate in, contribute to, and enjoy economic, social, cultural and political development, in which all human rights and fundamental freedoms can be fully realized". Note too that the mandate of the UN High Commissioner for Human Rights includes this subject.

62 See the Preamble to the Desertification Convention where the Parties express that they are "Conscious that sustainable economic growth, social development and poverty eradication are priorities of affected developing countries."

63 See Principles 8-14 of the Stockholm Declaration (1972) and Principle 5 of the Rio Declaration (1992).

The Brundtland Commission described the destructive effects of poverty and the links between it and the global economic system:

> [Present] inequities represent great differences not merely in the quality of life today, but also the capacity of societies to improve their quality of life in the future. Most of the world's poorest countries depend for increasing export earnings on tropical agricultural products that are vulnerable to fluctuating or declining terms of trade. Expansion can often only be achieved at the price of ecological stress. Yet diversification in ways that can alleviate both poverty and ecological stress is hampered by disadvantageous terms of technology transfer, by protectionism, and by declining financial flows to those countries that most need international finance.[64]

Several international instruments recognise this overwhelming problem and the need for global cooperation to address it.[65]

As noted in Agenda 21, the eradication of poverty is at the same time a country or regionally specific phenomenon as well as a shared responsibility of all States.[66] Hence the idea of global partnership, which emphasizes international solidarity and unity of interest.[67] The global partnership envisaged involves working towards an equitable international economic order (Article 30(1) (Trade and Environment)) and appropriate development assistance to developing countries (see Article 46(2) (International Financial Resources)). Other elements of this partnership are technical cooperation (Article 41 (Development and Transfer of Technology)), information exchange (Article 43 (Information and Knowledge)) and appropriate institution building and strengthening.[68]

---

[64] The WCED Brundtland Report (1987), at p. 29, continues:

> Within countries, poverty has been exacerbated by the unequal distribution of land and other assets. The rapid rise in population has compromised the ability to raise living standards. These factors, combined with growing demands for the commercial use of good land, often to grow crops for exports, have pushed many subsistence farmers onto poor land and robbed them of any hope of participating in their nations' economic lives. These same forces have meant that traditional shifting cultivators, who once cut forests, grew crops, and then gave the forest time to recover, now have neither land enough nor time to let forests re-establish. So forests are being destroyed, often only to create poor farmland that cannot support those who till it. Extending cultivation onto steep slopes is increasing soil erosion in many hilly sections of both developing and developed nations.

[65] For example, Principles 8-13 of the Stockholm Declaration stress the need for rational development and assistance to developing countries. Principle 5 of the Rio Declaration is a direct precedent for this provision. The preambles to the Climate Change Convention and the Convention on Biological Diversity contain similar references. Also see Part I, paragraph 4 of the Stockholm Declaration (1972).

[66] Paragraph 3.1

[67] See Preamble of the Draft Covenant and Article 1(1) of the UN Charter.

[68] See Paragraph 3.10 of Agenda 21 (1992).

ARTICLE 10

CONSUMPTION PATTERNS AND DEMOGRAPHIC POLICIES

The elimination of unsustainable patterns of consumption and production and the promotion of appropriate demographic policies are necessary to enhance the quality of life for all humanity and reduce disparities in standards of living.

The elimination of unsustainable patterns of production and consumption and the promotion of appropriate demographic policies are necessary to enhance the quality of life for all humanity and reduce disparities in standards of living.

Article 10 flows from the Principles expressed in Article 8 (Right to Development) and Article 9 (Eradication of Poverty). It targets two fundamental requirements of sustainable development: elimination of unsustainable consumption patterns and recognition of demographic limits. It also reaffirms that the ultimate goal is to improve the quality of life of all humans, which would include, *inter alia*, reducing disparities in standards of living.

These goals and the means to achieve them form part of the "equity" elements of the conservation and sustainable use of natural resources, by seeking to enhance the quality of life of all people. They also have a mutually-reinforcing character, particularly when, as now, a growing world population exists in combination with the presence of unsustainable consumption patterns.[69]

This Article is modelled on Principle 8 of the Rio Declaration. The subjects of consumption patterns and demographic policies are operationalized in Article 28 (Consumption Patterns) and Article 29 (Demographic Policies), respectively.

The provision is aimed at, and relevant to, all States although the concept of "common but differentiated responsibilities" is clearly applicable. It is apparent that unsustainable production and consumption patterns are generally found in developed countries. In contrast, developing countries tend to have the fastest growing population levels. In recognition that States have different capacities for absorbing population growth, this provision entreats the promotion of "appropriate" demographic policies, building in flexibility for individual States. This is to be contrasted with the clearer objective of eliminating unsustainable consumption patterns.[70]

PART III. GENERAL OBLIGATIONS

Part III contains obligations that apply irrespective of environmental sectors or components and of different types of activities. In conformity with the title and the spirit of the Draft Covenant,

---

[69] *Cf.* Principle 6 of the Cairo Conference Programme of Action (1994).

[70] For comparable discussions, see Chapters 4 and 5 of Agenda 21 (1992).

it includes provisions on both environment and development. This Part articulates the rights and duties of Parties, all States (in cases where the provisions are declaratory of customary international law) and individuals. It sets forth a general framework from which the specific obligations of the Draft Covenant are derived and should be interpreted.

ARTICLE 11

STATES

1. States have, in accordance with the Charter of the United Nations and the principles of international law, the sovereign right to utilize their resources to meet their environmental and sustainable developmental needs, and the obligations:

(a) to protect and preserve the environment within the limits of their national jurisdiction; and

(b) to ensure that activities within their jurisdiction or control do not cause potential or actual harm to the environment of other States or of areas beyond the limits of national jurisdiction.

2. States have, in accordance with the Charter of the United Nations and principles of international law, the right to protect the environment under their jurisdiction from significant harm caused by activities outside their national jurisdiction. If such harm has occurred, they are entitled to appropriate remedies.

3. Parties shall take all appropriate measures to avoid wasteful use of natural resources and, in particular, to ensure the sustainable use of renewable resources.

4. Parties shall provide the public, including non-governmental organizations, local communities and indigenous peoples, with appropriate opportunities to participate during decision-making processes relating to the environment.

5. Parties who are members of international organizations undertake to pursue within such organizations policies that are consistent with the provisions of this Covenant.

6. Parties shall apply the principle that the costs of preventing, controlling and reducing potential or actual harm to the environment are to be borne by the originator.

Article 11 enunciates two fundamental principles relevant to all States under customary international law and details general obligations applicable to Parties to the Draft Covenant. These duties are derived from numerous international instruments and many of them can be considered declaratory of customary international law. They must be applied in the implementation of the more specific provisions of the Draft Covenant.

Paragraph 1, subparagraphs (a) and (b) apply, respectively, to the environment within and beyond national jurisdiction. The citation in the chapeau to the UN Charter (1945) and principles of international law refers to two fundamental items. First, each State's sovereign right to utilize its resources[71] is to be given effect in the broad framework of international law,[72] which includes obligations of good-neighbourliness,[73] cooperation, respect for human rights, peaceful settlement of disputes, and commitments to raise living standards, as well as other principles which now form the body of international environmental law. International law must be seen as an evolutionary process, so that earlier instruments which focused exclusively on matters of economic development should be read in conjunction with later ones imposing constraints on resource exploitation.[74] The development of international environmental law is indicative of the willingness of States to support such constraints with a view to sustainable development. Environmental law, both national and international, also falls within this broader legal structure. In addition, the chapeau gives effect to the objective of sustainable development by making it the goal of resource utilization.

Although the full scope of subparagraph (a), as such, is without precedent in treaty law, the essence of it is based on existing international law.[75] All recent developments in international

---

71 This is affirmed, e.g., in UN General Assembly Resolution 1803 on Permanent Sovereignty Over Natural Resources.

72 See e.g., UN General Assembly Resolution 3171 (28th session). That the basic elements of this provision form part of modern international law is evident from the UN Charter (1945) (see especially Article 103) and the Declaration of Principles of International Law (1970).

73 This principle was given expression to in the *Island of Palmas* and *Trail Smelter* cases.

74 As stated by the ICJ in the *Gabcikovo-Nagymaros Case*, "Throughout the ages, mankind has, for economic and other reasons, constantly interfered with nature. In the past, this was often done without consideration of the effects upon the environment. Owing to new scientific insights and to a growing awareness of the risks for mankind – for present and future generations – of pursuit of such interventions at an unconsidered and unabated pace, new norms and standards have been developed, set forth in a great number of instruments during the last two decades. Such new norms have to be taken into consideration, and such new standards given proper weight, not only when State contemplate new activities but also when continuing with activities begun in the past. This need to reconcile economic development with protection of the environment is aptly expressed in the concept of sustainable development" (para. 140).

75 See e.g., Article 192 of UNCLOS (1982), Preamble to the Convention on Biological Diversity (1992), and Article 1 of the ASEAN Agreement (1985), all of which apply within domestic jurisdiction. Many other conservation conventions, e.g., Ramsar Convention (1971), Convention on Migratory Species (1980), and Berne Convention on European Wildlife (1979). See also Stockholm Declaration, Rio Declaration and WCED Legal Principles, containing provisions aimed at the domestic environment. The reference in the chapeau to the UN Charter (1945) should be interpreted so that Article 2(7) of that instrument does not restrict the scope of this provision: see the Advisory Opinion in the *Nationality*

environmental law recognize that the global environment is an integrated whole.[76] The term "jurisdiction" is broader than "territory", and would include, for example, exclusive economic zones.

Subparagraph (b) codifies the all-important Principle 21 of the Stockholm Declaration[77] and Principle 2 of the Rio Declaration, and is declaratory of customary international law.[78] These provisions have been included in Article 194(2) of UNCLOS (1982) and in Article 3 of the Convention on Biological Diversity, as well as in other instruments.[79] Article 7 of the Watercourses Convention similarly provides that watercourse states shall take all appropriate measures to prevent the causing of significant harm to other watercourse states and that where harm is caused, the State causing the harm shall take all appropriate measures to eliminate or mitigate such harm and discuss the question of compensation. They constitute the foundation of much of contemporary international environmental law. By referring to "activities within their jurisdiction or control," this provision covers vessels flying national flags, activities within exclusive economic zones, and activities of each State's nationals.

Paragraph 2 expresses the right of each State under international law to take lawful action within its jurisdiction to avoid transboundary environmental harm. It flows from and applies the

---

Decrees issued in Tunis and Morocco case, where the PCIJ stated at p. 24 that "the question whether a certain matter is or is not solely within the jurisdiction of a State is an essentially relative question, it depends upon the development of international relations".

76 The obligation in this provision to protect and preserve is based on the global environment being a "common concern of humanity" (Article 3 of the Draft Covenant), and thus not a matter solely within the domestic jurisdiction of States.

77 See also UN General Assembly Resolutions 2995 and 2996 XXVII (1972) affirming that Principles 21 and 22 lay down the basic rules on this matter.

78 *Cf. Trail Smelter* case. Widespread acceptance of the norm led the International Court of Justice to recognize in an advisory opinion that "[t]he existence of the general obligation of states to ensure that activities within their jurisdiction and control respect the environment of other states or of areas beyond national control is now part of the corpus of international law relating to the environment." *Legality of the Threat or Use of Nuclear Weapons*, Advisory Opinion, I.C.J. Reports 1996, pp. 241-242, para 29. This statement was repeated in the Judgment concerning the *Gabcikovo-Nagymaros Project*, in which the Court also "recall[ed] that it has recently had occasion to stress ... the great significance that it attaches to respect for the environment, not only for states but also for the whole of mankind." September 25, 1997, para 53. See Covenant Articles 23 and 33.

79 See e.g., the Preamble to the LRTAP Agreement (1979) and Article 20 of the ASEAN Agreement (1985). Article 2(2) of the Danube Convention (1994) similarly requires States Parties to take all legal and technical measures to at least maintain and improve the current environmental and water quality conditions of the Danube River and the waters in its catchment area and prevent and reduce, as far as possible, adverse impacts and changes occurring or likely to be caused. Article 3(2) subjects to the Convention activities and on-going measures as far as they cause or likely to cause transboundary impacts. Article 5 specifies the measures necessary to prevent, control and reduce transboundary impact. Transboundary impact is defined Article 1(c) as harm affecting life and property, safety of facilities and the aquatic ecosystems.

preventive and precautionary approaches (Article 6 and Article 7). It generalizes rules developed respecting to the marine environment where the coastal state is adversely affected.[80] The right expressed in paragraph 2 extends to measures to ensure the conservation of renewable resources. See Article 23 of the Straddling Stock Agreement which provides that a port state has the right and the duty to take measures, in accordance with international law, to promote the effectiveness of sub-regional, regional and global conservation and management measures. It may inspect documents, fishing gear and catch on board vessels in ports as well as prohibit landings and trans-shipments when the particular catch undermines the effectiveness of the measures (para. 1- 3). This right of protection must be exercised in conformity with the existing framework of general international law, in particular principles embodied in the UN Charter. It does not entitle the affected State to interfere unreasonably with the sovereignty of other States. The protection contemplated by this provision is to be proportional to the risk of harm and in most cases will involve implementing Article 15 (Prevention of and Response to Emergencies) of the Draft Covenant. The right to appropriate remedies alludes to Part IX of the Draft Covenant and includes the notion of "effective access" (see Article 12 (Persons)).

Paragraph 3 flows from Paragraph (1)(a) but particularizes natural resources. Both elements, namely the conservation of all resources and the sustainable use of renewable ones, are drawn from general international environmental law.[81] The Paragraph should also be read in conjunction with Article 10 (Consumption Patterns and Demographic Policies) and Article 28 (Consumption Patterns) of the Draft Covenant.

The participatory rights of the public, including local communities, non-governmental organizations and indigenous peoples included in this provision embody current human rights and environmental law.[82] They reflect democratic values and recognize the specialized knowledge these

---

80 See e.g., Intervention Convention (1969) (expanded to cover other forms of pollution other than oil by a 1973 Protocol), Article 221 and 234 of UNCLOS (1982) and Article 9 of the Salvage Convention (1989).

81 See e.g., UNCLOS (1982), Convention on Biological Diversity (1992), LRTAP Convention (1979). International Tropical Timber Agreement (1994) (calling for sustainable utilization and conservation of timber producing forests and genetic resources); Straddling Stocks Agreement, Article 5 (States shall adopt measures to ensure long-term sustainability of straddling fish stocks and highly migratory fish stocks and promote the objective of their optimum utilization. Measures should be designed to maintain or restore stocks at levels capable of producing the maximum sustainable yield, as qualified by relevant environmental and economic factors, including the requirements of developing states, taking into account fishing patterns, interdependence of stocks, and any generally recommended international minimum standards, whether sub-regional, regional or global); Danube Convention, Article 2(5) (1994) (States Parties should cooperate to achieve sustainable water management).

82 See e.g., Preamble and Article 23(5) of the Convention on Biological Diversity (1992), Article 4(2)(h) of the Basel Convention (1989), ILO Indigenous Peoples Convention (1989), Chapter 27 of Agenda 21 (1992), and Principles 10 and 22 of the Rio Declaration (1992). Articles 3 and 5 of the Desertification Convention (1994); Article 3(4) of the Aarhus Convention on Information, Participation and Redress (1998) requires that each Party provide for appropriate recognition of and support to associations,

groups can bring into the decision-making process.[83] It is thus desirable, if not necessary, to include them as partners in the implementation of this Draft Covenant. The provision requires Parties to involve non-governmental groups in decision-making processes that concern the implementation of this Draft Covenant, both nationally and internationally. The precise modalities of this involvement are left to the discretion of the Parties involved, although at a minimum information and opportunities to comment should be provided. A noteworthy example at the international level is the UNCED negotiating process, whereby a wide consultation with NGO's occurred in relation to each of the instruments adopted.

Paragraph 5 guides Parties in their actions as members of international organizations, in recognition of the importance and power of some of these bodies, such as multilateral development banks. This provision purposely does not directly govern the acts of such organizations; international law in this area is not yet ripe for a general rule which would allow international organizations to become party to treaties in their own right.[84] This is reflected in the fact that the only provision made in the Draft Covenant for international organizations to become party are those that are regional economic integration organizations.[85] The undertaking sought by this provision is for Parties to use their best efforts to influence the behaviour of such organizations, if necessary seeking to amend any relevant statutes accordingly. Article 3(7) of the Aarhus Convention (1998) supports this provision; it requires that each Party promote the application of the principles of the Convention in international environmental decision-making processes and within the framework of international organizations in matters relating to the environment. Similarly, Article 12(1) of the Straddling Stocks Agreement (1997) calls for States to apply goals of public information and participation within international organizations: "States shall provide for transparency in the decision-making process and other activities of sub-regional and regional fisheries management organizations and arrangements."

Paragraph 6 expresses the so-called "polluter-pays principle," but uses "originator" to make it clear that it encompass potential as well as actual environmental harm. Similar provisions can be found in several international texts to date.[86] If fully implemented, it should eliminate many non-tariff barriers to trade. The provision creates a long-term objective, because it is unrealistic at

organizations or groups promoting environmental protection and ensure that its national legal system is consistent with this obligation.

83 See generally, Agenda 21 (1992), which emphasizes the important role of grass-roots efforts.

84 Note, for example, the fact that the Convention on the Law of Treaties between States and International Organizations (1986) has not yet entered into force.

85 See Part XI.

86 See e.g., Principle 16 of the Rio Declaration (1992); Article 130(r) of the EC Treaty (1957), as amended, OECD Recommendation on Guiding Principles Concerning International Economic Aspects of Environmental Policies (1972), OECD Council Recommendation on the Implementation of the Polluter-Pays Principle (1974), Article 2(2)(b) of the North-East Atlantic Convention (1992), and the Preamble to the ECE Industrial Accidents Convention (1992).

present to expect that all "external" costs associated with preventing, controlling and reducing harm to the environment can be borne by the originator. There are significant social choices to be made and regardless of level of economic development, most Parties are not in a position immediately to implement this fully. More conceptual work is needed on how to quantify these costs and on the best means to achieve this result. Nonetheless, it is clear that direct subsidies should be phased out and *de facto* subsidies, such as rules that are not fully enforced, should be eliminated. This provision also relates to cases where harm has taken place, where domestic and international rules of responsibility and liability are triggered.[87]

ARTICLE 12

PERSONS

1. **Parties undertake to achieve progressively the full realization of the right of everyone to an environment and a level of development adequate for their health, well-being and dignity.**

2. **All persons have a duty to protect and preserve the environment.**

3. **All persons, without being required to prove an interest, have the right to seek, receive, and disseminate information in respect to the environment, subject only to such restrictions as may be provided by law and are necessary for respect for the rights of others, for the protection of national security or for the protection of the environment.**

4. **All concerned persons have the right to participate effectively during decision-making processes at the local, national and international levels regarding activities, measures, plans, programs and policies that may have a significant effect on the environment.**

5. **All persons have a right of effective access to administrative and judicial procedures, including for redress and remedies, to enforce their rights in respect to the environment, under national and international law.**

6. **Parties shall respect and ensure the rights and the fulfillment of the duties recognized in this Article and shall devote special attention to the satisfaction of basic human needs, in particular the provision of potable water.**

7. **Parties shall develop or improve mechanisms to facilitate the involvement of indigenous peoples and local communities in environmental decision-mak-**

[87] In cases of transboundary harm, see *Trail Smelter* case.

ing at all levels and shall take measures to enable them to pursue sustainable traditional practices.

Article 12 sets out a series of specific human rights relevant to the objective of the Draft Covenant. Parties shall provide for these. As indicated in Paragraph 5, this Article complements Article 11 (States).

Paragraph 1 affirms everyone's entitlement to an adequate environment and level of development.[88] Because sustainable development includes environmental conservation and economic development, both are guaranteed here. The Stockholm Declaration first established the link between two fundamental objectives of the present world: respect for human rights and protection of the environment. The phrase "health, well-being and dignity" reflects the totality of human rights protections: civil, political, economic, social and cultural rights. Also of note is that many rights are not absolute but may be limited for the protection of other humans, other species (Article 2 (Respect for All Life Forms)), future generations (Article 5 (Inter-generational Equity)), or the environment as a whole (Article 3 (Common Concern of Humanity)). This is also linked with

---

[88] According to Stockholm Declaration (1972), Principle 1:

> Man has the fundamental right to freedom, equality and adequate conditions of life, in an environment of a quality that permits a life of dignity and well-being, and he bears a solemn responsibility to protect and improve the environment for present and future generations.

The right to environment is explicitly guaranteed and proclaimed in human rights treaty law, including Article 24 of the African Charter of Human Rights (1981) and Article 11 of the Additional Protocol to the American Convention on Human Rights (1988). Clauses concerning the protection of the environment, either as a duty of States, the implementation of which can be claimed by individuals, at least in principle, or as an individual right, can be found in the Constitutions of more than 50 States. For example, the Constitution of India, as amended in 1976, imposes a general duty on both the State and the individual to protect and improve the environment (Articles 48A and 51A). See vast Indian case law on this subject, e.g., *Rural Litigation and Entitlement Kendra v. State of Uttar Pradesh* (1987), *M.C. Mehta v. Union of India* (1987), *Bangalore Medical Trust v. B.S. Muddappa* (1991), *M.C. Mehta v. State of Orissa* (1992), *Murali Purushothaman v. Union of India* (1993), *People United for a Better Living in Calcutta v. State of West Bengal* (1993), and *Nizam v. Jaipur Development Authority* (1994); see also *Columbian Constitutional Court case Fundepublico v. Mayor of Bugalagrande and Others* (1992) and Pakistan Supreme Court case *Ms. Shahla Zia vs. WAPDA* (1994). Practically no Constitution or constitutional modification adopted since the beginning of the 1970s ignores this issue: see e.g., Political Constitution of Chile of 1980, Section 19 of the Constitution of Ecuador of 1984, Article 16 of the 1986 Constitution of the Philippines, Article 79 of the Constitution of Colombia, 1991, and Article 35 of the Constitution of the Republic of Korea year. See also the European Charter on Environment and Health (1989), Draft ECE Charter on Rights and Obligations, UNGA Resolution 45/94 (1990), Principle 1 of the WCED Legal Principles (1986), the Sierra Club Draft Declaration on a Human Right to the Environment, and the Preamble to the Draft Covenant.

Regarding economic development, see Article 25(1) of the Universal Declaration of Human Rights (1948) and Article 11(1) of the Covenant on Economic, Social and Cultural Rights (1966). See also Principle 5 of the Rio Declaration and Article 9 (Eradication of Poverty) of the Draft Covenant.

Paragraph 2. In addition, although this provision expresses individual rights, the exercise of collective rights is not precluded.[89]

Paragraph 2 reiterates individual responsibility for the protection of the environment.[90] Most human rights instruments contain limitation clauses; some articulate express duties,[91] but human rights are not to be considered as conditional or dependant upon fulfilment of duties in a reciprocal manner.[92] Rather, states could apply this provision on human duties to society in the form of criminal responsibility, both nationally[93] and internationally,[94] including for intentionally causing serious environmental harm. Another application is in the corresponding right of individual citizens in some countries to seek remedies for environmental harm.[95] The Aarhus Convention on Information, Participation and Redress explicitly recognizes the rights and duties of individuals in its Preamble where it states that "every person has the right to live in an environment adequate to his or her health and well-being, and the duty, both individually and in association with others, to protect and improve the environment for the benefit of present and future generations."

---

89 The Vienna Declaration (1993) indicates

> All human rights are universal, indivisible, interdependent and intimately connected. The international community must treat human rights globally ...

See, in addition, Articles 11(1) and 12(1) of the Covenant on Economic, Social and Cultural Rights (1966). Note, as well, Article 6(1) of the Covenant on Civil and Political Rights (1966) (right to life) and Article 8 of the European Human Rights Convention (1950) (right to privacy) and Article 1 of its Protocol 1 (right to possessions and property) may apply in cases where environmental degradation is such as to threaten human life. Case law, however, indicates that this might only apply to extreme circumstances (see e.g., UN HRC Decision No. 67/180 (1990), dismissed on account of non-exhaustion of local remedies, and *Powell and Rayner v. United Kingdom* (1990)).

90 See Principle 1 of Stockholm Declaration (1972); the EC Fifth Environmental Action Programme; and the Declaration on Human Duties (1993). Also see various national constitutions, e.g., Article 97 of the Constitution of Guatemala (1985), which defines duties of the State, municipalities, and all inhabitants regarding the environment and ecological balance.

91 E.g., Articles 27-29 of the African Charter on Human Rights (1981); Article 105 of the General Law on the Environment (Honduras); Article 17 of the Act on the Environment (Czech Republic) and Articles 4, 5 and 6 of the Basic Environmental Policy Act (Korea).

92 E.g., Article 29 of the Universal Declaration of Human Rights (1948).

93 See e.g., Article 106 of the General Law on the Environment (Decree 104-93 of 8 June) 1993 (Honduras); Chapter 1 of Decree 180 of 4 March 1993 (Cuba); Article 85 of Ley 99, 22 December 1993, Crecion del Ministerio del Medio Ambiente (Colombia) and Articles 27, 28 and 30 of the Act on the Environment, 5 December 1991 (Czech Republic).

94 See Article 19(3)(d) of the ILC Draft on State Responsibility (1980) and Article 26 of the ILC Draft Code of Crimes Against the Peace and Security of Mankind (1991). See Article 9(2) of the Bamako Convention (1991) which deem the illegal transfer of hazardous waste to be a criminal offence.

95 See e.g., *Sierra Club v. Morton (1972), Australian Conservation Foundation v. Commonwealth of Australia* (1980), and *R. v. Secretary of State for the Environment ex Parte Rose Theatre Trust Ltd.* (1990).

Paragraph 3 expresses the right of access to information. The right to receive information on the general state of the environment and special information on projects which potentially affect the environment of humans is well known to both national[96] and international law (see also Article 43 (Information and Knowledge) and Article 44 (Education, Training and Public Awareness)). "The language of paragraph 3 conforms to the requirements of international human rights texts and treaties on environmental protection."[97] The provision specifies that the right to information does not require that the requesting person prove an interest. This finds support in international and national law.[98] The right can imply pro-active measures by the State to acquire and disseminate information on the state of the environment and on any emergencies that might arise as well as adequate product information to enable consumers to make informed environmental choices.[99]

Paragraph 4 guarantees the right of public participation to all concerned persons. Public participation in the decision-making process concerning the environment is now considered to be a fundamental ingredient of sustainable development (see also Article 28(e) (Consumption Patterns), Article 33(c) (Transboundary Environmental Effects), and Article 37(3) (Environmental Impact Assessment)),[100] and, more generally, to be a necessary component of a demo-

---

96 See e.g., Act respecting Environmental Rights in Ontario (Canada) (1994).

97 The right to seek and disseminate information appears in all human rights texts, such as Article 19 of the Universal Declaration of Human Rights (1948), Article 19 of the Covenant on Civil and Political Rights (1966), Article 10 of the European Human Rights Convention (1950), and Article 9 of the African Charter on Human Rights (1981). In addition, numerous environmental texts mandate the provision of specific information on the environment, e.g., the European Union which has adopted a series of texts which provide for the information of individuals, the most general of which is the Directive on Freedom of Access to Information on the Environment (90/313/EEC) (1990), but others require specific information of the public on pollution or on potential risks to be disseminated (see e.g., Article 6 of EC Council Directive 84/360/EEC on the Combatting of Air Pollution from Industrial Plants (1984); and Articles 13-15 of EC Council Directive 90/219/EEC on the Contained Use of genetically modified Micro-organisms (1990). Almost all recent international treaties related to environmental protection include provisions concerning this issue: Article 6 of the Convention on Climate Change (1992), Article 3(8) of the Espoo Convention (1991); Article 16 of the ECE Transboundary Watercourses Convention (1992); Article 9 of the North-East Atlantic Convention (1992); Articles 14-16 of the Council of Europe Civil Liability Convention (1993). See also Principle 16 of the World Charter for Nature (1982), Principle 10 of the Rio Declaration (1992), and Principles 2(c) and (d) of the Forests Principles (1992). Article 14 Danube Convention (1994) (States shall make available information concerning the state or the quality of riverine environment in the basin to any natural or legal person in response to any reasonable request, without the person having to prove an interest); Aarhus Convention (1998).

98 See e.g., Article 4(1)(a) of the Aarhus Convention (1998).

99 See, Article 5 Aarhus Convention (1998).

100 The process leading up to the Rio Conference itself was an important step in encouraging the participation of non-governmental organizations and the representatives of economic interest. Principle 10 of the Rio Declaration (1992) recognizes a general right to public participation and Principles 20-22

cratic society.[101] Local and non-governmental actors are essential in the implementation of environmental rules and the best protection will be achieved by involving as many people as possible in the initial decision-making. Often these actors can bring new and useful perspectives to the process. This provision does not seek to prescribe the precise venues for such participation because these will vary. For example, full public hearings may be appropriate for issues of widespread community or national concern, whereas in other instances simply a notice-and-comment period might be sufficient. Capacity-building in developing countries should take place where implementing this provision might cause undue administrative and financial difficulties.[102]

Paragraph 5 expresses the right to effective access to judicial and administrative proceedings, which is a natural complement of the right to environment and well settled in international human rights and environmental law.[103] It includes international norms on non-discrimination,[104] and is intended to apply both domestically and internationally. With regard to redress and remedy for environmental harm, this provision should be read in conjunction with Article 11(6) (States) and Article 53(1) (Recourse Under Domestic Law and Non-Discrimination), whereas the other procedures contemplated here include those in connection with Article 12(3), Article 33(c) (Transboundary Environmental Effects) and Article 37(3) (Environmental Impact Assessment).

Paragraph 6, as indicated above, is necessary to ensure that the rights guaranteed in this provision are enforceable. Implicit in this provision is that States will take affirmative steps to support the exercise of these rights ("ensure"), for example by providing appropriate financial and other assistance. In recognition of the link between environmental rights and development, Paragraph 5 highlights the importance of basic human needs, especially potable water (see, *inter alia*,

---

stress the participation of different components of the population. Public participation also is emphasized throughout Agenda 21 (1992). See, further, Principle 23 of the World Charter for Nature (1982); Article 5 of the Desertification Convention; Article 6 of the Aarhus Convention (1998).

101 See e.g., Article 21 of the Universal Declaration of Human Rights (1948), Article 25 of the Covenant on Civil and Political Rights (1966), Article 3 of the 1954 Paris Protocol I of the European Human Rights Convention, Article 13 of the African Charter on Human Rights (1981), and Article 23 of the American Convention on Human Rights (1969).

102 See also Articles 44(2) (Education, Training and Public Awareness) and 46(1)(b).

103 E.g., Article 2 of the Covenant on Civil and Political Rights (1966); Article 6 of the European Convention on Human Rights (1950); Article 8 of the American Convention on Human Rights (1969). See also Article 2 of the 1909 Boundary Waters Treaty (1909); Article 5(3) of the Convention on Jurisdiction and Enforcement of Judgments in Civil and Commercial Matters (1968); *Mines de Potasse d'Alsace (1976)* case; Article 3 of the Nordic Convention (1974); Article 2(6) of the Espoo Convention (1991), and Articles 19 and 23 of the Council of Europe Civil Liability Convention (1993). See also OECD Council Recommendation on Implementation of a Regime of Equal Right of Access and Non-Discrimination in Relation to Transfrontier Pollution (1977), and Principle 20 of WCED Legal Principles (1986).

104 E.g., Article 26 of the Covenant on Civil and Political Rights (1966).

Article 8 (Right to Development), Article 9 (Eradication of Poverty), and Article 29 (Eradication of Poverty).

Paragraph 7 seeks to promote the continuation of sustainable traditional practices of local communities and indigenous peoples. This is increasingly considered a significant aspect of sustainable development[105] and is particularly important in relation to the use of natural resources, as has been recognized in international law.[106]

ARTICLE 13

INTEGRATING ENVIRONMENT AND DEVELOPMENT

1. **Parties shall pursue sustainable development policies aimed at the eradication of poverty, the general improvement of economic, social and cultural conditions, the conservation of biological diversity, and the maintenance of essential ecological processes and life-support systems.**

2. **Parties shall ensure that environmental conservation is treated as an integral part of the planning and implementation of activities at all stages and at all levels, giving full and equal consideration to environmental, economic, social and cultural factors. To this end, Parties shall**

   (a) **conduct regular national reviews of environmental and developmental policies and plans;**

   (b) **enact effective laws and regulations which use, where appropriate, economic instruments; and**

   (c) **establish or strengthen institutional structures and procedures to fully integrate environmental and developmental issues in all spheres of decision-making.**

---

105 See e.g., Principle 22 of the Rio Declaration (1992), Paragraph 26.3 of Agenda 21 (1992) and Articles 4(1) and 7(3)(4) of the ILO Indigenous Peoples Convention (1989). See also the Declaration on the Establishment of the Arctic Council (1996). A major feature of the Council is the involvement of indigenous peoples as Permanent Participants, based on "recognition of the special relationship and unique contributions to the Arctic of indigenous peoples and their communities" (Preamble). The category of Permanent Participation is created "to provide for active participation and full consultation with the Arctic indigenous representatives within the Arctic Council."

106 E.g., Article IV of the Whaling Convention (1946), Article V(2)(d) of the North Pacific Seals Convention (1957), Article III(1)(d) and (e) of the Polar Bears Agreement (1973), Article 12 of the Protocol to the East African Marine Environment Convention Concerning Protected Areas and Wild Fauna and Flora (1985), and Article 3 of the EC Council Directive Concerning the Importation of Skins of Certain Seal Pups (1983).

Article 13 provides substantive and procedural guidance for giving effect to the concept of sustainable development, which requires integrating environmental and developmental policies.[107] Although long recognized as essential,[108] only relatively recently has the term "sustainable development" become widely used.[109] As stated earlier, it encompasses the reality that environmental conservation and economic development are mutually supportive and should be pursued nationally and internationally.[110]

Paragraph 1 contains the substantive contents of sustainable development. Many of these elements are given further operational detail in subsequent provisions of the Draft Covenant. The list is not exhaustive, although each objective is mandatory and all are interdependent and of equal importance. The requirement "to pursue" demands best-efforts to comply; clearly the individual capacity of each Party will determine the results that can be achieved.

Paragraph 2 details the mechanisms for integrating environmental and developmental ends, obligating Parties to take specific actions. The reference to "planning and implementation" in the chapeau connotes integrated processes and activities "at all levels" international and national (i.e. national, regional, and local). The core obligation in the chapeau is for "full and equal consideration" of environmental, economic, social, and cultural factors, meaning that each imperative is considered in a fair manner without priority of one over another. The subparagraphs that follow list specific procedural steps to be taken. Subparagraph (a) might be achieved in the context of national action plans required under Article 35 (National Action Plans); subparagraph (b) calls on Parties to enact laws and regulations that are effective to achieve this integration and the reference to "economic instruments" can be considered in the context of implementing Article 11(6) (States) and Article 45(2) (National Financial Resources); and subparagraph (c) requires that governmental decision-making be structured to fully integrate these issues.

ARTICLE 14

TRANSFER OR TRANSFORMATION OF ENVIRONMENTAL HARM

Parties shall not transfer, directly or indirectly, harm or hazards from one area to another or transform one type of environmental harm to another.

Article 14 seeks to ensure that efforts to protect the environment lead to net improvements. National environmental policies initially were developed in a piecemeal fashion, often geared to-

107 See also Article 1 (Objective).

108 See e.g., Principles 8-14 of the Stockholm Declaration (1972).

109 See e.g., Chapter 9 of the World Conservation Strategy (1980), WCED Brundtland Report (1987), Principle 4 of the Rio Declaration (1992) and Chapter 8 of Agenda 21 (1992).

110 See e.g., Article 2 of the ASEAN Agreement (1985) and Article 7 of WCED Legal Principles (1986).

wards specific sectors like air or water. This had a major impact on the development of international environmental law. An increased awareness of the complex inter-relationship among different components of the environment has shifted the philosophical underpinnings of environmental thinking towards an ecosystem approach and a holistic view.[111] This provision is equally applicable to domestic and international environment policy.[112]

The provision lays down procedural and substantive means to achieve a substantive end. The substantive element is a prohibition on the transfer of environmental harm to other areas or environmental media (air, water, soil), or to other forms of harm.[113] It would be inappropriate, for example, to install scrubbers that reduce air emissions but produce waste water that can transfer toxic substances to the aquatic environment. The procedural element requires a comprehensive assessment of environmental measures to ensure that the substantive objective is reached.

This provision follows from the essential purpose of the Draft Covenant; i.e., to create an integrated set of obligations to afford the highest possible level of protection for the environment as a whole. It is premised on the fundamental principle that nature as a whole warrants respect (see Article 2 (Respect for All Life Forms)), and thus rejects the notion that some forms of environmental harm are less undesirable than others.

Among the legal antecedents of this provision, most prominent is the injunction of UNCLOS (1982) that "[i]n taking measures to prevent, reduce and control pollution of the marine environment, States shall act so as not to transfer, directly or indirectly, damage or hazards from one area to another or transform one type of pollution into another."[114] This goes further than merely enjoining the substitution of more detrimental environmental harm,[115] in that even the transfer of an equiva-

---

111 See e.g., Principle 7 of the Rio Declaration (1992).

112 As regards international policy, see e.g., the North East Atlantic Convention (1992) which formalizes the administrative reality whereby the secretariats of the Oslo Marine Pollution Convention (1972), which deals with dumping of wastes, and the Paris Marine Pollution Convention (1974), which addresses land-based sources of marine pollution, operate jointly to regulate the same geographic area.

113 For a similar prohibition, see Article 6 of the Cairo Guidelines on Hazardous Wastes (1987).

114 Article 195. See also Articles 207-212 of UNCLOS (1982), Article 6 of the Paris Marine Pollution Convention (1974), Article 6 of the Baltic Sea Convention (1974), and Article 4 of the 1980 Athens Protocol on the Protection of the Mediterranean Sea Against Pollution from Land-Based Sources to the Barcelona Convention (1976). Article 23 of the Watercourses Convention (1997) (States Parties shall take all measures with respect to an international watercourse that are necessary to protect the marine environment, including estuaries).

115 See e.g., Article III(e) of the Kuwait Regional Convention (1978), which states: "The Contracting States shall use their best endeavour to ensure that the implementation of the present Convention shall not cause transformation of one type of pollution to another which could be more detrimental to the environment."

lent level of harm is prohibited. It would, however, permit the transfer or substitution of lesser forms of harm.[116]

Achieving compliance with this provision entails a cross-sectoral and multi-media approach to solving environmental problems. The concept of "integrated pollution control" (IPC) has been applied on a limited basis in some industrialized countries[117] and the European Union.[118] IPC has several characteristics, including a comprehensive and unified system of permits, a mandatory high standard of emissions control, and regulatory consideration of the entire life-cycle of products.[119] IPC presupposes the use (not necessarily exclusively) of environmental quality objectives, bearing in mind point, non-point, and mobile sources of pollution in all media.

The present provision contemplates broader action than IPC, signalled by the use of the term "environmental harm" and the reference to the rehabilitation of ecosystems and natural resources. Ideally Parties would adopt comprehensive ecosystem-based management plans, which would take into account all potential threats.[120] This might require institutional adjustments to support integrated and coordinated decision-making, inspection and enforcement.[121]

An integrated approach can better identify environmental priorities, allow more interaction between environmental policy and other policy sectors, and lead to more rational use of institutional resources.[122] Setting cross-sectoral standards and targets will also assist in reducing the risks of environmental harm because risk analysis methods will be harmonized and there will be less danger of different departments regulating the same substances using different methods and criteria.

---

116 This is expressed, for example, in the note to Guideline 6 of the Montreal Guidelines for the Protection of the Marine Environment Against Pollution from Land-Based Sources (1985).

117 See especially the New Zealand Resource Management Act (1991) which integrates all aspects of resource management. And see also the Pollution Control Act (1981) of Norway; Environment Protection Act (1969) of Sweden; and Federal Emission Control Act (1990) of Germany.

118 See Commission Proposal for a Directive on Integrated Pollution Control (1993).

119 This is referred to as the "cradle to grave" concept, and is recommended in Article 1(a) of the OECD Council Recommendation on Integrated Pollution Prevention and Control (1991).

120 See e.g., Section 208(a) of the US Clean Water Act.

121 This is advocated by the OECD Council Recommendation on Integrated Pollution Prevention and Control (1991), Appendix, Article 6(e), although in the more limited context of pollution control.

122 The World Commission on Environment and Development pointed out that "The integrated and interdependent nature of the new challenges and issues contrasts sharply with the nature of the institutions that exist today. These institutions tend to be independent, fragmented, and working to relatively narrow mandates with closed decision processes. Those responsible for managing natural resources and protecting the environment are institutionally separated from those responsible for managing the economy. The real world of interlocked economic and ecological systems will not change; the policies and institutions concerned must." WCED Brundtland Report (1987) at p. 310.

ARTICLE 15

EMERGENCIES

1. **Each Party shall, without delay and by the most expeditious means available, notify potentially affected States and competent international organizations of any emergency originating within its jurisdiction or control, or of which it has knowledge, that it may cause harm to the environment.**

2. **A Party within whose jurisdiction or control an emergency originates shall immediately take all practicable measures necessitated by the circumstances, in cooperation with potentially affected States, and where appropriate, competent international organizations, to prevent, mitigate and eliminate harmful effects of the emergency.**

3. **Parties shall develop joint contingency plans for responding to emergencies, in cooperation, where appropriate, with other States and competent international organizations.**

Article 15 addresses sudden, unforeseen threats to the environment resulting from intentional or negligent human conduct or from natural causes. Recognising that emergencies cannot always be prevented or controlled, the provision contains obligations of conduct rather than result. To some extent, the wording derives from the two IAEA treaties concluded after the 1986 Chernobyl nuclear accident.[123]

Paragraph 1 contains fundamental requirements in cases of emergency, namely, notification of potentially affected States and relevant international organizations. "Emergency" should be thought of as any situation which causes, or poses an imminent threat of causing, serious harm to the environment of other States or areas beyond national jurisdiction.[124] Notification is an obligation rooted in customary international law and is connected with each State's due diligence obligation to prevent harm to another State's environment and to areas beyond national jurisdiction (see Article 11(1)(b) (States)).[125] The duty to warn has been codified in several international treaties and has been extended to include incidents of which a State has knowledge even where located outside

[123] Nuclear Notification Convention (1986) and Nuclear Assistance Convention (1986). See also Oil Pollution Preparedness Convention (1990).

[124] Article 28(1) of the Watercourses Convention (1997) makes clear that the emergencies including situations arising from natural causes and that the duty is to notify potentially affected states and competent international organizations "without delay and by the most expeditious means available."

[125] See also, e.g., the *Corfu Channel* case, where the Court held that the obligation to notify other ships in their waters of the existence of a minefield was also based on the "elementary considerations of humanity".

its territory.[126] Because of this status, the obligation to notify includes an obligation to give notice to States not party to the Draft Covenant. Implicit in this obligation is a requirement that each Party establish a sufficiently effective monitoring system of activities under its jurisdiction so as to be able to notify others in a timely manner.[127] Notification is to take place immediately upon learning of the emergency. The "most expeditious means available" are those which are the most rapid. Once initial notification of the incident is completed, Parties should, to the best of their ability, continue to notify those affected, or potentially affected, of further details of the incident so as to allow those notified to take mitigating measures. The notifying Party should also indicate what mitigating measures it has taken.[128]

The obligation contained in Paragraph 2 follows upon the first, and requires all potentially affected Parties, including the Party of origin, to cooperate in dealing with the emergency. For the Party of origin, this again stems from the duty not to knowingly cause harm to the environments of other States or of areas beyond national jurisdiction. The requirement that other Parties cooperate in this regard follows from the obligation on Parties to the Covenant to take measures to protect their own environment (Article 11(1)(a) (States)) and from the general international legal duty to cooperate, which is why the provision also calls for cooperation with States not party to the Draft Covenant and with relevant international organizations. The substance of the obligation in this context has been codified in treaty law.[129] Parties are required to cooperate only to the extent that their capabilities so permit, and to their best abilities.

Paragraph 3 applies the principles of prevention and precaution (Articles 6 and 7), based on provisions in a number of international instruments.[130] It requires States to evaluate the potential

---

126 See e.g., Article 13 of the Basel Convention (1989); Article 198 of the UNCLOS (1982); Article 11 of the Rhine Chemical Convention (1976); Article 9(2) of the Barcelona Convention (1976); Article 11(2) of the Wider Caribbean Marine Environment Convention (1983) and Article 9(b) of the Kuwait Regional Convention (1978). Also see Principle 18 of the Rio Declaration (1992). Articles 16 and 17 Danube Convention (1994). The duty to warn may extend also to the public that may be affected by an emergency. See Article 5(c) of the Aarhus Convention (information on emergencies "which could enable the public to take measures to prevent or mitigate harm arising from the threat" must be disseminated immediately and without delay to members of the public who may be affected.")

127 See also Article 39 (Monitoring of Environmental Quality).

128 See Article 7 of the ILA Montreal Rules on Transfrontier Pollution (1982).

129 See e.g., Article 199 of UNCLOS (1982); Article 5 of the LRTAP Convention (1979); Article 7 of the North-Sea Oil Pollution Agreement (1983); Article 7 of the Oil Pollution Preparedness Convention (1990); Article 9 of the Barcelona Convention (1976); Article XI of the South-East Pacific Hydrocarbons Agreement (1981); Article 6 of the Protocol Concerning Cooperation in Combatting Marine Pollution in Cases of Emergency (1985) to the Eastern African Marine Environment Convention; Article 1 of the North-East Atlantic Pollution Convention (1990). See also Principle 18 of the Rio Declaration (1992).

130 For domestic environmental emergencies, see Article 14(1)(e) of the Convention on Biological Diversity (1992). Regarding transboundary environmental emergencies, see e.g., Article 199 of the UNCLOS

for environmental emergencies stemming from activities under their jurisdiction. Where risk exists, they must cooperate with all potentially affected States, including non-Parties, and relevant international organizations to develop contingency plans for such an emergency. Compliance with this obligation also requires compliance with Article 33 (Transboundary Environmental Effects) and Article 37 (Environmental Impact Assessment) for potential emergencies in a State's own environment. In the case of potential transboundary environmental harm, cooperation with other States should flow from the notification and consultation process which each Party is required to initiate (Article 33(b) (Transboundary Environmental Effects)).

PART IV. OBLIGATIONS RELATING TO NATURAL SYSTEMS AND RESOURCES

Part IV concerns all the components and resources of the earth. Although these are dealt with in separate Articles for clarity of legal obligations, the components are interrelated and indivisible aspects of the unity of the biosphere. The sectoral approach reflected in this Part formed the essence of early measures of environmental protection. Because of the potential harm that may result from treating each sector in isolation, all the provisions of this Part should be read in light of Article 14.

ARTICLE 16

STRATOSPHERIC OZONE

Parties shall take all appropriate measures to prevent the depletion of stratospheric ozone. To that end, Parties shall restrict human activities which modify or are likely to modify the stratospheric ozone layer in ways that adversely affect human health and the environment.

Article 16 is largely based on the international legal regime for protection of the stratospheric ozone layer,[131] established by the Vienna Convention on the Ozone Layer (1985), its Montreal Protocol (1987), and recent adjustments thereto.[132] This regime was established in the aftermath of the discovery of an alarming rate of loss of stratospheric ozone, largely due to human introduction

(1982); Article 7 of the North Sea Oil Pollution Convention (1983); Articles 19 and 20 of the ASEAN Agreement (1985); Article 12 of the West and Central African Marine Environment Convention (1981); Article 7 of the Nuclear Assistance Convention (1986); and Article 6 of the 1983 Protocol Concerning Cooperation in Combatting Oil Spills in the Wider Caribbean Region to the Wider Caribbean Marine Environment Convention.

131 Article 1(1) of the Vienna Convention on the Ozone Layer (1985) defines the ozone layer as that layer of atmosphere ozone above the planetary boundary layer.

132 Note that the customary law "no-harm" proscriptions are also applicable here (see also Article 11(1)(b)).

into the atmosphere of chlorofluorocarbons (CFCs), halons, and other chlorine-based substances. The persistent problem of ozone depletion requires global action and a specific provision to this effect is thus included in the Draft Covenant. This provision is an application of the principle that the safeguarding of the global environment is a "common concern" of humanity (Article 3).

The primary goal of this provision is to prevent the depletion of the ozone layer, thereby protecting human health and the environment. The means for accomplishing this goal are the restriction of certain human activities. The regime outlined in the Montreal Protocol, which contains lists of substances to be phased out over an agreed time period, should be the basis of action so long as it remains effective.

While the current regime gives effect to principles of prevention and precaution (Article 6 and Article 7), the Draft Covenant goes further by requiring States to take all appropriate measures to prevent depletion of stratospheric ozone.[133]

The second sentence of this provision mandates specific action by Parties, namely the restriction of human activities. This should be understood in the sense of requiring Parties to "control, limit, reduce or prevent human activities" which have or are likely to modify the ozone layer.[134] Further elaboration of this notion appears in the detailed regime of the Montreal Protocol for the phasing out of ozone-depleting substances, including their consumption and production.[135] In order to prevent "free riders", it would also encompass import and export restrictions on controlled substances listed in the Montreal Protocol,[136] as well as trade restrictions on items produced with such substances.[137] These trade restrictions should comply with Articles 30(2)(a) and (d) (Trade and Environment).

Article 16 requires Parties to take a broad range of measures. In order to prevent a universal restriction on ozone-depleting substances from interfering with the right to sustainable development in accordance with Article 8 (Right to Development), environmentally-sound technology should be transferred from the industrialized to the developing world.[139] This is because developing countries might be denied substances which have played an important role in the industrial development of OECD States and because it would compensate the developing world for the damage caused by

---

133 The comparable provision of the Vienna Convention on the Ozone Layer (1985), Article 2(2)(b) states that "Parties shall ... adopt appropriate legislative or administrative measures and co-operate in harmonizing appropriate policies to control, limit, reduce or prevent human activities under their jurisdiction..."

134 This is what is required under Article 2(2)(a) of the Vienna Convention on the Ozone Layer (1985).

135 See Articles 2 and 3.

136 Articles 4(1) and (2).

137 This is what is contemplated by Article 4(4) of the Montreal Protocol (1987).

138 See also Article 41 (Development and Transfer of Technology).

using ozone-depleting substances, acknowledging that the vast majority of such substances have been emitted from the industrialized world. Another important strategy in this regard will be to alter consumption patterns in industrialized countries, thereby giving effect to Article 28 (Consumption Patterns).

ARTICLE 17

GLOBAL CLIMATE

Parties shall take all appropriate measures to achieve the stabilization of concentrations of greenhouse gases in the atmosphere at a level that prevents dangerous anthropogenic interference with the climate system. Such a level should be achieved within a time frame sufficient to allow ecosystems to adapt naturally to climate change, to ensure that food production, essential ecological processes, and biological diversity are not threatened, and to enable economic development to proceed in a sustainable manner.

Article 17 is designed to regulate anthropogenic influences on the climate system caused by emissions of greenhouse gases.[139] It is modelled on the Convention on Climate Change, and is best applied on a multilateral basis, with due recognition of common and differentiated responsibilities. Accordingly, the Draft Covenant should be thought of as a "related legal instrument" referred to in Article 2 of the Climate Change Convention (1992). The present provision is based on the concept of critical load: i.e., that a certain threshold of acceptable emissions exists.[140] Its wording reflects scientific evidence that current levels of greenhouse gas emissions can not be considered safe.[141] In fact, the lack of full scientific certainty on the causes of what may turn out to be a catastrophe means that the application of this provision should be done in the spirit of precaution (Article 7).

The language of this provision is taken almost verbatim from Article 2 of the Climate Change Convention, although in the Draft Covenant the provision is stated as an immediate obligation, rather than an "objective" as in the earlier Convention. Article 17 calls on Parties to take action within certain time-periods, which if implemented multilaterally, will require agreed timetables for emissions reductions.[142] Parties should act immediately, recognising the need to ensure that the enumerated processes are not threatened, notwithstanding that "to allow eco-systems to adapt naturally to climate change" might suggest a longer time-frame. The reference to "economic development" reaffirms the integration of environment and development objectives (Article 13 (Integrating

---

139 See Article 1(5) of the Climate Change Convention (1992) for a definition of greenhouse gases.

140 See e.g., LRTAP Convention (1979) and Protocols thereto.

141 See also Article 3(3) of the Climate Change Convention (1992).

142 See the Kyoto Protocol (1997).

Environment and Development)). It should be understood in a global sense, acknowledging that some developing countries may be required to follow development patterns in the short term which are less sustainable than in those of industrialized countries (see Article 9 (Eradication of Poverty)). As such, Article 17 should be read in conjunction with other provisions of the Draft Covenant which are designed to assist all developing countries in attaining sustainable development.[143]

ARTICLE 18

SOIL

Parties shall take all appropriate measures to ensure the conservation and where necessary the regeneration of soils for all living systems by taking effective measures to prevent soil erosion, to combat desertification, to safeguard the processes of organic decomposition and to promote the continuing fertility of soils.

Elements of Article 18 can be derived from existing international instruments at the global level,[144] but soil conservation *per se* is only addressed in regional treaties.[145]

Protection and restoration of soils is essential to many natural systems and resources, as well as to biological diversity.[146] By the same token, soil conservation is affected by the operation of other natural systems, such as forests.[147] As such, this provision refers to "all living systems",

---

143 E.g., Articles 40-46.

144 See e.g., FAO Soil Charter (1981), the European Soil Charter (1972) and Articles 10 and 11 of the Desertification Convention (1994), Article 8(3)(b) in the Annex for Africa and Article 4(c) in the Annex for Latin America. See also, generally, Chapters 10 and 14 of Agenda 21.

145 See Articles II and IV of the African Convention (1968), Article 7 of the ASEAN Convention, and Article 2(d) of the Convention on the Protection of Alpes (1991). A protocol on soils to the latter Convention was concluded 16 October 1998.

146 Recommendation 92(8) of the 1992 Council of Europe Soil Protection Policy, adopted on 18 May 1992, states,

> Soils are integral parts of the earth's ecosystems and are situated at the interface between the earth's surface and the bedrock. They are subdivided into successive layers with specific physical, chemical and biological characteristics and different functions. From the standpoint of history of soil use and from an ecological and environmental point of view, the concept of soil also embraces porous sedimentary rocks and other permeable materials, together with the water which these contain and reserves of underground water. Soils so defined may reach considerable depths and therefore, in some contexts, includes the concept of land.

147 See e.g., Paragraph 11.10 of Agenda 21. Note in this regard that Article 1(e) of the Desertification Convention refers to "land" as meaning the terrestrial bio-productive system that comprises soil, vegetation, other biota, and the ecological and hydrological processes that operate within the system."

indicating the importance of soil beyond agricultural or silvicultural needs. In this regard, the need for conservation is stressed, and where this fails or has failed, restoration is prescribed. "Conservation" in this provision is a preventive concept, emphasized by the words "prevent," "combat," and "safeguard" which follow. Both the structural aspects of soil, indicated in the reference to "erosion," and the maintenance of soil quality including processes of organic decomposition and continuing fertility, are necessary.

Article 7(2) of the ASEAN Agreement (1986) is particularly instructive in achieving the objective of this provision. It calls for (a) the establishment of "land use policies aimed at avoiding losses of vegetation cover, substantial soil losses, and damages to the structure of the soil"; (b) the control of "erosion, especially as it may affect coastal or freshwater ecosystems, lead to siltation of downstream areas such as lakes or vulnerable ecosystems such as coral reefs, or damage critical habitats, in particular that of endangered or endemic species;" and (c) the rehabilitation of soil "affected by mineral exploitation." Article IV of the African Convention (1968) requires that land-use plans be "based on scientific investigations (ecological, pedological, economic, and sociological) and, in particular, classification of land-use capability" and that agricultural practices and agrarian reforms be implemented so as to "improve soil-conservation and introduce farming methods which ensure long-term productivity of the land".

It is clear from Agenda 21 that the gathering and exchange of data is especially important in the case of soil conservation.[148] Also important in soil conservation are local communities and individuals. As such, Parties should increase public awareness of the issues surrounding soils conservation (Article 44 (Education, Training and Public Awareness)),[149] so that individuals can act sustainably and public participation in decision-making can be meaningful (Article 12(3) (Persons)).[150] Capacity-building of developing countries in all these matters should be a high priority.[151]

Implementation of Article 18 is linked to other provisions in the Draft Covenant, such as Article 24 (Pollution), particularly with regard to pollution from agricultural run-off resulting from pesticides and other dangerous chemicals,[152] and Article 25(1) (Waste).[153] Given the importance of

---

148 See Paragraphs 10.11 and 10.12. Accordingly, Articles 39-41 and 43 of the Draft Covenant are relevant in this context.

149 See Paragraph 10.9 of Agenda 21 (1992).

150 See Paragraph 10.10 of Agenda 21 (1992).

151 Paragraph 10.17 of Agenda 21 (1992).

152 See e.g., FAO Code on the Distribution and Use of Pesticides and the UNEP London Guidelines for the Exchange of Information on Chemicals in International Trade; also see General Regulation of Pesticides and Related Products of Agricultural Use (Ecuador).

153 See e.g., EC Council Directive 86/278/EEC of 12 June 1986 on the Protection of the Environment, and in particular of the Soil, when Sewage Sludge is used in Agriculture.

soil, Parties should consider soil conservation in the establishment of protected areas, especially in the context of complying with Article 20 (Natural Systems) and Article 21 (Biological Diversity).[154]

Decision-making regarding soil, and more generally land-use, should be based on environmental and socio-economic considerations,[155] for example, regarding land-tenure rights.[156] The conservation of soils must be an integral consideration in the physical planning of Parties and Article 18 should be read together with Article 36 (Physical Planning). In addition to urban and other land use planning, Parties should consider the effect on soils of other infrastructure planning, such as tourist areas, roads, and railways. Further, agricultural and silvicultural planning must have soil conservation as an objective,[157] in addition to the provision of food security.[158] All of this may require improved coordination between the relevant government agencies.[159]

ARTICLE 19

WATER

Parties shall take all appropriate measures to maintain and restore the quality of water, including atmospheric, marine, ground and surface fresh water, to meet basic human needs and as an essential component of aquatic systems. Parties also shall take all appropriate measures, in particular through conservation and management of water resources, to ensure the availability of a sufficient quantity of water to satisfy basic human needs and to maintain aquatic systems.

Water is essential for life on earth. Article 19 seeks to protect aquatic systems in a comprehensive manner, taking into account the hydrologic cycle by which most water is in constant motion. Because of the interrelationship of the various forms of water, one form of pollution can easily be transformed into another, such as is the case when sulphur dioxide in the atmosphere falls to the earth as acid deposition and pollutes water bodies.[160]

---

154 Protected areas include areas where human activities are permitted so long as they support the aims of the protected area.

155 See Paragraph 10(3) of Agenda 21 (1992).

156 See e.g., Paragraph 14.9(c) of Agenda 21 and Agricultural Land Tenure Act, as amended in 1993 (Bulgaria).

157 See generally Chapter 14 of Agenda 21 (1992).

158 See Article 29(b) (Eradication of Poverty) of the Draft Covenant.

159 See Paragraph 10.18 of Agenda 21 (1992).

160 See also Article 14 (Transfer or Transformation of Environmental Harm).

Article 19 is based on a general obligation in international law to protect the quality[161] and quantity of water, for anthropocentric ("basic human needs") and eco-centric (aquatic ecosystems) purposes.[162] "Basic human needs," should be understood within the context of the Universal Declaration of Human Rights and other human rights instruments,[163] so that special attention is paid to providing sufficient water to sustain human life both for drinking and for producing food. International law is well developed concerning atmospheric,[164] marine,[165] and surface fresh water,[166] all of which are specifically highlighted in this provision. This provision also addresses ground water, the conservation of which is less well developed in international law.[167]

---

161 The London Protocol on Water and Health (1999) to the Convention on the Protection and Use of Transboundary Watercourses and International Lakes (1992) reflects this approach. The Protocol Parties are to pursue aims of access to drinking water and provision of sanitation to everyone and sustainable use of water resources. To achieve these goals, each party is to establish, publish and periodically revise national or local targets on the basis of national or local water-management plans. Article 6 details the contents of the targets, which shall cover the water quality standards, the need for improvement in supply of drinking water and sanitation, performance standards, good management practices, waste water quality, treatment of sewage sludge, and public information procedures. Intermediate or phased targets must be set where a long process of implementation is foreseen for the achievement of a target.

162 E.g., Articles 192 and 194(1) of UNCLOS (1982) and Articles 2(2)(b) and (d) of the ECE Transboundary Watercourses Convention (1992).

163 See e.g., Article 11 of the Covenant on Economic, Social and Cultural Rights (1966); Vienna Declaration on Human Rights (1993) and African Charter on Human Rights (1981). Article 24, Convention on the Rights of the Child (1989). See also Article 10 of the Watercourses Convention (1997) which provides: "In the absence of agreement or custom to the contrary, no use of an international watercourse enjoys inherent priority over other uses." Paragraph 2 continues: "In the event of a conflict between uses of an international watercourse, it shall be resolved with reference to articles 5 to 7, with special regard being given to the requirements of vital human needs." A statement of understanding accompanying the text of the Convention indicates that "in determining 'vital human needs,' special attention is to be paid to providing sufficient water to sustain human life, including both drinking water and water required for production of food in order to prevent starvation."

164 See e.g., the regional acid-rain regime embodied in the LRTAP Convention (1979) and the Protocols thereto: Programme for Monitoring and Evaluation of the Long-Range Transmission of Air Pollutants in Europe (EMEP) (1984); Reduction of Sulphur Emissions or their Transboundary Fluxes (1985); Control of Emissions of Nitrogen Oxides or their Transboundary Fluxes (1988); Control of Emission of Volatile Organic Compounds or their Transboundary Fluxes (1991).

165 See e.g., Part XII of UNCLOS (1982)

166 See e.g., ECE Transboundary Watercourses Convention (1992) and the numerous international (regional and bilateral) river treaties.

167 See however, Article 20 of the Watercourses Convention (1997) calls for an ecosystem approach and article 2(a) of the same treaty which defines watercourse to mean a system of surface waters and groundwaters constituting by virtue of their physical relationship a unitary whole and normally flow-

It requires the establishment of specific standards, especially internationally agreed standards, which is the approach adopted by all modern instruments (e.g., the Great Lakes and Rhine regimes; also see Article 38 (Environmental Standards and Controls)), and is necessary because of the generality of global norms. This is because it is almost impossible to provide adequate protection for shared water resources or those beyond areas of national jurisdiction through individual state action: first, it is difficult to know the effects of a Party's activity on other States and the global commons; second, the actions of other States may frustrate the efforts of one State acting alone.

ARTICLE 20

NATURAL SYSTEMS

1. **Parties shall take appropriate measures to conserve and, where necessary and possible, restore natural systems which support life on Earth in all its diversity, including biological diversity, and to maintain and restore the ecological functions of these systems as an essential basis for sustainable development, including *inter alia*,**

   (a) **forests as natural means to control erosion and floods, and for their role in the climate system;**

   (b) **freshwater wetlands and floodplains as recharge areas for groundwaters, floodwater buffers, filters and oxidizing areas for contaminants;**

   (c) **marine ecosystems, in particular coastal ecosystems including barrier islands, estuaries, mangroves, sea grass beds, coral reefs and mudflats as natural defenses against coastal erosion and essential habitats for the support of fisheries.**

2. **Parties shall, within their jurisdiction, manage natural systems as single ecological units. In particular they shall,**

   (a) **manage aquatic systems as entire units covering the full extent of the catchment area, and**

   (b) **manage coastal systems as entire units covering both aquatic and terrestrial components.**

---

ing into a common terminus. Article 1(b) of the European Criminal Law Convention (1999) also defines water as "all kinds of groundwater and surface water including the water of lakes, rivers, oceans and seas.

Article 20 aims to protect the natural systems necessary to support the global ecosystem,[168] i.e. the conjunction of processes that make life on Earth possible.[169] "Natural systems" include the main ecosystems as well as their individual components (physical, chemical, and biological).[170] The Article applies to all natural systems, including those in relation to areas beyond national jurisdiction,[171] such as the high seas and Antarctica.

While there is some overlap between this provision and Article 21 (Biological Diversity), "life on Earth in all its diversity" should not be confused with biological diversity; the former is broader and covers both quantitative and qualitative aspects. Whereas "biological diversity" is an attribute of life, which is a qualitative concept, this provision requires that the elements of these natural systems be present in sufficient numbers so as to sustain their continued existence. In addition to encompassing human life and health, the present provision also concerns, *inter alia*, production of sufficient quantities of food, fibre, and wood and as well as the capacity of ecosystems sustainably to produce renewable natural resources such as game, fish and timber. It also includes biological diversity.

In Paragraph 1, "conserve" means to manage human-induced processes and activities which may be damaging to natural systems in such a way that the essential functions of these systems are maintained.[172] This obligation must be implemented through application of Part VIII of the Draft Covenant, especially Article 36 (Physical Planning) and Article 37 (Environmental Impact Assessment).[173] Indeed, the main means of implementing this provision is through physical planning, while the purpose of EIAs in this context is to reveal in the physical planning process all potentially adverse effects. "Restore" means the re-establishment of lost or impaired ecological functions.

---

168 There is no direct precedent for this provision in international law, but see Article 3(a) of the WCED Legal Principles (1986) and, generally, Climate Change Convention (1992).

169 This notion is well reflected in "soft law": see Principle 3 of the Stockholm Declaration (1972), which states, "The capacity of the earth to produce vital renewable resources must be maintained and, wherever practicable, restored or improved"; Principle 1 of the World Charter for Nature (1982), which calls on nature to be respected and for "its essential processes shall not be impaired"; and Principle 7 of the Rio Declaration (1992), which calls on States to cooperate to "conserve, protect and restore the health and integrity of the Earth's ecosystem."

170 Section 2 of the *World Conservation Strategy* (1980) identifies three main "life support" systems: agricultural, forests, and coastal and freshwater. The latter fall within the scope of this Article, while agricultural systems are addressed by other provisions of the Draft Covenant, such as Article 18 (Soil), Article 21 (Biological Diversity) and Article 36 (Physical Planning).

171 See also Article 58.

172 This notion is reflected in Article 10(f) of the ASEAN Agreement (1985).

173 See also Articles 34 (Transboundary Natural Resources) and 39 (Monitoring of Environmental Quality).

This paragraph singles out for special attention three major types of natural systems – forests,[174] freshwater wetlands,[175] and marine and coastal ecosystems.[176] According to the *World Conservation Strategy* (1980), forests are particularly important in the upper catchment and source areas of rivers, while wetlands and coastal ecosystems are critical for the maintenance of genetic diversity and for the sustainable harvesting of fishing.[177] The list is not exhaustive, either in terms of major types of natural system falling within the ambit of this provision, or in each of their main functions.

Paragraph 2 is premised on the view that the optimal management of a natural system (i.e. its conservation, maintenance and restoration) occurs when it is treated as a single ecological unit. The paragraph addresses the specific case of where a natural system crosses administrative divisions, both geographic and substantive, within a Party. Note that Article 34(a) (Transboundary Natural Resources) addresses natural systems that cross national boundaries. "Jurisdiction" covers terrestrial, marine and atmospheric areas. This holistic approach can be undermined by administrative and other jurisdictional divisions covering different aspects of the same system. Accordingly, this provision requires the coordination between different agencies or entities within a Party so that managing these systems can be subject to integrated and cross-sectoral strategies, plans, programmes, and policies. Subparagraphs (a) and (b) identify the scope of two significant natural systems:

---

174 Regarding the sink function of forests, see Article 3(3) of the Climate Change Convention (1992) ("policies and measures should cover ... sinks and reservoirs of greenhouse gases) and Article 4(d) ("Parties shall ... promote sustainable management ... in the conservation and enhancement, as appropriate, of sinks and reservoirs of greenhouse gases ... including ... forests and oceans as well as other terrestrial, coastal and marine ecosystems"). For the general ecological value of forests, see Forest Principles (1992) especially Preambular paragraphs (f) ("all types of forests embody complex and unique ecological processes which are the basis for their present and potential capacity to provide resources to satisfy human needs as well as environmental values ...") and (g) ("forests are essential to economic development and the maintenance of all forms of life").

175 The crucial role played by wetlands is apparent in the both the content and the wide subscription to the Ramsar Convention (1971) (see especially the Preamble: "Considering the fundamental ecological function of wetlands as regulators of water regimes" and Article 3: "The Contracting Parties shall formulate and implement their planning so as to promote ... as far as possible the wise use of wetlands in their territory").

176 See especially Article 192 of UNCLOS which provides that "States have the obligation to protect and preserve the marine environment", covering all jurisdictional zones, including territorial sea and internal waters which form part of the coastal environment. See also Article 193 of UNCLOS (1982); the first preambular paragraph of Antarctic Marine Living Resources Convention (1980): "Recognizing the importance of safeguarding the environment and protecting the integrity of the ecosystem of the seas surrounding Antarctica"; Articles 2 and 3 of the 1991 Madrid Protocol on Environmental Protection to the Antarctic Treaty, and generally Chapter 17 of Agenda 21 (1992).

177 See section 5.

aquatic[178] and coastal.[179] Article 24 of the Watercourses Convention defines management to means planning the sustainable development of an international watercourse throughout its catchment area and providing for the implementation of any plans adopted and otherwise promoting the rational and optimal utilization, protection and control of the watercourse.

ARTICLE 21

BIOLOGICAL DIVERSITY

1. Parties shall take all appropriate measures to conserve biological diversity, including species diversity, genetic diversity within species, and ecosystem diversity, especially through in situ conservation. To this end, Parties shall:

(a) integrate conservation of biological diversity into their physical planning systems,

(b) establish a system of protected areas, where appropriate with buffer zones and inter-connected corridors, and

(c) prohibit the taking or destruction of endangered species, protect their habitats, and develop recovery plans for such species.

2. States shall regulate or manage biological resources with a view to ensuring their conservation, sustainable use, and where necessary and possible, restoration. To this end, Parties shall:

(a) develop and implement conservation and management plans for harvested biological resources;

(b) prevent a decrease in the size of harvested populations below the level necessary to ensure stable recruitment;

(c) safeguard and restore habitats essential to the continued existence of the species or populations concerned;

(d) preserve and restore ecological relationships between harvested and dependant or associated species or populations; and

(e) prevent or minimize incidental taking of non-target species and prohibit indiscriminate means of taking.

178 *Cf.* Articles 66, 207 and 212 of UNCLOS (1982) and Paragraph 18.9 of Agenda 21 (1992).

179 *Cf.* Articles 66, 207 and 212 of UNCLOS (1982) and Paragraph 17.5 of Agenda 21 (1992).

Article 21 deals with conservation of biological diversity (Paragraph 1) and sustainable use of biological resources (Paragraph 2), which are interlinked. The importance of biological diversity, for its intrinsic value and for the benefit of future generations, is now widely recognized and led to adoption at Rio de Janeiro of the Convention on Biological Diversity (1992).[180] "Biological diversity" should be understood in the same broad sense as in that Convention.[181]

Paragraph 1 indicates that the preferred method of conserving biological diversity is through *in situ* conservation.[182] *Ex situ* (off site) conservation, such as botanic gardens or zoos, should occur when *in situ* conservation cannot be achieved. As provided in Article 9 of the Convention on Biological Diversity, these efforts should complement *in situ* efforts. The paragraph lists three techniques to implement the obligation to conserve.[183] This is not an exhaustive list, but it is mandatory; all three types of measures must be used, because they are not alternatives.

Subparagraph (a) requires of *in situ* conservation be incorporated into the physical planning system, through appropriate zoning and restructuring, and by generally taking it into consideration when allocating land uses. This provision is to be read in conjunction with Article 36 (Physical Planning), especially Article 36(3).

In subparagraph (b), "protected areas" are those areas specifically managed for the *in situ* conservation of biological diversity and where human activities are restricted to the extent neces-

---

180 Note that the Preamble of the Convention on Biological Diversity (1992) recognizes the conservation of biological diversity as a common concern of humankind (see also Article 3 (Common Concern of Humanity) of the Draft Covenant).

181 Article 2 of the Convention on Biological Diversity (1992) provides the following definition:

the variability among living organisms from all sources including, *inter alia*, terrestrial, marine and other aquatic ecosystems and the ecological complexes of which they are part; this includes diversity within species, between species and of ecosystems.

182 This conforms to Article 2 of the Convention on Biological Diversity (1992) which defines *in situ* conservation as "conservation of ecosystems and natural habitats and the maintenance and recovery of viable populations of species be in their natural surroundings." For domesticated or cultivated species this means in the surroundings "where they have developed their distinctive properties."

183 The main basis of this provision is Convention on Biological Diversity (1992), which crystallizes earlier law, but see also the many precursors which have dealt with the conservation of species and ecosystems for the sake of conservation, e.g., Paris Birds Convention (1902), Convention on the Preservation of Fauna and Flora (1933), the Western Hemisphere Convention (1940), African Convention (1968), ASEAN Agreement (1985) and others. In addition, four global sectoral treaties exist: the Ramsar Convention (1971) (wetlands especially as waterfowl habitat), World Heritage Convention (1972) (outstanding areas), CITES (1973) (trade in endangered species), Convention on Migratory Species (1980)(migratory species). Finally, the national legislation of many countries provides for protection of endangered species (e.g. Endangered Species Act (USA) and for protected areas (e.g. National Integrated Protected Area System Law (Philippines). See also important "soft law" instruments, such as Principle 2 of the Stockholm Declaration (1972); Principles 2 and 3 of the World Charter for Nature (1982).

sary to achieve this end. There are many kinds of protected areas and Parties should use their legal systems to afford the flexibility needed to design appropriate ones. The relevant consideration is their effectiveness in conserving biological diversity. "Buffer zones" are special areas surrounding protected areas, designed to preserve them from harmful outside influences. Activities that do not have adverse affects on the protected area may be allowed to continue. "Interconnected corridors," created through land-use regulations or private contracts and other incentives, are necessary to allow genetic exchanges to occur between protected areas. Scientific research has shown that if gene flow is impeded, protected areas will soon lose a part of their biological diversity. Corridors can be linear, such as along river banks if natural vegetation is maintained, or may consist of stepping stones, such as strings or patches of natural vegetation from which animals (and plants) can move one to another.

In subparagraph (c), the "taking" of endangered species includes the direct targeted taking as well as the incidental taking of non-targeted species, such as the unintended capture of marine mammals and sea turtles in drift nets. "Destruction" should be understood as killing, whether deliberate or not, which might result from an otherwise authorized or legitimate activity, such as land clearing. Destruction must be limited if endangered species are to be saved. The provision also contemplates the protection of habitats, which requires controlling both the factors causing habitat destruction and those modifications which make the habitat unsuitable for the species concerned. "Recovery plans" are those developed by a conservation authority aimed at eliminating threats to an endangered species. Recovery plans may be binding or non-binding.

Paragraph 2 deals with the conservation and sustainable use of biological resources, concepts which have deep roots in international environmental law.[184] "Biological resources" means the same as in Convention on Biological Diversity, and includes all biotic components of ecosystems with actual or potential use or value for humanity.[185] In practice this encompasses any harvested species or population, including game, fish, forest products, and medicinal plants. "Sustainable use" also has the same meaning as in Convention on Biological Diversity,[186] and entails several important considerations: (i) taking should be at a level that does not lead to longterm decline; (ii)

---

184 See e.g., Articles 8(c) and 10 of the Convention on Biological Diversity (1992). See also Articles 61(2), 117, 119(1) of UNCLOS (1982). Before these major conventions, taking regulations were required under other conservation treaties, e.g., African Convention (1968), Berne Convention on European Wildlife (1979), CITES (1973), Whaling Convention (1946) and many additional regional treaties. Among these earlier agreements, however, the Antarctic Marine Living Resources Convention (1980) was unique in its concentration on habitat preservation. See too UNGA Resolution 44/225 (1989) and the South Pacific Driftnets Convention (1989), which restrict the use of driftnets in fishing. Note as well that sustainable use is referred to in Principle 4 of the World Charter for Nature (1982), which prohibits species use likely to endanger the integrity of a coexisting species. In addition, regulation of taking is embodied in the domestic legislation of most countries.

185 Article 2.

186 Article 2 defines sustainable use as the use of components of biological diversity in a way and at a rate that does not lead to a long term decline in biological diversity, thereby maintaining its potential to meet the needs and aspirations of present and future generations.

methods of taking may affect other factors essential to the species concerned; and (iii) species other than target species should not be threatened. This provision requires both regulation, being the imposition of restrictions on taking such as close seasons, prohibited taking methods, quotas, etc., and management, which is a broader control of factors other than taking, e.g., pollution or habitat destruction. The obligation to regulate or manage applies to all biological resources, whether terrestrial, freshwater or marine, and wherever located.[187]

This paragraph lists, in a non-exhaustive but mandatory manner, five specific measures that States must take to implement their obligations. The primary obligation is set out in subparagraph (a) which calls for the development and implementation of conservation and management plans. These plans should address all relevant factors that may affect the conservation and sustainable use of the resource concerned. The measure outlined in subparagraph (b), preventing a decrease in harvested populations below that necessary for stable recruitment, should be the primary objective of the plan referred to in subparagraph (a). The third measure, subparagraph (c), places emphasis on an essential, often neglected, aspect of the conservation of biological resources, namely the maintenance and conservation of habitats. Indeed, if critical habitats are not safeguarded, taking restrictions will be insufficient to save a resource. Subparagraphs (d) and (e) address problems beyond the target species, by seeking to protect dependent[188] and associated[189] species, particularly important in the context of fishing,[190] and by seeking to prevent incidental taking.[191]

---

[187] See Article 5 of the Straddling Stocks Agreement, which provides that States Parties must protect biodiversity in the marine environment taking into account the interests of artisanal and subsistence fishers and by the use of selective environmentally safe and cost-effective fishing gear and techniques. See also Article 34 (Transboundary Natural Resources) and Article 58 (Areas Beyond the Limits of National Jurisdiction).

[188] "Dependent species" mean species ecologically linked to the target species, e.g., predators or prey. If the target species is overexploited, predators with less food available may also decline; on the other hand prey species of target species may have a population boom. In both cases there may occur a disruption of the ecological balance. To avoid this it may be necessary to exploit target species below the maximum sustainable yield level.

[189] "Associated species" may not have ecological relationship with target species but are present at the same place and are taken incidentally with target species. If taking level is to high, non target species will decline. Measures must, therefore, be taken to limit incidental take, e.g., by changes in design of fishing gear.

[190] "Incidental" taking is meant to cover species neither dependant nor associated with the target species. Indiscriminate means of taking, a major cause of incidental taking, includes, for instance, the use of nets for the taking of game birds or of drift nets in the sea where many non-target species may get caught. This is particularly serious if these are endangered species.

[191] E.g., associated and dependant species are referred to in UNCLOS (1982), where the obligation is to maintain or restore populations of such species above levels at which their reproduction may become seriously impaired (by implication in Article 61(2) for exclusive economic zones (EEZ) and expressly in Article 119(1) for the high seas). See also the Antarctic Marine Living Resources Convention (1980) (Article II(2)(b)) which requires ecological relationships between harvested, dependent and related populations to be maintained.

ARTICLE 22

CULTURAL AND NATURAL HERITAGE

Parties shall take all appropriate measures to conserve or rehabilitate cultural and natural monuments, and areas, including Antarctica, of outstanding scientific, cultural, spiritual, or aesthetic significance and to prevent all deliberate measures and acts which might harm or threaten such monuments or areas.

The main object of Article 22 is to protect monuments and areas of outstanding importance for geological, physiographical, paleontological or other scientific reasons, or for aesthetic purposes. The importance of conserving such monuments and areas is on account of their outstanding and irreplaceable nature, which is in the interest of humanity as a whole.[192] Major cultural monuments and areas, including ancient cities and cultural landscapes, as well as natural areas that are important because of their scenery or scientific value are included. Some of these areas may be significant for their biological diversity.

The central obligation outlined in this provision is for each Party to conserve such monuments and areas as may exist on its territory,[193] as well as Antarctica.[194] This entails preventing deliberate action such as pollution that may harm or threaten these objects. In addition, activities under the control of a Party should not be exercised so as to harm such objects in the territory of other Parties.[195] Implementation of this provision might involve international cooperation, such as the provision of financial and technical assistance. To be noted is that this Article applies both in times of peace as well as armed conflict.[196]

---

192 See also Article 3 (Common Concern of Humanity) of the Draft Covenant.

193 The primary precedent in international law is provided by the World Heritage Convention (1972). The preamble says that parts of the cultural or natural heritage are of outstanding interest and, therefore, need to be preserved as part of the World Heritage of Mankind as a whole. Article 4 recognizes the duty of each party to ensure the identification, protection, conservation, preservation and transmission for future generations of such World Heritage situated on its territory. Article 6 each party undertakes not to take any deliberate measure which might damage directly or indirectly cultural or natural heritage situated on the territory of other Parties.

194 See Antarctic Treaty, generally, and Article 2 of the 1991 Madrid Protocol to the Antarctic Treaty which states that "the Parties commit themselves to the comprehensive protection of the Antarctic environment and dependent and associated ecosystems and hereby designate Antarctica as a natural reserve, devoted to peace and science".

195 See e.g., Article 6(3) of the World Heritage Convention (1972). This obligation refers largely to transboundary harm, but also to the activities of transnational corporations and the provision of foreign aid.

196 See also Article 32(3) (Military and Hostile Activities) of the Draft Covenant; Hague Cultur al Property Convention (1954) and the Additional Protocol I (1977).

PART V. OBLIGATIONS RELATING TO PROCESSES AND ACTIVITIES

Environmental harm is caused by processes and activities that involve or are generated by the use of substances and technologies. Processes are the physical, chemical or biological phenomena that directly cause of the harm, while activities are the human actions that apply the processes.[197] While different activities may generate the same process, using different substances and technologies,[198] the same activity may result in different processes.[199]

Special attention must be placed on processes although prevention and control of environmental harm requires control of both processes and activities. Each process must be identified, monitored, regulated, and managed on the basis of all substances, technologies and activities which generate it. When the same substance, technology, or activity is the origin of different processes, and has been identified as such, it must be monitored, regulated and managed with regard to all processes concerned.

In Part V, Article 23 (Prevention of Harm) lays down the general rule, while Article 24 (Pollution), Article 25 (Waste), and Article 26 (Introduction of Alien and Modified Organisms) set forth more specific rules with regard to certain well identified activities. The ability of each State to comply with the provisions herein will be dependant on its individual capacities and on the provision of assistance to developing countries.[200] Although each of these provisions addresses individual processes and activities, they should each be applied in accordance with Article 14 (Transfer or Transformation of Environmental Harm) to ensure that they are addressed in an integrated manner. The focus of the obligations in this Part is on intervention at an early stage to prevent environmental harm from occurring.

---

197 E.g., the depletion of ozone layer is caused by chemical reaction which breaks up the ozone molecules ("process") due to presence of certain substances (CFC gases) in upper atmosphere. These substances are used in certain technological applications ("activities") such refrigerators, air conditioners, fire extinguishers, aerosol sprayers, etc. Another example is the use of drift-nets: the "process" is the excess mortality of certain species through incidental taking in these nets whereas the "activity" is high seas fishing.

198 E.g. climate change (is the process) caused by emission of different greenhouse gases resulting from very different technologies and activities, including power production and deforestation.

199 E.g. activities releasing CFCs into the atmosphere, which affect both climate change and the ozone layer.

200 See also Part VIII (Implementation and Cooperation) of the Draft Covenant.

ARTICLE 23

PREVENTION OF HARM

Parties shall identify and evaluate substances, technologies, processes and categories of activities which have or are likely to have significant adverse effects on the environment. They shall systematically survey, regulate or manage them with a view to preventing any significant environmental harm.

Article 23 establishes the basis upon which action can be taken to prevent environmental risks caused by damaging substances, technologies, processes and activities. It requires their identification and evaluation, and mandates the taking of measures to prevent significant environmental harm.[201] The process of identification and evaluation is an active one, so that Parties should be constantly initiating such activities. The substance of this provision is broad; it includes both direct and indirect causes of environmental harm. Many rules of international law already exist to control these causes.[202]

It is to be expected that further causes of environmental harm will continue to be discovered, and as such this provision is forward looking, by requiring the surveillance, regulation, and management of processes and activities that may cause significant environmental harm. The Article places a duty on Parties to work toward such discovery and to assess risks associated with human activities.

While no specific rules are provided about methods to be used to identify or evaluate, the former can be achieved through comprehensive EIAs (Article 37 (Environmental Impact Assessment)) and the latter through application of Article 39 (Monitoring of Environmental Quality). Regulation and management will occur as a result of adopting and implementing standards (Article

[201] See also Articles 6 (Prevention), 7 (Precaution), and 11(1)(a) and (b) (States) of the Draft Covenant.

[202] For the regulation and management of processes, see the Vienna Convention on the Ozone Layer (1985) and its Montreal Protocol (1987), the first completely process-oriented international instruments establishing an international management system. The most explicit obligation in this regard is contained in Articles 7(c) and 8(b) of the Convention on Biological Diversity (1992). Also of note are the Climate Change Convention (1992) and the Desertification Convention (1994), both of whose objective is the management of all causes of the relevant processes. See too Article 7 of the Cairo Guidelines on Hazardous Waste (1987) (concerning the promotion of low-waste technologies and recycling), and Principle 11 of the World Charter for Nature (1982) which states that "activities which might have an impact on nature shall be controlled, and the best available technologies that minimize significant risks to nature or other adverse effects shall be used." Contrast Article 27 of the Watercourses Convention (1997) provides that watercourse states shall, individually and, where appropriate, jointly take all appropriate measures to prevent or mitigate conditions that may be harmful to other watercourse states whether resulting from natural causes or human conduct, such as flood or ice conditions, waterborne diseases, siltation, erosion, salt-water intrusion, drought or desertification.

38 (Environmental Standards and Controls)), but the ideal method would be through the elaboration of process management plans.[203]

ARTICLE 24

POLLUTION

Parties shall take, individually or jointly, all appropriate measures to prevent, reduce, control, and eliminate to the fullest extent possible, detrimental changes in the environment, in particular from radioactive, toxic, and other hazardous substances. For this purpose, they shall use the best practicable means at their disposal and shall endeavor to harmonize their policies.

The purpose of Article 24 is to prevent, reduce, and control pollution from all sources. It reflects existing conventional and customary international law[204] and is modeled on Article 194(1) of UNCLOS (1982), making it applicable to all parts of the environment. The provision applies generally, whether or not the pollution is of a transboundary nature, although in the latter case multilateral cooperation is urged. For example, this provision would encourage Parties to cooperate in further strengthening the relatively underdeveloped legal regime pertaining to land-based sources of marine pollution. This provision should be read in conjunction with Article 38 (Environmental Standards and Controls). "Pollution" should be understood as:

> the introduction by man, directly or indirectly, of substances or energy into the environment resulting or is likely to result in such deleterious effects as harm to living resources, ecosystems, and other forms of life, hazards to human health, and impairment or interference with amenities and other legitimate uses of natural resources.[205]

---

203 E.g., The Australian Federal Endangered Species Act of 1992, for instance, provides for the listing of processes threatening endangered species and for the development of Threat Abatement plans. These plans are binding on federal authorities and may be made subject of contracts between federal government and Australian States or private persons.

204 The international legal precedents for pollution control are numerous: e.g., MARPOL Convention (1973), London Convention (1972), LRTAP Convention (1979), Part XII of UNCLOS (1982), Vienna Convention on the Ozone Layer (1985), Climate Change Convention (1992), US-Canada Air Quality Agreement (1991).

205 This is adapted from Article 1(4) of UNCLOS (1982) and Part A (Annex) of the OECD Council Recommendation on Transfrontier Pollution (1974). Article 23 of the Watercourses Convention similarly defines pollution and includes a duty to prevent, reduce and control pollution that may cause significant harm to other water course states or their environment, including harm to human health or safety, to the use of the waters for any beneficial purpose or to the living resources of the watercourse.

The order of the wording in Article 24 is important; the emphasis is on Prevention (see Article 6). Reduction and control are supplementary to the duty to prevent and should only be resorted to if prevention is not possible. The comprehensive nature of this obligation will involve the use of planning procedures, such as EIAs (Article 37 (Environmental Impact Assessment)) and licensing, as well as consistent monitoring of the environment (Article 39 (Monitoring of Environmental Quality)). There are many legal techniques in use for regulating pollution; a common international method is to categorize substances by degree of toxicity, so that the discharge of those at the upper end is completely prohibited, while those less toxic are either permitted or permitted in certain circumstances.[206] Environmental quality,[207] product[208] and technological[209] standards also can be effective. "Of any part of the environment" from whatever source requires Parties to consider the effects of pollution on all environmental media, suggesting that an integrated pollution control strategy is the most effective (see Article 14 (Transfer of Transformation of Environmental Harm)). The specific listing of radioactive, toxic and other hazardous substances is intended to highlight those forms of pollution which are particularly harmful, and the list is not meant to be exhaustive.

The standard set by this provision is "best practicable means at their disposal," which is intended to introduce into this obligation a high level of protection based on the customary international law concept of "due diligence". The result is that individual national capacities are to be taken into account in determining the precise application of this provision in each context.

The final element, harmonization of policies, is the natural outcome of international cooperation.[210] It is intended to encourage Parties to reach international agreement on the most appropriate means for tackling environmental problems. Doing so will increase transparency during the regulatory process, allowing all relevant actors to participate effectively, and can help eliminate non-tariff barriers to trade. By not making this obligation absolute, the Draft Covenant affirms that ecological differences between States exist, necessitating higher or different standard-setting than that set internationally. However, harmonization should attempt to take a high level of environmental protection as its base.[211]

---

206 E.g., London Convention (1972), Article IV and Annexes I and II.

207 See e.g., EC Directives such as the Directive on Pollution Caused by Certain Dangerous Substances Discharged into the Aquatic Environment of the Community (1976), Directive on Air Quality Limit Values and Guide Values for Sulphur Dioxide and Suspended Particulates (1980), Directive on a Limit Value for Lead in the Air (1982).

208 E.g., European Detergent Agreement (1968).

209 See e.g., MARPOL Convention (1973) and SOLAS Convention (1974), as amended.

210 See Article 23 of the Watercourses Convention.

211 See e.g., Article 100a of the EC Treaty (1957), as amended.

ARTICLE 25

WASTE

1. **Parties shall ensure that the generation of waste is reduced to a minimum, particularly through the use of non-waste technology.**

2. **Waste shall be reused, recovered, and recycled to the fullest extent possible.**

3. **Waste which cannot be reused, recovered, or recycled, shall be disposed of in an environmentally sound manner, to the fullest extent possible in the source Party.**

4. **Under no circumstances shall there be any export of waste where the exporting Party has reason to believe that it will not be managed in an environmentally sound manner or to a place where waste import has been banned. If a transboundary movement cannot be completed in compliance with these requirements, the exporting Party shall ensure that such waste is taken back if alternative environmentally sound arrangements cannot be made.**

Article 25 concerns a major cause of environmental harm, namely, the generation and improper disposal of waste. Waste is a by-product of modern life, but regulatory control can minimize the problems it causes. This provision also recognizes that wastes are a matter of concern at both the national and international levels.[212] Wastes should be thought of as anything that might be disposed of in the natural environment, whether by its nature or as a requirement of national law.[213] It is a form of pollution, and therefore should be read together with Article 24 (Pollution).

Paragraph 1 expresses the primary obligation on Parties to deal with wastes at the national level. Applying the principles of Prevention (Article 6) and Precaution (Article 7), the first obligation is to minimize waste generation.[214] This requirement should be realized partly through compliance with Article 28 (Consumption Patterns), which calls on Parties to encourage recycling and reuse as far as possible and to promote product designs that as far as possible eliminate waste.[215] In

---

[212] E.g., there are several precedents at the international level concerning dumping of wastes at sea, see London Convention (1972), Oslo Marine Pollution Convention (1972), and Article 210 of UNCLOS (1982).

[213] This definition is adapted from Article 2(1) of the Basel Convention (1989). See also Article 1 of the Cairo Guidelines on Hazardous Wastes (1987).

[214] See Paragraph 21.10 of Agenda 21.

[215] These have become standard features in the national legislation of many countries. One of the most noteworthy attempt is the German Packaging Regulation (1991), which requires the seller to either take back the packaging of any items sold or to establish private sector methods of collecting this waste; see also EC efforts.

addition, the Article also contemplates use of "clean" technology, which can be achieved through technology and technology-forcing emissions standards,[216] and a "cradle-to-grave" approach to regulation.[217] In this regard, both traditional command-and-control mechanisms as well as economic incentives (Article 13(2)(b) (Integrating Environment and Development)) will be appropriate.

Paragraph 2 requires that once waste is generated, all efforts should be made to dispose of it at source through recovery, recycling and reuse. The purpose of this provision, a common feature of international law, is to reinforce and encourage the minimal generation of waste.[218] The third paragraph calls for disposal should occur in an environmentally sound manner. This requires that disposal occurs in a manner that protects human health and the environment from the adverse effects which could arise from such disposal.[219]

Compliance with this provision will depend on the particular capabilities of each State. Reference should therefore be made to Articles 41 (Development and Transfer of Technology) and 46 (International Financial Resources), which should assist developing countries to meet these obligations.

Paragraph 4 of this provision, addressing transboundary movement, is activated when disposal at source is not possible. It applies to the dangerous wastes.

In concert with other international instruments, Paragraph 4 requires exporting Parties to prohibit export where the Party has reason to believe that hazardous wastes will not be handled in an environmentally sound manner. This requirement imposes implicit obligations on both the State of export and that of import. The exporting Party must be in regular communication with the authorities of the importing State about management and disposal of hazardous wastes, including the state of available facilities and the level of technology.[220] Second, the importing Party must

---

216 See, generally, US Clean Water and Clean Air Acts.

217 See Article 14 (Transfer of Transformation of Environmental Harm).

218 See e.g., Article 4(2)(a) of the Basel Convention (1989); Article 3(c) of Bamako Convention (1991); Article 7 of the Cairo Guidelines on Hazardous Wastes (1987); Principle 3 of the annex to the OECD Recommendation on Waste Management (1976). See also Case C-2/90 *EC Commission v. Belgium*, where the principle of "proximity" was affirmed.

219 See Article 2(8) of the Basel Convention (1989) and Article 1(10) of the Bamako Convention (1991). See also Article 12 of the Cairo Guidelines on Hazardous Wastes (1987). Article 1 of the Forum Island Hazardous Waste Convention (1995) defines environmentally sound management to mean "taking all practicable steps to ensure that hazardous wastes are managed in a manner which will protect human health and the environment against the adverse effects which may result from such wastes." See also Covenant Article 33 Bis.

220 See Article 6(3)(b) of Basel Convention (1989); Articles 6(8) and 10(2)(a) of Bamako Convention (1991); and Article 26 of the Cairo Guidelines on Hazardous Wastes (1987).

establish a system of monitoring the management and disposal of hazardous waste under its jurisdiction. Finally, so as to ensure the environmentally sound management or disposal of such wastes, Paragraph 4 places the responsibility on the exporting Party to either make alternative arrangements or reimport the wastes if the transboundary transaction cannot be completed in accordance with the arrangements made pursuant to this provision.[221] The duty to reimport also applies to the case of wastes which have been subject to transboundary movement in violation of the terms of this provision.[222]

ARTICLE 26

INTRODUCTION OF ALIEN OR MODIFIED ORGANISMS

1. **Parties shall prohibit the intentional introduction into the environment of alien or modified organisms which are likely to have adverse effects on other organisms or the environment. They shall also take the appropriate measures to prevent accidental introduction or escape of such organisms.**

2. **Parties shall regulate and manage the risks associated with the development, use and release of modified organisms resulting from biotechnologies which are likely to have adverse effects on other organisms or the environment.**

3. **Parties shall take all appropriate measures to control and, to the extent possible, eradicate introduced alien or modified organisms when such organisms have or are likely to have a significant adverse effect on other organisms or the environment.**

Article 26 addresses the risks to humans, biological diversity, and economic interests associated with the introduction of alien or modified species.[223] Introductions have caused extinctions and are currently threatening many species by predation, competition, hybridization with native

---

221 Article 8 of Basel Convention (1989); Article 27 of the Cairo Guidelines on Hazardous Wastes (1987).

222 Article 9(2) of Basel Convention (1989).

223 See e.g., the Convention on Biological Diversity (1992), especially Article 8(h) for alien species and Article 8(g) for modified organisms; Article 196 of UNCLOS (1982) for alien or new species: "States shall take all measures necessary to prevent, reduce and control ... the intentional or accidental introduction of species, alien or new, to a particular part of the marine environment, which may cause significant and harmful changes thereto" ("new" species are to be understood in this context as modified organisms); and Article 4 of Annex II to the 1991 Madrid Protocol to Antarctic Treaty (containing very strict provisions on introductions). Introductions into the marine environment are also the subject of a code of practice by the International Council in Exploration of the Sea (ICES) which in its 1994 version also covers genetically modified organisms. Introduction of alien and new species is also governed by Article 22 of the Watercourses Convention (1997).

forms, transmission of diseases and parasites. This impacts on not only the particular affected species, but others and can cause major economic damage.[224] Should a harmful introduction spread or be likely to spread to another Party or to areas beyond national jurisdiction, the provisions of the Draft Covenant relating to transboundary issues apply (see Part VII). It should be noted that the precise extent of the risks associated with modified organisms is still relatively unknown, as there are few records of damage from this new technology. However, since the existence of the risk is widely accepted, this is an appropriate instance to adopt a precautionary approach (Article 7 (Precaution)).

Paragraph 1 contains an absolute prohibition against intentional introductions which are likely to be harmful to other organisms or the environment. It also calls on Parties to control the risk of accidental introductions. "Alien organism" means any organism unmodified by human action which does not occur naturally in a particular ecosystem. This is not limited to species but can also be sub-species or genetically distinct populations belonging to any taxonomic group (fauna, flora, micro-organisms). "Modified organism" means any organism which has been genetically modified by human action, whether by biotechnology, selective breeding or otherwise. The reference to "other organisms" that may be affected should be understood to include humans, other domesticated or cultivated organisms, and wild organisms. The reference to the "environment" is intended to be broad and includes effects on human activities and interests. "Introduction into the environment" is any introduction at any place other than a confined environment from which the organisms cannot escape.[225] In taking action to control the risk of accidental introductions, Parties should take a broad view of "escapes" so as to include escape from captivity and inadvertent importation by ships, aircrafts or other means.[226]

Paragraph 2 specifically addresses modified organisms resulting from biotechnologies. This is intended to cover the development and use of such organisms in a confined environment as well as release into the general environment. Regulatory techniques to meet the objectives of this provision include classification of modified organisms, prior assessment of environmental and health risks, prior notification and consent procedures (for packaging, labelling, handling and use), public consultation, emergency planning, and information exchange.[227]

---

224 One notable example is the introduction (presumably through ship ballast waters) of the zebra mussel from eastern Europe into American Great Lakes (damage caused by widespread colonization of water pipes and other structures).

225 E.g., this would also apply to introductions of an organism within the country of origin but into an area in which it does not occur naturally.

226 E.g., ballast waters have now been identified as a major pathway for such organisms. Introductions through ballast waters and sediments carried by ships is now in the forefront of international concern (see IMO Resolution No. 774 (18) (1993) which lays down guidelines on this; also the IMO is expected to adopt in the future an Annex to the MARPOL Convention (1973) on the matter).

227 See EC Directives 20/219/EEC of 23 April 1990 on the Contained Use of Genetically Modified Micro-Organisms and 90/220/EEC of 23 April 1990 on the Deliberate Release into the Environment of Genetically Modified Organisms.

Paragraph 3 addresses the consequences of unwanted and potentially harmful introductions of alien or modified organisms, requiring that such organisms be eradicated, or if eradication is impossible, controlled. "Control" should involve limiting the increase in numbers and spread of the organism by appropriate elimination, removal, or other measures.[228] It is important to note, however, that it may not be possible to determine in advance with full scientific certainty if significant adverse effect is likely to occur, and, accordingly, Article 7 (Precaution) should apply unless no such risk exists.

PART VI. OBLIGATIONS RELATING TO GLOBAL ISSUES

Part VI deals with different societal activities that directly or indirectly affect environmental protection and thus sustainable development. They reflect the variety of structural problems and root causes throughout the world and the need to address these at the global level in a spirit of solidarity, reflecting the concept of common but differentiated responsibilities. The full transition to sustainable development will not be achieved unless the global issues identified in this Part are dealt with on a world-wide scale.

ARTICLE 27

ERADICATION OF POVERTY

Parties, with the assistance of and in cooperation with other States and international organizations as appropriate, shall seek to take measures which will, directly or indirectly, contribute to the eradication of poverty, including measures to:

(a) enable all individuals to achieve sustainable livelihoods;

(b) promote food security and, where appropriate, food self-sufficiency in the context of sustainable agriculture;

(c) rehabilitate degraded resources, to the extent practicable, and promote sustainable use of resources for basic human needs;

(d) provide potable water and sanitation; and

(e) provide education.

---

228 The need for controlling introductions of alien species has been recognized by several conservation conventions which set forth obligations to control introductions, whether intentional or accidental e.g., Article 11.2 of the Berne Convention on European Wildlife (1979); Articles 8(h) and 8(g) of the Convention on Biological Diversity (1992); and Article 196 of UNCLOS (1982).

Article 27 is designed to implement the principle set forth in Article 9 (Eradication of Poverty) of the Draft Covenant. This provision is addressed to all Parties, recognizing that no State is yet free from the challenge of eliminating poverty within its boundaries and on a global basis. Cooperation with non-party States, envisaged here, includes North-South transfers of resources, cooperation among developing countries *inter se*, and action among industrialized countries. Since the causes of poverty are often regionally or nationally specific and may be complex, this provision is drafted so as to allow maximum flexibility in action to achieve its ends.

The Article lists a series of specific objectives which Parties must seek to achieve. The enumerated subparagraphs are based on existing international human rights and environmental standards.[229] The obligations are also related to other provisions in the Draft Covenant, particularly Article 12(1) (Persons), but are emphasized here in the context of eliminating poverty. The means for achieving these ends are many and involve all sectors of society.

ARTICLE 28

CONSUMPTION AND PRODUCTION PATTERNS

Parties shall seek to develop strategies to eliminate unsustainable patterns of consumption and production. Such strategies shall be designed, in particular, to meet the basic needs of the poor and to reduce use of non–renewable resources in the production process. To this end, Parties shall:

(a) collect and disseminate information on consumption patterns and develop or improve methodologies for analysis;

(b) ensure that all raw materials and energy are conserved and used as efficiently as possible in all products and processes;

(c) require reusing and recycling of used materials to the fullest extent possible;

(d) promote product designs that increase reuse and recycling and as far as possible eliminate waste; and

---

[229] See generally the Covenant on Economic, Social and Cultural Rights (1966). For subparagraph (a) see Article 25 of the Universal Declaration of Human Rights (1948) and Article 7 of the Covenant on Economic, Social and Cultural Rights (1966); for subparagraph (b) see Article 25 of the Universal Declaration of Human Rights (1948); for subparagraph (c) see FAO Code of Conduct on the Distribution and Use of Pesticides (1985); for subparagraph (d) Article 24(2)(c) of the Convention on the Rights of the Child (1989); and for subparagraph (e) see Article 26 of the Universal Declaration of Human Rights (1948), Article 13 of the Covenant on Economic, Social and Cultural Rights (1966), and Article 17 of the African Charter on Human Rights (1981).

(e) **facilitate the role and participation of consumer organizations in promoting more sustainable consumption patterns.**

(f) **ensure that sufficient product information is made available to the public in a manner that enables consumers to make informed environmental choices.**

Article 28 elaborates on and provides operational details for the principle contained in Article 10 (Consumption Patterns and Demographic Policies) relating to consumption and production. In view of the tremendous challenge facing all States, not just industrialized ones, that seek to eliminate unsustainable consumption patterns, the essence of the obligation is to make best efforts, in good faith, to develop strategies to make such changes. This is in the expectation that developing these strategies will be a first step toward making new patterns supportive of sustainable development. Given the complexity of socio-economic factors underlying these patterns, it is not expected that all developing countries will have the capacity to develop strategies to the same effectiveness as in industrialised countries. Accordingly, the provision does not contain an absolute obligation to develop such strategies. However, industrialized Parties should assist developing countries in building their capacity in this regard (e.g., by implementing Articles 40-46); once the capacity exists, these strategies should be developed.

These strategies are envisaged to make production patterns more sustainable while aiming to meet the basic needs of the poor.[230] The latter condition sets limits on the extent to which consumption patterns can be changed. The reference to production processes derives from the fact that a successful transition to sustainable development cannot be simply consumer driven. In particular, Parties must reduce use of non-renewable resources; this forms part of inter-generational, as well as intra-generational, equity.[231]

Subparagraphs (a) to (f) list specific obligations, although Parties have the discretion to take additional steps. Subparagraph (a) provides the basis for the development of strategies for changing consumption patterns, by encouraging the acquisition and analysis of relevant data. The requirement that this data be disseminated encourages meaningful public participation in decision-making and is related to subparagraph (d).[232] Subparagraph (b) aims at making the production process sustainable by requiring efficient use of natural resources and energy. Subparagraph (c) flows from subparagraph (b) by focusing on the recycling and reuse of the inputs into the production process, to the maximum extent each Party can achieve this result. As in subparagraph (b), the use of appropriate economic instruments should be considered. Subparagraph (d) calls for affirmative measures to encourage "green" technology in product design. This result can either be achieved through traditional command-and-control regulation or through economic instruments which encourage voluntary compliance.[233] Different Parties will achieve different results, depending on

---

230 See also Article 9 (Eradication of Poverty).

231 See also Article 5 (Inter-Generational Equity).

232 See also Article 11(3) (States).

233 See also Article 13(2)(b) (Integrating Environment and Development).

their individual capacities. Subparagraph (e) is related to both subparagraph (a) and Article 12(3) (Persons), but goes further by requiring each Party to not only remove obstacles to the effective functioning of consumer organizations, but to act in a supportive manner. One concrete application of this provision would be to disseminate the data referred to in subparagraph (a) in a non-technical and easily accessible manner. Subparagraph (f) is a specific application of the regime of environmental information. See Covenant Article 12(3).

ARTICLE 29

DEMOGRAPHIC POLICIES

Parties shall develop or strengthen demographic policies in order to achieve sustainable development. To this end, Parties shall:

(a) conduct studies to estimate the size of the human population their environment is capable of supporting and develop programs relating to population growth at corresponding levels;

(b) cooperate to alleviate the stress on natural support systems caused by major population flows;

(c) cooperate as requested to provide a necessary infrastructure on a priority basis for areas with rapid population growth; and

(d) provide to their populations full information on the options concerning family planning.

Article 29 is intended to give effect to Article 10 (Consumption Patterns and Demographic Policies) of the Draft Covenant, by requiring that Parties adopt demographic policies that are supportive of sustainable development.[234] This provision favours action by each Party on an individual basis, with assistance from other Parties only when requested. Sustainable development is to be understood as an individual goal of each Party. It is to this end that "appropriate" demographic policies are to be developed and strengthened (see Article 10 (Consumption Patterns and Demographic Policies)).

The provision includes four mandatory actions, although the list is not exhaustive. Subparagraph (a) contains a two-fold obligation for each Party: the first is to conduct a regular census of its population and then on the basis of the results to estimate the carrying capacity of its environment; the second is to develop or strengthen appropriate programmes adapting population growth accord-

[234] This Article is based on the precautionary approach (Article 7 (Precaution)). See also Principle 6 of the Cairo Conference Programme of Action (1994).

ingly. The means of so doing are left to the discretion of each Party, consistent with other international obligations. Subparagraph (b) addresses the specific problem of population flows creating stress on natural systems. It calls for cooperation between States because of the transboundary environmental problems that may result, although it would also cover the situation where other States could also assist in coping with the unmanageable population flows, for example by resettlement. In this context, subparagraph (c) provides for assistance in cases where rapid population growth outpaces the necessary infrastructure to support it. Other States are only required to contribute to establishing such an infrastructure, not to ensure a specific result. Subparagraph (d) gives effect to individual choice by requiring full information to be provided on the options concerning family planning consistent with international human rights obligations.[235] In view of cultural differences concerning this issue, the intent of the provision is to require the Party to provide information on those options that are available in the particular Party; it is not intended to dictate which forms of family planning are acceptable.[236]

ARTICLE 30

TRADE AND ENVIRONMENT

1. Parties shall co-operate to establish and maintain an international economic system that equitably meets the developmental and environmental needs of present and future generations. To this end, Parties shall endeavor to ensure that:

(a) trade does not lead to the wasteful use of natural resources nor interfere with their conservation or sustainable use;

(b) trade measures addressing transboundary or global environmental problems are based, as far as possible, on international consensus;

(c) trade measures for environmental purposes do not constitute a means of arbitrary or unjustifiable discrimination or a disguised restriction on international trade;

(d) unilateral trade measures by importing Parties in response to activities which are harmful or potentially harmful to the environment outside the jurisdiction of such Parties are avoided as far as possible or occur only after consultation with affected States and are implemented in a transparent manner; and

---

235 See Principle 8 and Paragraph 7.14(a) of the Cairo Conference Programme of Action (1994).

236 *Cf.* Article 12(1) of the Convention on the Elimination of All Forms of Discrimination Against Women (1979).

(e) **prices of commodities and raw materials reflect the full direct and indirect social and environmental costs of their extraction, production, transport, marketing, and, where appropriate, ultimate disposal.**

2. **As regards biological resources, products and derivatives, Parties shall endeavor to ensure that:**

(a) **trade is based on management plans for the sustainable harvesting of such resources and does not endanger any species or ecosystem; and**

(b) **Parties, whose biological resources cannot be exported due to prohibitions imposed by a multilateral environmental agreement, shall receive appropriate compensation for losses suffered due to non-compliance by any other party to that agreement.**

Article 30 is concerned with reconciling environmental protection and the international trade regime, a topic that has been high on the international agenda, particularly since UNCED. The latter regime is based free-trade objectives[237] based on the assumption that the well-being of all increases when goods and services move freely across national boundaries. However, this system is increasingly perceived as permitting unsustainable practices.

Despite of the free trade mandates, trade restrictions for environmental purposes have long been used to restrict markets for environmentally hazardous products and for items produced unsustainably.[238] However, many countries have been suspicious of attempts to impose trade restrictions for environmental purposes, fearing they are disguised instruments of protectionism. Article 30 strikes the balance between environmental protection and free trade goals in favour of environmental protection, while establishing safeguards to prevent abusive unilateral trade restrictions.[239] In so doing, it reverses the current presumption in favour of free trade and against environmental norms.[240] As a result Parties may have to work towards ensuring that the rules of international economic law are supportive of this end.[241]

Paragraph 1 sets out the duty to cooperate to establish and maintain an international economic system that ensures inter- and intra-generational equity, giving effect to the principles enun-

[237] This is apparent from two key provisions of GATT (1947), reflecting the principles of "most-favoured nation" (Article I) and "non-discrimination" (Article III).

[238] See CITES (1973); Montreal Protocol (1987); Basel Convention (1989).

[239] Indeed, Agenda 21 (1992) calls for improved access for export markets of developing countries.

[240] This presumption currently exists as a result of several GATT Panel rulings on the interpretation of GATT Article XX.

[241] Conflicts with the GATT (1947) as currently interpreted may arise with respect to instruments which further the ends of the Draft Covenant.

ciated in Articles 5 (Inter-generational Equity) and 8 (Right to Development) of the Draft Covenant. This duty has been recognized in recent international instruments as being an essential component of sustainable development.[242] It is manifest that developing countries cannot develop sustainably unless the global rules of trade are supportive of sustainable development (or at least are not an obstacle).[243] The subparagraphs contain a non-exhaustive list of actions Parties should take to achieve the system foreseen in the first sentence of Paragraph 1.

Subparagraph (a) states that international trade should not be an obstacle to sustainable use and conservation of natural resources. As such, it should be read along with Article 11(2) (States) of the Draft Covenant. Its wording is stronger than the prescription in Agenda 21 that international trade and environmental policies be consistent[244] or that trade and environment be mutually supportive.[245] The general application of this provision implements the obligation of Parties to protect and preserve their own environments (Article 11(1)(a)) as well as that of areas beyond national jurisdiction (Article 11(1)(b)).

Subparagraph (b) expresses the objective that trade measures concerned with international (global or transboundary) environmental matters be based on multilateral consensus, if possible. This is because international problems invite international solutions and also because this approach facilitates effective enforcement and eliminates free riders. In addition, this obligation is in accordance with the general requirement under international law that States cooperate with each other in good faith. The presumption against unilateral action on these matters has been recently expressed in international law. While this provision does not require that every Party subscribe to such trade measures, it seeks to ensure that instances of economic coercion are minimized. Widely adhered to multilateral environmental treaties that employ trade measures would not be in violation of this provision even where applied against non-parties.[246] Where a single Party or group of Parties seek

242 See generally, WTO Agreement (1994). See also Principle 12 of Rio Declaration (1992); Paragraph 2.9 of Agenda 21 (1992).

243 See, generally, Chapter 2 of Agenda 21 (1992). Examples of current obstacles are the lack of market access in developed countries for manufactured products, thereby increasing dependence in developing countries on resource extractive industries; heavy international debt pressure on developing countries to over-exploit their natural resources in order to get hard currency; and developed country dumping of agricultural surpluses (the result of protectionist policies) which devalue commodities important to the export economy of developing countries.

244 Paragraph 2.20.

245 See Paragraph 2.19 of Agenda 21 (1992). In fact, international trade involving ecologically unsound consequences could be seen as an activity that has or is likely to have significant adverse effects on the conservation of biological diversity and sustainable use of biological resources, which Parties to the Convention on Biological Diversity (1992) are required to identify (Article 7(c)) and to regulate or manage (Article 8(c)).

246 E.g., CITES (1973), Montreal Protocol (1987), Basel Convention (1989). Note Article 104 of the NAFTA (1992) which, in certain circumstances, permits those treaties to override its provisions.

to impose a trade restriction that may adversely affect developing countries, all concerned should cooperate to find a solution. Such a solution could be reached by transferring technology to the affected developing countries, so as to allow them to comply with the relevant environmental standard (see also Article 41 (Development and Transfer of Technology)), or by compensating them for any undue hardship (see also Article 46 (International Financial Resources)). Finally, it should be noted that products as well as production processes and methods may be "environmental problems" as contemplated by this provision.

Subparagraph (c) is intended to protect the integrity of the international free trade system, as well as the integrity of trade-related environmental measures. This provision does not contain any qualifying language, indicating its importance. It is consistent with Agenda 21[247] and GATT (1947)[248] in seeking to eliminate protectionism and/or discriminatory trade barriers disguised as environmental measures.[249]

Subparagraph (d) is intended to limit the exercise of unilateral trade measures for environmental purposes. They may be used to protect the environment of areas beyond national jurisdiction[250] only if affected States have been consulted and the measures are implemented in a transparent manner. Unlike subparagraph (b) permitting multilateral trade barriers for international environmental purposes, subparagraph (d) calls for avoidance of unilateral measures. This is indicative of the general undesirability of unilateral trade measures. However, in extreme circumstances, unilateral trade restrictions may be the only effective means of protecting, for example, the global commons. Article 58 (Areas Beyond the Limits of National Jurisdiction), read in conjunction with Article 11 (States), allows Parties pursue this objective. There must, however, be some nexus between the action taken by the acting Party and the objective of environmental protection. "Consultation" should be understood both in the sense of attempting to negotiate a consensus and in the sense of informing affected States of the environmental issue at stake. The obligation of "transparency" is to ensure that such unilateral measures are not employed for improper purposes and to enable all affected States to understand the nature of the measures taken and how to comply with them.[251]

---

247 Paragraph 39.3(d).

248 Chapeau to Article XX of GATT (1947).

249 GATT jurisprudence reveals an overriding concern with preventing permissable exceptions from being abused for protectionist purposes (see e.g., *GATT Panel Report: Canada - Measures Affecting Exports of Unprocessed Herring and Salmon* (1987); *GATT Panel Report: Thailand - Restrictions of, and International Taxes on, Cigarettes case* (1990); *GATT Tuna I* case (1991); and *GATT Tuna II* case (1994). See also, Stockholm Recommendation 103 (1972), discouraging the use of environmental concerns as pretexts for discriminatory trade policies.

250 *Contra*, the *GATT Tuna I* case (1991).

251 For example, in the *GATT Tuna I* (1991) case, Mexico claimed that US regulations on taking of tuna were not transparent because the allowable foreign quotas were determined in an unpredictable manner.

Subparagraph (e) imposes an obligation on Parties to influence the market, both domestically and internationally, so that commodity and raw material prices reflect all social and environmental costs. As such, it is related to Article 11(6) (States) and 13(2)(b) (Integrating Environment and Development), and is an application of the "originator-pays principle". It is highlighted for special mention in this Article because of the particularly detrimental effect international trade can have. The objective of the provision is already partially realized in most States,[252] although the differing extent to which this is so gives rise to non-tariff barriers. This provision also encourages Parties to limit their subsidization of private enterprises, both those which operate in an unsustainable manner and those which seek state aid in meeting environmental requirements. Although the global trade regime already discourages the use of subsidies (see Article XVI of the GATT (1947) and, generally, the Uruguay Round Agreement on Subsidies and Countervailing Measures (1994)), full implementation of this provision will entail a broader interpretation of the concept of "subsidy" than is currently in use and would include, e.g., agricultural subsidies (which under the Uruguay Round Agreement on Agriculture are still permitted to exist) or *de facto* subsidies which accrue due to lack of stringent environmental regulation. As such, full implementation of this policy will eliminate the need for any environmentally related trade restrictions, and as such will preserve the integrity of the free trade system. It should be noted that implementation of this provision is no substitute for reducing the external costs of environmental harm as far as possible.

Paragraph 2 focuses on biological resources[253] because of their particular vulnerability to the adverse effects of international trade. It is especially important that States structure their trade relations so as not to place these resources in danger.[254] Subparagraph (a) is directly concerned with the sustainable harvesting of biological resources that are traded. The Convention on Biological Diversity identifies the elaboration of management plans as a particularly effective means for ensuring the conservation of biological resources.[255] Paragraph 2 takes this notion further by encouraging Parties to base trade on such management plans on the conservation of ecosystems as well as species.[256]

Subparagraph (b) covers a special situation, best exemplified by CITES (1973). States that comply with their obligations to restrict the trade in endangered species are "punished" or deprived of benefits from these species in cases when the endangered status of the species in question is

---

252 This is the result of much environmental regulation, for example the enactment of emissions standards, product standards, and environmental taxes, fees and levies.

253 Article 2 of the Convention on Biological Diversity (1992) defines biological resources as including "genetic resources, organisms or parts thereof, populations, or any other biotic component of ecosystems with actual or potential use of value for humanity."

254 See, generally, CITES (1973), as well as Article IX of the African Convention, Article 5(1)(b) of the ASEAN Agreement (1985), and Article 3(2)(c) of the South Pacific Driftnets Convention (1990).

255 Article 8(b), (c), and (f).

256 This provision is also based on the scheme established by CITES (1973) which establishes trade restrictions in accordance with a species' conservation status.

maintained due to other States not complying with such treaties.[257] The 19th IUCN General Assembly requested that possibilities for compensating such States, as well as the precise modalities of compensation, be explored.

ARTICLE 31

ECONOMIC ACTIVITIES OF FOREIGN ORIGIN

1. Parties shall require, from all economic entities and in regard to activities of foreign origin conducted within their jurisdiction, information on:

(a) potential or actual harm to the environment resulting from their activities;

(b) the relevant environmental legal requirements and standards applicable in the State of origin;

(c) the techniques in use in the State of origin to comply with such requirements and standards; and

(d) reasonably available data and information concerning the state-of-the-art techniques to prevent environmental harm.

2. The Party of origin shall, upon request of the host Party,

(a) provide it with all relevant information on applicable environmental requirements and standards within the limits of its jurisdiction; and

(b) enter into consultations with the host Party to enable the host Party to take appropriate measures regarding such activities.

3. The Party of origin shall ensure that, in the absence of equally strict or higher environmental standards in the host Party or express agreement by the host Party to the contrary, it shall cause its nationals to apply the relevant standards of the Party of origin.

Article 31 aims to ensure that economic activities of foreign origin, primarily those of transnational corporations, are conducted in a manner that does not cause environmental harm. It

[257] This provision is primarily aimed at the application of CITES (1973), but also would be relevant to the application of other regional treaties with similar regimes, such as Article IX of the Western Hemisphere Convention (1940), Article IX of the African Convention (1968), and Article 5 of the ASEAN Agreement (1985).

encompasses and develops the concept of prior informed consent in the regulation of these activities, and adds a new choice of law principle in requiring application of the best environmental laws.

The scope of the provision governs individuals, private or State-owned enterprises and corporations, and other business organizations of foreign origin. The latter term includes individuals of foreign nationality, enterprises having the nationality of another State and corporations that are not incorporated in the State where the activities are occurring.[258] It also includes transnational corporations that are incorporated in the State where the activity is occurring but which are wholly or in majority owned by foreign nationals. "Origin" in this Article refers to home nationality of the activity of foreign origin, while "host" refers to where the activity takes place, other than at the origin.

The principle of territorial sovereignty in international law permits a State generally to control the entry of foreigners to its territory and to subject them to its domestic laws while their are present. In addition to being subject to the territorial laws where they do business, corporations are governed by the laws of the State of incorporation, as the International Court of Justice held in the *Barcelona Traction* case.

According to Paragraph 1, Parties must require foreign economic actors to provide information regarding potential adverse environmental effects of their activities and the ways and means to avoid them. The Party in receipt of such information should accord any confidential business information with any reasonable and normally applicable safeguards to protect that confidentiality.[259]

In terms of the information that must be provided to the host Parties, subparagraph (a) implies that the entities will conduct an environmental impact assessment[260] if needed in order to report on the environmental harm of their activities.[261] Subparagraph (b) requires information on relevant legislation and regulations in the State of origin.[262] Subparagraphs (c) and (d) provide for sharing of information on commonly used and state-of-the art industrial techniques to prevent environmental harm.[263]

---

258 Under international law, nationality refers not only to the place of incorporation, but also where effective control lies.

259 See Article 54 of the Code of Conduct of Transnational Corporations.

260 An EIA may be already required under Article 37 (Environmental Impact Assessment) if there is a risk of significant environmental harm, but even this is not the case, the provisions of that Article should be applied where appropriate.

261 See Articles 44 (and generally Article 47(a)) of the Draft Code of Conduct on Transnational Corporations and Article 3 of the OECD Guidelines for Multinational Enterprises. See also "Responsible Care Code" approved by the US Chemical Manufacturers Association in 1988.

262 See Paragraph 44 of the Draft Code of Conduct on Transnational Corporations.

263 Id.

Paragraph 2 creates a parallel obligation requiring the Party of origin to provide additional information on its environmental requirements and standards (subparagraph (a)), and to enter into consultations if requested (subparagraph (b)).

Paragraph 3 calls for the Party of origin to impose its own standards of conduct on its nationals operating outside its territory,[264] where these standards are more stringent than in the host Party, except where both Parties agree otherwise. The provision is structured so as not to interfere with the sovereign rights of the host Party to regulate as it sees fit. This provision will discourage the relocation of activities harmful to the environment to countries with weak environmental standards.[265] By not allowing economic entities to escape more stringent rules, this provision may also remove the inducement to have weak standards to attract environmentally harmful activities and thus should enhance overall environmental protection.

ARTICLE 32

MILITARY AND HOSTILE ACTIVITIES

1. **Parties shall protect the environment during periods of armed conflict. In particular, Parties shall:**

   (a) **observe, outside areas of armed conflict, all national and international environmental rules by which they are bound in times of peace;**

   (b) **take care to protect the environment against avoidable harm in areas of armed conflict;**

   (c) **not employ or threaten to employ methods or means of warfare which are intended or may be expected to cause widespread, long–term, or severe harm to the environment and ensure that such means and methods of warfare are not developed, produced, tested, or transferred; and**

   (d) **not use the destruction or modification of the environment as a means of warfare or reprisal.**

2. **Parties shall cooperate to further develop and implement rules and measures to protect the environment during international armed conflict and es-**

---

264 The direct regulation of a State's nationals abroad is recognized under international law. See e.g., Article 19(4) of the Convention on Biological Diversity (1992), which requires a Contracting Party to require of any person under its jurisdiction to provide information on the safety and use of living modified organisms which is required in that Contracting Party to the Contracting Party into which the organisms are to be introduced.

265 This draws on Principle 14 of the Rio Principles relating to relocation by transnational enterprises.

tablish rules and measures to protect the environment during non-international armed conflict.

3. **All Parties involved in armed conflicts shall take the necessary measures to protect natural and cultural sites of special interest, in particular sites designated for protection under applicable national laws and international treaties, as well as potentially dangerous installations, from being subject to attack as a result of armed conflict, insurgency, terrorism, or sabotage. Military personnel shall be instructed as to the existence and location of such sites and installations.**

4. **Parties shall take measures to ensure that persons are held responsible for the deliberate and intentional use of means or methods of warfare which cause widespread, long–term, or severe harm to the environment.**

5. **Parties shall ensure that military personnel, aircraft, vessels and other equipment and installations are not exempted in times of peace from rules, standards, and measures for environmental protection.**

Article 32 responds to the widespread sentiment that international law should provide better protection for the environment during armed conflict, both by enforcing existing norms and developing new ones.[266] It seeks to offer as much environmental protection as is reasonably possible during armed conflict, based on the presumption under customary international law that the environment, *per se*, which is not a military objective, is entitled to protection.[267] Conflicts such as the 1991 Gulf War and those in regions of the former Yugoslavia have aroused international consciousness about the potential to cause grave harm to the environment.[268] Environmental protection in this context is particularly difficult and complex, due to the axiom that all warfare is harmful to the environment. As such, the law on this issue can only limit rather than eliminate the environmental damage.[269]

---

[266] This is implied by Principle 24 of the Rio Declaration (1992) and Paragraph 39.6 of Agenda 21. See also UNGA Resolution 47/37.

[267] See e.g., ICRC Guidelines (1994).

[268] See the United Nations Claims Commission created in the aftermath of the 1991 Gulf War (UN Security Council Resolution 687/1991) and *Bosnia-Herzegovina* v. *Yugoslavia (Serbia and Montenegro)* (1993) where the applicants claimed compensation, *inter alia*, for damages to the environment.

[269] Note the customary principles of the law of war, "proportionality", "discrimination", and "military necessity" as well as treaty law, especially the ENMOD Convention (1976), Additional Protocol I (1977), and Inhumane Weapons Convention (1980). In addition several arms control treaties are relevant (notably the Geneva Gas Protocol (1925); Biological Weapons Convention (1972); and the Chemical Weapons Convention (1993)).

The first sentence of Paragraph 1 calls for the environment to be protected during armed conflict, and the following subparagraphs are a non-exhaustive list of measures to achieve this end. This general rule is largely a restatement of international law,[270] and implies that all peacetime obligations relating to environmental protection continue upon the outbreak of hostilities, so long as they do not interfere with the exercise of lawful self-defence.[271] As between belligerents and third parties, the Draft Covenant provision is an application of the customary principle of "neutrality". As between belligerents themselves, two reasons justify the continuance of environmental treaties during wartime: first, there exists a global interest in the integrity of the environment,[272] given the ecological reality of interdependence and interrelation, i.e., the consequences of most environmental damage will not be confined to the belligerents alone; and second, most environmental treaties do not contain express provisions limiting their application during wartime.

Subparagraph (a) explicitly requires the continued application by Parties of national and international environmental rules during armed conflict to areas outside the conflict, and follows from the aforementioned reasoning. As above, this provision encompasses environmental rules derived from customary and treaty law.

Subparagraph (b) sets out a second basic obligation to which Parties must adhere during armed conflict. The first part of this provision builds on the requirements set out in the World Charter for Nature,[273] which in addition to requiring nature to "be secured against the degradation caused by warfare or other hostile activities," states that "military activities damaging to nature are to be avoided." Additional Protocol I (1977) also requires that care be taken to protect the natural environment as a whole against "widespread, long-term and severe damage."[274]

Subparagraph (c) contains a threshold of permissable harm that departs from existing precedents, with the particular elements to be understood in accordance with their ordinary

---

270 See Articles 35(3) and 55(1) of Additional Protocol I (1977). See also Principle 24 of the Rio Declaration (1992).

271 To be noted is that most environmental treaties are silent about the consequences of armed conflict. The one exception is the Article XIX of the OILPOL Convention (1954), which expressly provides for the treaty's suspension during armed conflict. This treaty, however, has been superseded by the MARPOL Convention (1973), which does not contain any reference to armed conflict. The other environmental treaties which contemplate armed conflict are those which exempt operators from liability, such as Article 9 of the Paris Nuclear Liability Convention (1960); Article IV.3(a) of the Vienna Nuclear Liability Convention (1963); and Article III(2)(a) of the Oil Pollution Civil Liability Convention (1969). Finally, note should be made of Article 6(3) of the World Heritage Convention (1972) which prohibits deliberate measure from being taken which might directly or indirectly harm designated sites.

272 This is also reflected in Article 3 (Common Concern of Humanity) of the Draft Covenant.

273 Principle 5 of the World Charter for Nature (1982).

274 Articles 35(3) and 55(1).

meaning.[275] This provision is expressed in the disjunctive ("or") along the lines of ENMOD Convention (1976),[276] as compared with the conjunctive ("and") in Additional Protocol I (1977),[277] although "long-term" (from Additional Protocol I) is used instead of "long-lasting" (from ENMOD).[278] This provision is intended to reinforce the requirement set forth in subparagraph (b) by regulating the means and methods of warfare. Its prohibition on the methods or means of warfare which "are intended or may be expected" to cause damage, echoes the language of Articles 35(3) and 55(1) of Additional Protocol I, suggesting that its breach is not dependant on a finding that the attacker intended to cause the resulting damage. The final clause of this subparagraph is intended to give effect to preventive and precautionary approaches (Articles 6 and 7) by ensuring that means and methods of warfare which exceed the threshold of permissable harm are not available to the combatants.[279] This safeguard is in recognition of the temptation to which desperate commanders in the heat of battle may succumb using such means and methods even if prohibited. Comprehensive assurance of compliance with this requirement entails sophisticated institutional and verification support.[280]

Subparagraph (d) seeks to protect the environment from being used as a means of warfare, restating current international law. This is certainly the intent of ENMOD. In addition, Additional Protocol I has been interpreted as protecting the environment *per se*, thereby precluding its use as a weapon in many instances. Indeed, the drafting history of Additional Protocol I clearly reflects an intent to prevent a belligerent from even using its own environment as a technique of warfare. The proscription of reprisals against the environment is a repetition of the requirement of Article 35(3) of Additional Protocol I and is a progression on the state of customary international law in this context.

---

275 The Conference of the Committee of Disarmament (CCD), the body under whose auspices ENMOD was negotiated, transmitted to the UN General Assembly an Understanding on Article I of ENMOD, which stated that "widespread" encompasses an area on the scale of several hundred square kilometres and "severe" involves serious or significant disruption or harm to human life, natural and economic resources or other assets. During the Diplomatic Conference which adopted Additional Protocol I, the general understanding was that "long-term" meant several decades.

276 Article 1.

277 Article 35(3).

278 Since ENMOD Convention (1976) was negotiated at the same time as Additional Protocol I (1977), it is clear that their thresholds, which are worded slightly differently, are meant to be different.

279 This, for example, is what the Chemical Weapons Convention (1993) seeks to do. The Convention on Anti-Personnel Land Mines (1997) mentions the environment and requires that each State Party report to the Secretary General of the United Nations within 180 days of the entry into force of the Convention including information on the status of programs to destroy mines details of the methods to be used, the location of destruction sites and the applicable safety and environmental standards. Note also that the Comprehensive Nuclear Test Ban Treaty (1996) in its Preamble states that "the views expressed in this treaty could contribute to the protection of the environment."

280 See e.g., the institutional and verification scheme afforded by the Chemical Weapons Convention (1993).

Paragraph 2 aims at the further development of the law on this subject, both to deal with international armed conflict and non-international armed conflict. In the latter case, there is a dearth of law which must be remedied.[281]

Paragraph 3 is intended to provide protection to sites and installations of particular importance. It is derived from existing international law,[282] although is stronger in not providing an exhaustive list or permitting exceptions. In addition, the provisions on demilitarized zones and non-defended localities in Additional Protocol I could encompass the protection of natural and cultural sites. The requirement that military personnel be specially instructed responds to a general perception that armed forces personnel generally do not appreciate the environmental effects of their actions or the relevant law on this matter. This concern is evident in UNGA Resolution 47/37, passed unanimously, which calls for, *inter alia*, improved awareness by armed forces of environmental provisions of the law of war. This perception is also behind the efforts of the ICRC to develop guidelines for military manuals on environmental protection requirements.[283]

Paragraph 4 strengthens existing international law by requiring the imposition of individual criminal responsibility for actions which exceed the threshold of permissable harm outlined in Paragraph 1(b) above.[284] In so doing, it echoes the recent efforts of the UN International Law Commission, reflected in its Draft Code of Crimes Against the Peace and Security of Mankind.[285] The intention of the provision is to satisfy the demands of deterrence and retribution by signalling that individuals will be held accountable for breaches of Paragraph 1(b). To be noted, however, is that only those offenders who act in a deliberate and intentional manner are to be so punished. Collateral damage not foreseen would, therefore, not be covered. The discretion is left to individual Parties as to how to implement this obligation. Joint action, for example through the United Nations, could be undertaken.

---

281 E.g., Additional Protocol II (1977), which applies during non-international armed conflict, parallels the obligations of Additional Protocol I (1977) in several respects, save for the complete absence in the former of provisions directly protecting the environment.

282 The duty to protect cultural sites during wartime derives from the regime established under the Hague Cultural Property Convention (1954). Article 6(3) of the World Heritage Convention (1972) extends this protection to natural sites by requiring that states refrain from taking any deliberate actions which may directly or indirectly harm the designated sites of other States. The obligation to protect potentially dangerous installations draws on the substance of Article 56 of Additional Protocol I. Article 29 of the Watercourses Convention (1997) provides that "international watercourses and related installations, facilities and other works shall enjoy the protection accorded by the principles and rules of international law applicable in international and non-international armed conflict and shall not be used in violation of those principles and rules."

283 Also see ICRC Guidelines (1994).

284 See ICRC Guidelines (1994).

285 Article 26 as adopted by the ILC in 1991, although to be noted is that the ILC's threshold is cumulative ("and") based on the wording of Article 55(1) of Additional Protocol I (1977). See also the Comprehensive Nuclear Test Ban Treaty (1996) that calls on Parties to establish jurisdiction over its nationals who violate the Treaty anywhere and over violations that occur within its territory or jurisdiction.

Paragraph 5 is intended to regulate the significant environmental threat posed by military activities during peacetime by placing them under the rubric of general environmental law. It is based on general rules of international law, according to which sovereign immunity only precludes a litigant from pursuing a cause of action against a sovereign or a party with sovereign attributes, but does not exempt such entities from the duty to respect national or international law.[286] Both the MARPOL Convention (1973) and UNCLOS (1982) require vessels with such immunity to comply as far as possible with the environmental provisions of each treaty.3[287] In other instances, environmental treaties are silent on the issue of sovereign immunity. Implementation of the Nuclear Notification Convention (1986) is noteworthy in that it has given rise to some State practice of including military submarines within its ambit despite no express requirement to do so. Moreover, domestic state practice in relation to military activities during peacetime reveals an increasing trend to take environmental considerations into account.[288]

PART VII. TRANSBOUNDARY ISSUES

The first rules of international environmental law emerged because of the need to address transboundary problems which result from the increasing human capacity to adversely affect the environment of other States.[289] The roots of the norms are traceable to both customary and treaty law. "Transboundary" in this Draft Covenant is intended to refer to matters which originate under the jurisdiction of one State and affect the environment of one or more other States,[290] or areas beyond national jurisdiction. Two central themes are apparent throughout the law. The first is the avoidance of transboundary harm and the second is the caring for transboundary natural resources, including their equitable and sustainable or reasonable use and management. Both themes are reflected in the provisions of the Draft Covenant and Commentary.

ARTICLE 33

TRANSBOUNDARY ENVIRONMENTAL EFFECTS

Parties shall take appropriate measures to prevent transboundary environmental harm. When a proposed activity may generate such harm, Parties shall:

(a) ensure that an environmental impact assessment is undertaken, as provided in Article 37;

286 E.g., Article VII (4) of the London Convention (1972).

287 Article 3(3) MARPOL Convention (1973), Article 236 UNCLOS (1982).

288 See e.g., Paragraph 32 of the Helsinki Summit Declaration of the Conference on Security and Cooperation in Europe (1992).

289 See e.g., *Trail Smelter* case.

290 This encompasses both the territory and other subjects of a State's jurisdiction (eg. vessels) and would include a State's exclusive economic zone.

(b) give prior and timely notification, along with relevant information, to potentially affected States, and consult in good faith with those States at an early stage; and

(c) grant potentially affected persons in other States access to, as well as due process in, administrative and judicial proceedings, without discrimination on the basis of residence or nationality.

Article 33 details the fundamental rule of international environmental law expressed in Article 11(b)(1) (States): that States have an obligation to prevent transboundary environmental harm.[291] This provision concerns both the actions required to avoid such harm and those required when the possibility of harm is determined to exist. As such, it is closely linked to the principle of prevention (Article 6 (Prevention)). When the harm may be significant or pose risks of irreversible harm, precaution (Article 7 (Precaution)) requires that measures be taken even if the scientific evidence is not conclusive.

The first sentence of Article 33 requires Parties to take "appropriate measures" to prevent transboundary harm, a requirement that Parties exercise "due diligence" in this regard. This obligation not only attaches to governmental activity, but implies the establishment of a framework for regulating private activities under a Party's control.[292] As the International Court of Justice stated in the *Corfu Channel* case, every State has an obligation "not to allow knowingly its territory to be used for acts contrary to the rights of other States." What constitutes due diligence will vary with each case; two relevant factors are the capabilities of the Parties and the foreseeability of the harm. To some extent, the second factor is dependant on the first, which itself is related to several other provisions of the Draft Covenant (e.g., Article 41 (Development and Transfer of Technology), Arti-

---

[291] The famous dictum laid down in the *Trail Smelter* case on the damage caused to the United States from a smelter in Canada states:

> [U]nder principles of international law ... no state has the right to use or permit the use of its territory in such a manner as to cause injury by fumes in or to the territory of another or the properties of persons therein, when the case is of serious consequence and the injury established.

Although technically *obiter dicta*, this statement has been widely accepted as a declaratory of customary international law (or else of a general principle of international law based on Article 38(1)(c) of the Statute of the International Court of Justice) and is based on the ancient principle of *sic utere iure tuo ut alienum non laedas*. See e.g., the comment made by the arbitral tribunal in the Lac Lanoux decision whereby a claim would exist against a State which pollutes a transboundary river; Article 194(2) of UNCLOS (1982); and Article 20(2) of the ASEAN Agreement (1985). See also Principle 21 of the Stockholm Declaration (1972); Principle 2 of the Rio Declaration (1992); Principle 3(3) of the UNEP Draft Principles of Conduct in the Field of the Environment for the Guidance of States in the Conservation and Harmonious Utilization of Natural Resources Shared by Two or More States (1978).

[292] This was the case, for example, in the *Trail Smelter* arbitration, where the tribunal found that Canada was responsible for regulating a private smelter under its jurisdiction. Article 192 of the UNCLOS (1982).

cle 43 (Information and Knowledge), and Article 46 (International Financial Resources)).[293] While due diligence implies that *de minimis* environmental harm is likely excluded, it does require best effort toward abatement once transfrontier harm is positively identified. This may not only involve action by the source Party, but also cooperative international action.[294] This may require Parties to cooperate with each other or with international organizations to deal with transboundary harm.[295] By seeking to also regulate threats to the environment beyond areas of national jurisdiction, this provision is reflective of the evolution of international environmental law.[296]

The second sentence of Article 33 lists the duties that arise once the risk of transboundary harm is determined to exist.[297]

The first duty, in subparagraph (a), is to undertake an environmental impact assessment (EIA) required under Article 37 (Environmental Impact Assessment). In many cases, an EIA may already have been carried out in accordance with existing rules of international law to determine whether the proposed activity could give rise to transboundary harm.[298] This will require, *inter alia*, involving the public in other affected States in the EIA process and ensuring that all concerned are advised of the final decisions and periodic reviews, in particular so that full exercise can be made of

---

293 See also Article 2 of the London Convention (1972) which links the obligation to taking effective measures with each parties' scientific, technical and economic capabilities. Also see Article 12 of the Climate Change Convention (1992), and Article 12 of the Convention on Biological Diversity (1992) which both condition fulfilment of environmental obligations by developing countries with the provision of financial resources by developed countries.

294 See also Article 15 (Prevention and Response to Emergencies) of the Draft Covenant.

295 See e.g., Article 199 of the UNCLOS (1982).

296 See e.g., Article 3 of the Convention on Biological Diversity (1992), which echoes Principle 21 of the Stockholm Declaration (1972), Principle 2 of the Rio Declaration (1992), and Article 30 of the Charter of Economic Rights and Duties of States (1974). For the marine environment, see e.g., Article 194(2) of UNCLOS (1982), and by implication other treaties aimed at protecting the marine environment by setting standards which seek to prevent, reduce, and control pollution (e.g., London Convention (1972) and MARPOL Convention (1973)). For other areas beyond national jurisdiction, see e.g., Antarctic Treaty (1959) and the Outer Space Treaty (1967); Article 1 of the Nuclear Test Ban Treaty (1963); Articles 4 and 5 of the Convention on Biological Diversity (1992); and Article 20 of the ASEAN Agreement (1985).

297 As illustrated in Article 4 of the ECE Industrial Accidents Convention (1992), positive measures, individually or jointly, may be required to identify the existence of such possibilities. Note also the inquiry procedure to be established under that Convention in cases of disagreement between parties.

298 E.g., pursuant to Article 2(7) of the Espoo Convention (1991); Article 206 of the UNCLOS (1982); Article 20(3)(a) of the ASEAN Agreement (1985); Article 12(2) of the Wider Caribbean Marine Environment Convention (1983); and Article 6 of the 1983 US-Mexico Agreement on Cooperation for the Protection and Improvement of the Environment in the Border Area. *Cf.* also Article 12 of the ILC Draft Articles on Liability (1994). Article 37 of the Watercourses Convention (1997) governs impact assessment.

any rights of judicial or administrative review. For this to be a meaningful input, a sufficient flow of information between the relevant States is necessary.[299]

The second requirement, in subparagraph (b), is to notify and consult. Notice is an important feature of international environmental law.[300] The most extensive notification provision appears in the Nordic Convention (1974). It requires that once a determination is made that a significant nuisance to another party may exist:

> ... the examining authority shall, if proclamation or publication is required in cases of that nature, send as soon as possible a copy of the documents of the case to the supervisory authority of the other State ...[301]

Article 33 requires that notification be given in a "prior and timely" fashion, which implies that the notification be given no later than that provided to a Party's own public.[302] This is perhaps best accomplished in a regular or institutionalized manner.[303] Relevant information is to accompany the notification so as to facilitate the appropriate response to the risk.[304]

---

299 See Articles 33(d) (Transboundary Natural Resources), 43 (Information and Knowledge), and 44 (Education, Training and Public Awareness) of the Draft Covenant.

300 See e.g., Article 11(b) of the Kuwait Regional Convention (1978); Article 20(3) of the ASEAN Agreement (1985); Article 4 of the ECE Industrial Accidents Convention (1992); Article V(2) of US-Canada Air Quality Agreement (1991); and Articles 14(1)(c) and (d) of the Convention on Biological Diversity (1992). See also Principle 19 of the Rio Declaration (1992); Article 15 of the ILC Draft Articles on Liability (1994). Article 4(a) of the Danube Convention (1994); Articles 11 and 12 of the Watercourses Convention (1997) require prior information on planned measures "which may have a significant adverse effect upon other watercourse states." Including available technical data and information and the results of any environmental impact assessment.

301 Article 5 of the Nordic Convention (1974).

302 See e.g., Article 2 of Annex III of the ECE Industrial Accidents Convention (1992); EC Council Directive on the assessment of the effects of certain public and private projects on the environment (1985).

303 See e.g., the role of the US-Canada International Joint Commission (established under the Boundary Waters Treaty (1909) and whose role was expanded in subsequent agreements on air and water quality); Article 12 of the River Niger Agreement (1964); and Article 3 of the Agreement between Spain and Portugal on Cooperation in Matters Affecting the Safety of Nuclear Installations in the Vicinity of the Frontier (1980).

304 Such information should include any reports on emergency planning, the factors leading to the decision on siting, information provided to the source Party's public, any preventive measures taken, as well as the results of the EIA. In cases of pollution, such information can include data on emissions and fluxes, relevant changes in national policy and industrial development, control technologies, projected cost of emission control, relevant meteorological, physicochemical, and biological data, and national, sub-regional, or regional policies on pollution control. See also the duty to exchange information in Article 43 (Information and Knowledge).

Consultation is also a fundamental element of conventional international environmental law.[305] It may be the first step to subsequent negotiations in order to equitably balance the interests of the affected Parties.[306] It may be done bilaterally or through competent international organizations.

Subparagraph (c) requires granting affected persons access to all relevant proceedings regarding the proposed activity. It is based on Article 12(4) (Persons) and is similar to Article 53 (Recourse Under Domestic Law and Non-discrimination) of the Draft Covenant. The difference is that this provision applies before plans for an activity are implemented, while Article 53 applies after the harm takes place. The proceedings in question may include administrative licensing hearings, appeals from a decision to proceed with an activity, applications for injunctions, etc. The prohibition against discrimination on the basis of residence or nationality ensures that those outside the State of origin have the same rights, both procedural and substantive, as those within that State.[307]

ARTICLE 33 BIS

PRIOR INFORMED CONSENT

Prior to the export of domestically prohibited hazardous substances and of hazardous waste, Parties shall require the prior informed consent of importing and, where appropriate, transit States.

Prior informed consent is increasingly required for trade in hazardous substances and products. In 1983, the United Nations General Assembly declared that:

> products that have been banned from domestic consumption and/or sale because they have been judged to endanger health and the environment should be sold abroad by companies, corporations or individuals only when a request for such products is

---

305 See e.g., Article 12 of the 1980 Athens Protocol to the Barcelona Convention; Article 4 of the ECE Industrial Accidents Convention (1992); Article 5 of the Espoo Convention (1991); Article 5 of the LRTAP Convention (1979); and Article 14(1)(c) of the Convention on Biological Diversity (1992). See also Lac Lanoux arbitration; Principle 19 of the Rio Declaration (1992); and Article 18 of the ILC Draft Articles on International Liability (1994).

306 See e.g., the scheme proposed by Articles 18 and 20 of the ILC Draft Articles on Liability (1994) and Article 12 of the WCED Legal Principles (1986).

307 The notion of equal access is most firmly developed in Article 3 of the Nordic Convention (1974), but also appears in the Article 2(6) of the Espoo Convention (1991), and Article XII of the Boundary Waters Treaty (1909). Article 32 of the Watercourses Convention. See also Covenant Article 52. It has been recommended in OECD Recommendations C(74) 224 and C(77) 28; UNEP Principle 14 of the 1978 Principles of Conduct in the Field of the Environment for the Guidance of States in the Conservation and Harmonious Utilization of Natural Resources Shared by Two or More States; Guideline 16(c) of the 1985 Montreal Guidelines for the Protection of the Marine Environment Against Pollution from Land-Based Sources; and Article 20 of WCED Legal Principles (1986).

received from an importing country or when the consumption of such products is officially permitted in the importing country.[308]

UNEP's London Guidelines for the Exchange of Information on Chemicals in International Trade (1987) defines prior informed consent as

> the principle that international shipment of a chemical that is banned or severely restricted in order to protect human health or the environment should not proceed without the agreement, where such agreement exists, or contrary to the decision, or the designated national authority in the importing country.

The Rotterdam Convention on the Prior Informed Consent Procedure for Certain Hazardous Chemicals and Pesticides in International Trade, 10 September 1998, 998:68, requires that prior to the export of domestically prohibited goods or hazardous wastes or other internationally regulated hazardous substances, Parties shall seek the prior informed consent of importing and, where appropriate, transit states. The principle is also included in treaties governing trade in hazardous waste.

ARTICLE 34

TRANSBOUNDARY NATURAL RESOURCES

Parties shall co-operate in the conservation, management and restoration of natural resources which occur in areas under the jurisdiction of more than one State, or fully or partly in areas beyond the limits of national jurisdiction. To this end,

(a) Parties sharing the same natural system shall manage that system as a single ecological unit notwithstanding national boundaries. They shall co-operate on the basis of equity and reciprocity, in particular through bilateral and multilateral agreements, in order to develop harmonized policies and strategies covering the entire system and the ecosystems it contains. With regard to aquatic systems, such agreements shall cover the entire catchment area, including the adjoining marine environment.

(b) Parties sharing the same species or population, whether migratory or not, shall treat such species or population as a single biological unit. They shall cooperate, in particular through bilateral and multilateral agreements, in order to maintain the species or population concerned in a favorable conservation status. In the case of a harvested species or population, all the Parties that are range states of that species or population shall cooperate in the de-

[308] UNGA res. 37/137 (1983), para. 1.

velopment and implementation of a joint management plan to ensure the sustainable use of that resource and the equitable sharing of the benefits deriving from that use.

Article 34 aims at achieving better protection for transboundary natural resources. It addresses two situations: shared natural resources and resources beyond national jurisdiction. The international challenge of coordination between the relevant actors, is more complicated in the case of resources beyond national jurisdiction where the potential for new entrants is always present.

Where no regulation exists, particularly in areas beyond national jurisdiction, natural resources are vulnerable to a phenomenon popularly referred to as the "tragedy of the commons." Resources become depleted or exhausted as each State, due to the pressures of international competition, seeks to maximize its own benefit by exploiting the resources. International cooperation is required to prevent this result. Unilateral action to protect these resources cannot succeed.

In establishing the basis for cooperative efforts, this provision attempts to conserve natural resources to ensure their sustainable exploitation and to protect their integrity *per se*. Existing international law on this vital issue is piecemeal and uneven, dealing mostly with the issue of transboundary waters[309] and their living resources.[310] Recent treaties have been concluded on the management of air quality[311] and migratory species.[312] But effective regulation of transboundary resources must cover activities affecting all environmental media and sectors. A general "soft law" instrument on this topic was drawn up under the auspices of UNEP in 1978.[313]

---

309 E.g., ECE Transboundary Watercourses Convention (1992); Boundary Waters Treaty (1909); Rhine Chemicals Convention (1976). See the Watercourses Convention (1997) and the Danube Convention (1994) which in Article 1 defines Danubian States as states "sharing a considerable part of the hydrological catchment area of the Danube River." A considerable part is presumed if it exceeds 2000 square kms of the total hydrological catchment area. Catchment area means the hydrological river basin. There has also been a substantial amount of international litigation on international waterways, e.g., *River Oder*, *River Meuse*, and *Lac Lanoux* cases.

310 See e.g., Articles 63 and 64 of UNCLOS (1982); and generally Rhine Fishing Convention (1885); Whaling Convention (1946); Antarctic Marine Living Resources Convention (1980); *Behring Seals* arbitration, *Fisheries Jurisdiction* case.

311 Climate Change Convention (1992); the 1987 Montreal Protocol to the Geneva Convention on the Ozone Layer; LRTAP Convention (1979); and US-Canada Air Quality Agreement (1991).

312 Convention on Migratory Species (1980), Berne Convention on European Wildlife (1979), Birds Convention (1950), EC Council Directive on the Conservation of Wild Birds (1979), Polar Bears Agreement (1973), and the Convention on Biological Diversity (1992).

313 Draft Principles of Conduct in the Field of the Environment for the Guidance of States in the Conservation and Harmonious Utilization of Natural Resources Shared By Two or More States. See also Article 18 of WCED Legal Principles (1986), Principle 21 of Stockholm Declaration (1972) and Principle 2 of Rio Declaration (1992)).

At root, Article 34 stems from the general obligation of States to cooperate with each other, contained in Article 11(3) (States).[314] It balances the sovereign rights of States over their resources (Article 11(1)) with their duty to protect the global environment as a "common concern" (e.g., Article 3 (Common Concern of Humanity)). In this regard, it appears, on the basis of State practice, that a rule of customary international law has emerged requiring States to cooperate in the conservation and management of transboundary natural resources, although its operational aspects have not yet crystallized.[315]

Transboundary natural resources should be conserved and managed so as to yield sustainable benefit to present generations, while maintaining the potential to meet the needs and aspirations of future generations.[316] This entails preservation, maintenance, and enhancement of such resources. "Restoration" refers to action to rehabilitate, repair and return to former levels the resources covered by this Article. The most effective way to carry out each of these functions is to establish appropriate institutions.[317]

Subparagraph (a) requires Parties to manage shared natural systems as ecological units, through the conclusion of agreements that harmonise and develop policies and strategies. This entails protecting the integrity of each ecosystem as a whole as well as all its component parts. An "ecosystem" should be thought of as the complex of relationships between all living beings and their non-living environment. The focus on ecosystems[318] results from a recognition that rules on the component parts of the environment are bound to fail when the system as a whole breaks down. The components can only be conserved through protection of the entire supporting environment. One crucial factor in achieving such protection is the use of best available technologies for activities that impact on these resources.[319] One technique in the international protection of ecosystems is the establishment of "specially protected" or "particularly sensitive" areas.[320]

---

314 Article 5 of the Convention on Biological Diversity (1992) also echoes this sentiment.

315 See e.g., *Behring Sea Fur Seals and Fisheries Jurisdiction* cases. See also Article 8 of the WCED Legal Principles (1986).

316 See also Article 5 (Inter-generational Equity) of the Draft Covenant.

317 E.g., Commission for the Conservation of Antarctic Marine Living Resources and International Whaling Commission.

318 See, especially Articles I and II of Antarctic Marine Living Resources Convention (1980), but also see Article II of the Polar Bears Agreement (1973), Article 2(2)(d) of ECE Transboundary Watercourses Convention (1992), and, generally, the Convention on Biological Diversity (1992). See, in addition to the Treaties concerning Antarctica, the Convention Concerning the Protection of the Alps (1991) with its Protocols, and the Arctic Environmental Protection Strategy.

319 Principle 11 of the World Charter for Nature (1982).

320 Article III of the African Convention (1968); See also Western Hemisphere Convention (1940); ASEAN Agreement (1985); 1982 Geneva Protocol Concerning Mediterranean Specially Protected Areas to the Barcelona Convention; 1991 Madrid Protocol to the Antarctic Treaty.

Aquatic systems are singled out for special attention on account of their special significance, requiring agreements to cover entire catchment areas including the adjoining marine environment. The Watercourses Convention (1997) establishes a basic framework for cooperation. Article 5 requires equitable and reasonable utilization with a view to obtaining optimal and sustainable utilization thereof and benefits therefrom consistent with adequate protection of the watercourse." All watercourse states should participate in the use, development and protection of an international watercourse in an equitable and reasonable manner, which includes both the right to utilize the watercourse and the duty to cooperate in the protection and development thereof.

Regarding non-living resources, there is a long history of efforts at legal regulation. Numerous early bilateral treaties deal with international watercourses. In recent times, such efforts have expanded to include the high seas,[321] the atmosphere,[322] outer space,[323] and resources in Antarctica.[324] The international regulation of such resources is often bedeviled by social, political and scientific complexities. Hence, it has often proved advantageous to establish joint institutions, such as commissions, to handle day-to-day matters.[325] Such institutions not only provide a venue for the conduct of authoritative scientific research, they are a focal point for the international relations of the parties concerned, particularly for notification and consultation concerning uses which may pose risks to the resource, and for developing regimes of equitable utilization.[326] Such institutions can, in addition, help prevent international disputes, especially when conflicting uses require accommodation.

Subparagraph (b) focuses on shared species or populations, because cooperation between States in protecting migratory species is vital for their survival.[327] Maintaining such species or populations in a favourable conservation status requires that: (a) exploitation be permitted only on a rational basis taking into account scientific advice;[328] (b) the entire range of the species be regu-

---

321 E.g., UNCLOS (1982) and MARPOL Convention (1973).

322 E.g., LRTAP Convention (1979), Vienna Convention on the Ozone Layer (1985), the 1987 Montreal Protocol to the Vienna Convention on the Ozone Layer, and the Climate Change Convention (1992).

323 E.g., Nuclear Test Ban Treaty (1963), Outer Space Treaty (1967) and the Moon Treaty (1979).

324 Madrid Protocol (1991) to the Antarctic Treaty.

325 Examples of this are numerous: Canada-US Joint Commission, Rhine Commission, OSPAR Commission, River Niger Commission, and the committees established under the Antarctic Treaty system.

326 E.g., Article IX of the North Pacific Seals Convention (1957), where only the US and the USSR can seal, but a percentage of their take is to be delivered to Japan and Canada.

327 The obligation to cooperate is rooted in both customary and treaty law. Examples of the latter include especially the Convention on Migratory Species (1979) and Agreements adopted under it; Interim Convention on the Conservation of North Pacific Fur Seals, as amended; International Convention for the Conservation of Atlantic Tunas (1966); Article VII of the Western Hemisphere Convention (1940) and Article 10 of the Berne Convention on European Wildlife (1979). Also see UNGA Resolutions 2995(XXVII) and 2996(XXVII).

328 E.g., as done by the International Whaling Commission.

lated,[329] and (c) all ecological factors affecting species and habitat be considered.[330] Thus, compliance with this provision requires, for example, the conservation of wetlands in order to protect migratory waterbirds.[331]

It also requires that Parties jointly elaborate management plans in the case of harvestable transboundary biological resources, to ensure that these resources are exploited on a sustainable basis. The developing of management plans implies considering all threats to the resource. At a minimum, this will require consideration of the need to establish quotas and seasons for permissible taking, as well as the need to counter indirect threats, such as habitat loss, threats to associated species, and international trade. It is preferable that management plans be legally binding, but if this is not practicable in particular instances, States should nonetheless ensure that they are established in such a way as to command broad adherence. One method of creating popular legitimacy for the plan is to convene public hearings for communities and industries involved in the exploitation of the resources in question, permitting the public to have an input in the drafting process. Popular legitimacy for the process will be further enhanced if it is designed to lead to an equitable sharing of benefits.[332]

PART VIII. IMPLEMENTATION AND COOPERATION

This is the operational section of the Draft Covenant, setting forth the detailed national and international measures required of Parties. It includes legal procedures, scientific and management measures, and provisions for financial and technological sharing. Like other parts of the Draft Covenant, it affirms the need for public participation and information. All the measures are progressive and their implementation should keep pace with the evolution of environmental and developmental problems and conditions.

ARTICLE 35

NATIONAL ACTION PLANS

Parties shall establish action plans, with targets and time-tables, and update them as necessary, to meet the objective of this Covenant.

Article 35 mandates that each Party establish action plans to meet the objective of the Draft Covenant. Environmental management in many countries is based on local and regional action

---

329 See Article 2 of the Convention on Migratory Species (1980).

330 See Berne Convention on European Wildlife (1979) and EC Council Directive on the Conservation of Wild Birds (1979).

331 This is required under Article 3 of the Ramsar Convention (1971).

332 *Cf.* Article 42 (Sharing of Benefits).

plans.[333] The content of such plans must be systematic and specific, which explains the reference to targets and time-tables. The wording of this provision leaves open the issue of whether these targets and timetables are to be determined nationally or internationally. If the latter route is chosen, this might be done by way of the Review Conference (Article 63). Alternatively it may be decided by each individual Party in its discretion.[334] Whichever path the Parties to the Draft Covenant adopt, its effectiveness should be a matter taken up at each Review Conference. Elaborating action plans can facilitate effective and informed public participation (Article 12(3) (Persons)). Ideally, this process can help to consolidate a national consensus around implementing the Draft Covenant.[335] The plans can also form the basis of each Party's national reports (Article 60 (Reporting)). A further and fundamental benefit is that Parties may identify their sustainable developmental potential and needs. This determination will facilitate effective implementation of many of the Draft Covenant's obligations.

The necessity to update action plans emphasizes the dynamic character of this obligation. The title is not intended to exclude the possibility of international action plans where appropriate, of which the Stockholm Plan of Action (1972) and Agenda 21 (1992) are the leading examples. Bilateral or regional ones may also be appropriate.

ARTICLE 36

PHYSICAL PLANNING

1. **Parties shall establish and implement integrated physical planning systems, including provisions for infrastructure and town and country planning, with a view to integrating conservation of the environment, including biological diversity, into social and economic development.**

2. **In such planning, Parties shall take into account natural systems, in particular drainage basins, coastal areas and their adjacent waters, and any other areas constituting identifiable ecological units.**

---

333 Article 10 of the Desertification Convention (1994) calls for national actions plans and Article 11 calls for subregional and regional action plans.

334 There are precedents in international law for both approaches: (1) the 1987 Montreal Protocol clearly establishes targets and timetables in the body of its text and allows the Conference of the Parties to make adjustments as necessary; whereas (2) the Climate Change Convention (1992) leaves it to the discretion of each Party (see Article 4(2)). Note too the obligation in the Convention on Biological Diversity (1992) on Parties to develop strategies, plans or programmes on the conservation and sustainable use of biological diversity (Article 6(a)) and the recommendation in Agenda 21 (1992) and Principle 3 of the Forest Principles (1992) that governments adopt sustainable development strategies.

335 See also Paragraph 37.5 of Agenda 21 (1992).

3. Parties shall take into account the natural characteristics and ecological constraints of areas when allocating them for agricultural, grazing, forestry, or other use.

Article 36 requires Parties to establish physical planning systems as a means of integrating environmental and developmental objectives (see Article 13 (Integrating Environment and Development)). It is based on the assumption that sustainable development requires maintaining the functions and carrying capacities of natural systems.[336] As such, it calls for an integrated approach to land-use.[337]

Paragraph 1 lays down the basic principle underlying this Article and applies it to all forms of physical planning. To illustrate, two examples are mentioned on account of their particular significance. Planning should apply to all forms of infrastructures, such as highways, railways, waterways, dams, harbours, etc. Town and country planning includes land-use plans elaborated at all levels of government.

Paragraph 2 requires that ecological systems be taken into account. As stated in Article 20(2) (Natural Systems), natural systems constituting identifiable ecological units must be viewed as single units for purposes of physical planning, irrespective of administrative boundaries within a country.[338] Two examples are highlighted for special mention, namely drainage basins and coastal areas and their adjacent waters. Drainage basins, or watersheds, should be considered single planning units because events upstream have downstream effects.[339] Coastal areas and the adjacent waters also form ecological units, but often the administrative split between land and sea makes effective management of such areas as units difficult if not impossible. This paragraph aims to cure that situation.

Paragraph 3 is based on Paragraph 10.5 of Agenda 21, which seeks to "facilitate allocation of land to the uses that provide the greatest sustainable benefits and to promote the transition to a sustainable and integrated management of land resources."[340]

---

336 See e.g., Principles 7 and 16 of the World Charter for Nature (1982).

337 See Chapter 10 of Agenda 21 (1992).

338 This notion is contained in several legal precedents: Article 3(1) of the Ramsar Convention (1971); Article 6(b) of the Convention on Biological Diversity (1992) and most comprehensively in Article 12 of the ASEAN Agreement (1985). See also Paragraph 10.7(a) of Agenda 21 (1992). For transboundary natural systems see Article 34 of this Draft Covenant.

339 E.g., deforestation in the upper reaches of an estuary may cause siltation in the estuary of the main stream, and dams may adversely affect water regime or prevent siltation essential to the maintenance of deltas.

340 See also Principles 13 and 14 of the Stockholm Declaration (1972) and Principle 9 of the World Charter for Nature (1982).

ARTICLE 37

ENVIRONMENTAL IMPACT ASSESSMENT

1. Parties shall establish or strengthen environmental impact assessment procedures to ensure that all activities which are likely to have a significant adverse effect on the environment are evaluated before approval.

2. The assessment shall include evaluation of:

(a) cumulative, long-term, indirect, long-distance, and transboundary effects,

(b) the possible alternative actions, including not conducting the proposed activity, and

(c) measures to avert or minimize the potential adverse effects.

3. Parties shall designate appropriate national authorities to ensure that environmental impact assessments are effective and conducted under procedures accessible to concerned States, international organizations, persons and non-governmental organizations. Parties shall also ensure that the authority deciding on approval takes into consideration all observations made during the environmental impact assessment process and makes its final decision public.

4. Parties shall conduct periodic reviews both to determine whether activities approved by them are carried out in compliance with the conditions set out in the approval and to evaluate the effectiveness of the prescribed mitigation measures. The results of such reviews shall be made public.

5. Parties shall take appropriate measures to ensure that before they adopt policies, programs, and plans that are likely to have a significant adverse effect on the environment, the environmental consequences of such actions are duly taken into account.

Environmental Impact Assessments (EIAs) are a feature of modern domestic[341] and international[342] environmental law. First established in the United States under the National Environmen-

---

341 A large number of jurisdictions have either adopted legislation or guidelines on their use. See also the recommendation in the Business Charter for Sustainable Development.

342 See especially Espoo Convention (1991), which is the most comprehensive international instrument on EIAs. In addition other instruments make reference to EIAs: e.g., Article 14(1)(a) of the Conven-

tal Policy Act, EIAs are universally recognized as a fundamentally important process in the achievement of two results: (1) to inform decision-makers of the environmental consequences of their decisions[343] and (2) to integrate environmental matters into other spheres of decision-making.[344] The latter purpose recalls the obligations of integrating environment and development (Article 13 (Integrating Environment and Development)). A subsidiary but still important purpose of EIAs is to allow governments to inform, and hear the views of, the interested public on particular activities.[345] As such, this provision should be read in conjunction with the obligations to allow public participation (Article 12(3) (Persons)), and to provide environmental information (Article 43 (Information and Knowledge)), a prerequisite to meaningful public participation. The importance of EIAs was highlighted by the UNEP Legal Experts Group on the Montevideo Programme which added a programme area to promote the widespread use of EIAs.

EIAs are essential means of complying with the fundamental principles of Prevention (Article 6) and Precaution (Article 7). In addition, in the context of transboundary environmental harm, they form part of each State's obligation under general international law not to knowingly cause harm to other States.[346] As implementation of some of the EIA requirements demands significant resources, Article 46 (International Financial Resources) on transferring financial resources is relevant.[347] This is one notable area where States can seek to pursue policies expressed in this Draft Covenant in international organizations of which they are members (Article 11(5) (States)).[348]

Article 37 sets out differing requirements depending on whether the matter in question is an activity (or project), policy, or plan.

---

tion on Biological Diversity (1982); Article 4(1)(f) of the Climate Change Convention (1992), where it is a suggested means for complying with the provision; Article 206 of the UNCLOS (1982); Article XI of the Kuwait Regional Convention (1978); Article 13 of the West and Central African Marine Environment Convention (1981); Article 10 of the South-East Pacific Marine Environment Convention (1981); Article 14 of the ASEAN Agreement (1985). There are also several "soft law" instruments which call for EIAs: Principle 17 of Rio Declaration (1992). This is also complied in UNGA Resolution 2995 (XXVII) on Cooperation between States in the Field of the Environment (1972); Principles 11(b) and (c) of the World Charter for Nature (1982); UNEP Goals and Principles of Environmental Impact Assessment (1987); Note that Article 5 of the WCED Legal Principles (1986) suggests EIAs are an emerging principle of international law.

343 See e.g., UNEP Goals and Principles of Environmental Impact Assessment (1987).

344 This is identified in Paragraph 8.2 of Agenda 21 (1992) as an important objective and EIAs are pinpointed as a crucial means of achieving this.

345 E.g., Paragraph 8.4(f) of Agenda 21 (1992).

346 E.g., *Corfu Channel* case.

347 See also Article 202(c) of UNCLOS (1982).

348 Some international organizations already have EIA policies, see e.g., World Bank Operational Directive 4.00 (1989).

Paragraph 1 deals with activities, where the assessment requirements are most rigorous. This provision applies to both public activities and to private ones requiring governmental approval, whether on the territory of the particular State or otherwise.[349]

The triggering element for the EIA requirement is a determination that the activity is "likely to have significant adverse effect on the environment," in which case an EIA is to take place before each government grants approval. This standard was affirmed in the Rio Declaration,[350] after finding acceptance in some regional instruments.[351] Although "significant" is not defined, it involves consideration of both context and intensity,[352] and is less than serious but greater than *de minimis* or appreciable.

The provision allows individual Parties the discretion as to which method of determining the presence of the triggering element best suits them. This pattern is well-established and in effect sets up a two-step legal process for EIAs; the first determines whether the significant harm is likely, followed by a more extensive inquiry after such likelihood is found. State practice illustrates several possible options. One approach is to utilize a case-by-case procedure,[353] although this is prone to raise controversies over individual decisions and possible protracted litigation. Another is to make reference to lists of activities that are deemed to trigger the EIA requirement.[354] A third approach is to develop a list of sensitive areas or particularly pressing environmental problems. Any activity that adversely affects the area or exacerbates the problem will be deemed "significant."[355] A further approach is to create a presumption of significant environmental impacts for

---

349 Note that Article 6 of the Nordic Convention (1974) requires in certain circumstances each party to conduct an EIA for activities carried out in the territory of another party. See also Article 206 of UNCLOS (1982) on EIAs which applies to areas beyond national jurisdiction.

350 Principle 17 of the Rio Declaration (1992).

351 E.g., Article 14(1) of the ASEAN Agreement (1985); Article 12(2) of the Wider Caribbean Marine Environment Convention (1983) and; Article 2(2) of the Espoo Convention (1991). See also EC Council Directive on the assessment of the effects of certain public and private projects on the environment (1985)

352 See e.g., regulations implementing the National Environmental Policy Act, (USA) 40 CFR § 1508.27 (1992).

353 E.g., this is the model adopted by the US National Environmental Policy Act, which involves an initial quick and informal assessment to determine if the threshold is reached.

354 EC Council Directive on the assessment of the effects of certain public and private projects on the environment (1985) mixes these two approaches in that Annex I contains a list of projects where EIA's are required and Annex II is an illustrative list of projects where EIA's are not required unless they are found to have "significant effects on the environment".

355 See e.g., Article 1(b) of Appendix III of Espoo Convention (1991); Environmental Impact Assessment Act of 1990 of the Canary Islands; Act on Environmental Protection of 1986 of Greece; and Act on the Conservation of Natural Areas and of Wild Flora and Fauna of 1989 of France; and California Environmental Quality Guidelines.

activities that cross a monetary threshold.[356] Finally, it may be appropriate, in certain cases, to require EIAs when there is a change in ownership of an enterprise (activity).[357] Whichever approach, or combination of approaches, is adopted, EIAs should be conducted at an early stage of planning.[358]

Paragraph 2 contains a non-exhaustive list of factors which must be included in EIAs. Subparagraph (a) is drafted to ensure that all possible types of significant impacts are considered during the EIA process.[359] "Effects" includes all significant impacts on the environment as a whole, as well as its components.[360]

Experience has shown that the most difficult concept to incorporate into EIAs is "cumulative" effects. The term covers not only the incremental and synergistic impacts of several connected activities taken together, but also the aggregate effects of a single activity.[361] The focus should be on the connectedness of the impacts, rather than of the activities,[362] although it should include impacts from all related activities, even where individually the impacts would not be significant.[363] In this regard, the establishment of regional baselines as well as EIAs for programmes can be useful.

"Long-term" should be interpreted broadly, and is intended to be forward-looking over a period of several decades.[364] "Long-distance" can include transboundary[365] effects, but can also includes internal ones.

---

356 E.g., Article 2 of the French Law on the Protection of Nature (1976) and Decree (1977). Note that the legislation address the possibility of developers seeking to evade the EIA requirements by sub-dividing their projects into smaller monetary units. The US approach for preventing segmentation may be useful here, in which the connectedness of actions is defined (see 40 CFR § 1508.25(a)(1) (1992)).

357 See e.g., New Jersey Environmental Cleanup Responsibility Act (USA), which requires the filing of a cleanup plan which implicitly includes an EIA, for the transfer or closing of hazardous wastes sites which must be approved by the Government. See also Article 8(3) of the 1991 Madrid Protocol to the Antarctic Treaty which requires EIAs for any change in an activity.

358 See e.g., Principle 1 of the UNEP Goals and Principles of Environmental Impact Assessment (1987).

359 These effects are listed, *inter alia*, in Principle 4(d) of the UNEP Goals and Principles of Environmental Impact Assessment (1987) as among the minimum to be considered in an EIA.

360 Guidance is available from Article 1(vii) of the Espoo Convention (1991) which defines "impact" as:

> "any effect caused by a proposed activity on the environment including human health and safety, flora, fauna, soil, air, water, climate, landscape and historical monuments or other physical structures of the interaction among these factors; it also includes effects on cultural heritage or socio-economic conditions resulting from alterations to those factors."

361 This is the scope of the term provided for in the Regulations of the California Environmental Quality Act (USA).

362 As the US 5th Circuit Court did in *Fritiofson v. Alexander* (1985).

363 See e.g., *Kings County Farm Bureau v. City of Hanford* (USA).

364 The same expression appears in Articles 35(3) and 55 of the Additional Protocol I (1977) to the 1949 Geneva Conventions, and was intended to by the Diplomatic Conference adopting the Protocol to be

Subparagraph (b) requires Parties to consider alternatives to the activity in question. This means all reasonable alternatives,[366] including the option of not conducting the activity.[367] Subparagraph (c) requires the identification of so-called "mitigation measures." The grant of development permits should be conditional upon the carrying out of any such measures.

Paragraph 3 has several aspects. First, EIAs must be carried out in the desired manner by authority of some governmental institution, although the issue of who actually conducts the EIA is left to the individual Party. The provision requires that those concerned have access to the EIA procedure.[368] This will not require holding a full public hearing in every instance, but at minimum a sufficient notice and comment period is necessary to satisfy this provision. Also implicit in the term "accessible" is that all publicly available documents include a non-technical summary. This Paragraph also aims to ensure that the observations made during the EIA process are taken into account by the relevant decision-maker when determining whether the activity will proceed.[369] The requirement that the final decision be made public is to ensure public accountability, so that citizens can exercise any right of review, judicial or otherwise. The manner in which the decision is made public is left open, although in written form in official or mass media would likely have the widest audience.

Paragraph 4 requires periodic reviews in order to achieve two express goals: (1) measure compliance with the terms of the development permit; and (2) assess the adequacy of prescribed mitigation measures.[370] The former allows a State to follow up with enforcement or other compliance measures. The latter is more forward looking, designed to instruct future decision-makers which mitigation measures are likely to be effective. A third, unstated, objective is to evaluate whether environmental impacts have occurred as they have been predicted. The periodicity is to be determined by each State in accordance with the criteria of appropriateness and effectiveness. Consideration should be given to holding reviews at the request of the public or other States. Again, the public disclosure is designed to facilitate accountability.

---

interpreted as such. It is to be contrasted with the term "long-lasting" in the ENMOD Convention (1976), which was intended to refer to a period encompassing several months, possibly a season (see Understanding on Article I submitted by the Committee of the Conference on Disarmament to the UN General Assembly).

365 As in Part VII of the Draft Covenant, "transboundary" refers to effects which cross a national frontier, whether extending to another State or the global commons, as well as effects only in the global commons.

366 The Espoo Convention (1991) identifies locational or technological variations as possible reasonable alternatives (Appendix II).

367 This is an expressed alternative to consider in the Espoo Convention (1991) (Appendix II).

368 The inclusion of States and international organizations in this list is intended to be for cases of potential transboundary environmental harm (see Article 33 (Transboundary Environmental Effects)).

369 Article 6(1) of the Espoo Convention (1991) requires that "due account" be taken of the EIA.

370 This provision is modelled on Article 7 and Appendix V of the Espoo Convention (1991).

Finally, Paragraph 5 addresses policies, programmes and plans. These are not subject to as rigorous an assessment process as activities are, but in recognition of the significant environmental effects these may have, some evaluation before implementation is required.[371] The results of any evaluation should be considered at the decision-making stage and any mitigation measures identified should be implemented.

ARTICLE 38

ENVIRONMENTAL STANDARDS AND CONTROLS

1. **Parties shall co-operate to formulate, develop, and strengthen international rules, standards and recommended practices on issues of common concern for the protection and preservation of the environment and sustainable use of natural resources, taking into account the need for flexible means of implementation based on their respective capabilities.**

2. **Parties shall adopt, strengthen and implement specific national standards, including emission, quality, product, and process standards, designed to prevent or abate harm to the environment or to restore or enhance environmental quality.**

Article 38 concerns national and international standard-setting. The dynamic nature of this obligation is reflected in the use of the term "strengthen" in both paragraphs and the reference to enhancing environmental quality in Paragraph 2. The order of the paragraphs indicates that national standards should be based on international norms and that due account should be taken of non-binding recommendations and similar texts.

Like UNCLOS (1982) and other treaties,[372] Paragraph 1 of this Article obligates Parties to co-operate in the formulation of international rules and standards. There is a need for harmonization and coordination in addressing issues of common concern, in particular for protection of the global

---

[371] This notion is a new one, but which has been recognized in international environmental law, e.g., Article 14(1)(b) of the Convention on Biological Diversity (1992). Note also that the EC has committed itself to EIA its own plans and programmes (EC Fifth Environmental Action Programme *Towards Sustainability* (1993)), which has manifested itself, for example, in the 1992 Council Directive on the Conservation of Natural Habitats and of Wild Flora and Fauna. At the national level, France requires a "presentation report" for municipal land-use plans, which includes an initial analysis of the state of the environment and the effect of the plan on its evolution. In addition, the US has instituted assessments for grazing on Bureau of Land Management lands and Ontario has recently environmentally reviewed its forestry project.

[372] Article 197 of UNCLOS (1982); Article 4(2) of the Barcelona Convention (1976); Article 2(1 and 2) of the North-East Atlantic Convention (1992).

commons. This will avoid conflicts and competitive distortions and enhance the reduction or elimination of trade barriers. Although the norms to be adopted are to be jointly agreed, the needs of developing countries are taken into account in the call for flexible means of implementation. This corresponds to the concept of common but differentiated responsibilities enunciated at Rio. To be noted is that, as far as possible, international standards should be based on achieving a higher level of environmental protection.[373] Given their different ecological, social and economic circumstances, individual Parties should not be prejudiced in their right to set more stringent environmental standards, provided that they are not disguised barriers to trade (see Article 30(1)(c) (Trade and Environment)).

On the national level, addressed in Paragraph 2, measures should address causes of environmental deterioration (products, processes and emissions) and mandate environmental quality.[374] Standards should be both preventive and remedial.

ARTICLE 39

MONITORING OF ENVIRONMENTAL QUALITY

1. **Parties shall conduct scientific research and establish, strengthen, and implement scientific monitoring programs for the collection of environmental data and information to determine, *inter alia*,**

   (a) **the condition of all components of the environment, including changes in the status of natural resources; and**

   (b) **the effects, especially the cumulative or synergistic effects, of particular substances, activities, or combinations thereof on the environment.**

2. **To this end and as appropriate, Parties shall co-operate with each other and with competent international organizations.**

Scientific research is the basis of action for environmental protection. Reliable data on what is the environment, its status, its deterioration and the causes of such deterioration are indispensable for the adoption of the measures required by Article 38 (Environmental Standards and Controls) as well as for their effectively implementation. The primary obligation is to develop and strengthen research on the national level.[375] However, the dimensions of environmental problems are such that

---

373 See e.g., Articles 100A(3) and 130(r)(2) of the EC Treaty as amended by the Maastricht Treaty on European Union.

374 *Cf.* Principle 11 of the Rio Declaration (1992).

375 For a similar requirement in the context of waste management, see Article 19 of the Cairo Guidelines on Hazardous Wastes (1987).

international cooperation is necessary in many cases, such as long-range air or river pollution, the protection of the ozone layer, international trade in endangered species, and the condition of the seas. On the other hand, all the States concerned do not have the capacity to conduct research. Unless they have the assistance of other States and appropriate international organizations, they will be unable to fulfil this obligation. Thus the duty to co-operate is reiterated in Paragraph 2.

ARTICLE 40

SCIENTIFIC AND TECHNICAL COOPERATION

1. **Parties shall promote scientific and technical cooperation in the field of environmental conservation and sustainable use of natural resources, in particular with developing countries. In promoting such cooperation, special attention should be given to the development and strengthening of national capacities, through the development of human resources, legislation and institutions.**

2. **Parties shall:**

   (a) **cooperate to establish comparable or standardized research techniques, harmonize international methods to measure environmental parameters, and promote widespread and effective participation of all States in establishing such international methodologies;**

   (b) **exchange, on a regular basis, appropriate scientific, technical and legal data, information and experience, in particular concerning the status of biological resources; and**

   (c) **inform each other on their environmental conservation measures and endeavor to coordinate such measures.**

To facilitate the monitoring required in Article 39 (Monitoring of Environmental Quality), Article 40 calls for the cooperation of Parties in scientific research and the sharing of the results of research. This is not an innovation, because such co-operation exists in fact at the inter-governmental level, as well as in the academic and scientific communities of different countries. It is also required by numerous treaties on environmental protection and sustainable development.[376] Article 40 stresses the global nature of the obligation, particularly for the benefit of developing countries which may lack the human and material resources at present for scientific research and technological development. This also may include transfer of environmentally sound technology as dealt with in Article 41 (Development and Transfer of Technology).

---

376 See e.g., Article 4(1)(g) and (h) of the Climate Change Convention (1992); Article 200 of UNCLOS (1982) and Articles 7 and 8 of the LRTAP (1979).

Paragraph 1 is based on Article 18(2) of the Convention on Biological Diversity (1992). The emphasis on cooperation with developing countries is in recognition of the vast technological gap between the industrialized and developing worlds. The express intent of the provision is that developing countries can improve their national capacities through such cooperation.[377]

Paragraph 2 establishes essential aspects of scientific and technical co-operation. The rationale for subparagraph (a) is that it is impossible to adequately assess the state of the global environment and to remedy its deterioration without a degree of standardization and harmonization of research techniques, data, and methodologies.[378] Given the importance of this objective, the call for "widespread and effective participation of all States" implies the provision of financial and technical assistance e.g., to, allow developing countries to send qualified representatives to all the international meetings.[379] Secondly, subparagraph (b) sets forth the requirement that the exchange of general information must be regular, which suggests an ongoing and systematic process.[380] "Appropriate," in this case means in relation to the objective of the Draft Covenant. A formalized system of information exchange might, in some circumstances, prove the most effective.[381] Subparagraph (c) implies a slightly more stringent obligation than the previous subparagraph, in that the requirement to "inform" each other about environmental conservation measures suggests that this be done as soon as they are enacted.[382] Although Parties are left with the discretion as to the appropriate content and form of this information, the importance of the particular subject-matter should be a useful criterion. "Environmental conservation measures" should be interpreted broadly to encompass all measures relating to the Draft Covenant.[383]

---

377 See e.g., Article 5 of the Climate Change Convention (1992); Articles 202(a) and 203 of UNCLOS (1982); Article 7 of the WCED Legal Principles (1986); Principles 9 and 12 of Stockholm Declaration (1972) and Principle 9 of the Rio Declaration (1992).

378 See e.g., Article 18(2) of the ASEAN Agreement (1985), Basket 2(5) of the Helsinki Final Act (1975), Paragraphs 40.8 and 40.9 of Agenda 21 (1992). See also Article 39(2) (Monitoring of Environmental Quality) of the Draft Covenant.

379 See Article 200 of UNCLOS (1982).

380 Exchange of data is related to Article 43 (Information and Knowledge), and is a feature in many treaties, e.g., Article 7(1) of the Agreement between Poland and the USSR Concerning the Use of Water Resources in Frontier Waters (1964); Article VI of the Indus Waters Treaty Between India and Pakistan (1960); Article 2(c) of the River Niger Agreement (1964); Article 18(2)(d) of the ASEAN Agreement; Article 10 of the Basel Convention (1989). See also Principle 20 of the Stockholm Declaration (1972).

381 See e.g., Article 18(3) of the Convention on Biological Diversity (1992), which establishes a clearinghouse mechanism to promote and facilitate technical and scientific cooperation.

382 See Article 4(1)(h) of the Climate Change Convention (1992).

383 Accordingly, this provision also relate to others in the Draft Covenant, such as Articles 24 (Pollution), and 34 (Transboundary Natural Resources).

ARTICLE 41

DEVELOPMENT AND TRANSFER OF TECHNOLOGY

Parties shall encourage and strengthen cooperation for the development and use, as well as access to and transfer of, environmentally sound technologies on mutually agreed terms, with a view to accelerating the transition to sustainable development, in particular by establishing joint research programs and joint ventures.

Article 41 looks to the development and transfer of technology as a means to achieve sustainable development.[384] This technology is to be "environmentally sound" and should aim to reflect the state-of-the-art, although traditional technologies are also to be included. These technologies include "process," "product," and "end-of-pipe," and include know-how, procedures, goods, services, equipment, and managerial procedures.[385] Such transfer should be placed in the framework of joint research programmes and joint ventures, crafted to combine the strengths of the participants and builds capacity to strengthen areas of weakness.[386] All Parties should effectively draw on the experience and advice of the private sector, especially scientists, business, and non-governmental organizations, in determining their policies with regard to transfer of technology.

Effective technology transfer can be greatly enhanced by regular exchange of information, which allows Parties to know what is the state-of-the-art, as well as the sources and environmental risks of such technology.[387] Information clearinghouses can help Parties identify what their particular technological needs are and how they can be accommodated.[388] In addition, technical assistance should take place as appropriate in respect of assessing what each Party needs, what is "environmentally sound," and how specific technologies can be used.[389] Capacity-building should also take place so that developing countries can further develop technologies in which they have a comparative advantage, particularly through joint ventures with Parties in industrialized countries.[390]

---

384 This Article is standard in recent international environmental treaties: see e.g., Article 4(2) of the Vienna Convention on the Ozone Layer (1985); Article 5(2) of the 1987 Montreal Protocol; Article 4(5) of the Climate Change Convention (1992); Article 144 and Part XIV of UNCLOS (1982); and Article 10(d) of the Basel Convention (1989). Also see Articles 4 and 5 of the Cairo Guidelines on Hazardous Wastes (1987) which include specific provisions for international co-operation in the development and transfer of environmentally sound technologies. Article 17 of the Desertification Convention (1994).

385 Paragraphs 34.2 and 34.3 of Agenda 21 (1992).

386 See Article 40 (Scientific and Technical Cooperation). See also Article 18(5) of the Convention on Biological Diversity (1992).

387 See Paragraph 34.15 of Agenda 21 (1992).

388 See Paragraphs 34.16 and 34.17 of Agenda 21 (1992).

389 See Paragraphs 34.22 - 34.24 and 34.26 of Agenda 21 (1992)

390 See Paragraph 34.20 of Agenda 21 (1992). See also Paragraph 34.27 of Agenda 21 (1992), which emphasizes the positive roles multinational corporations can play in this regard.

Although not mentioned expressly, this provision contemplates the exchange of environmentally sound technologies between all Parties, but especially to developing countries. The phrase "encourage and strengthen" suggests that in respect of developing countries, the terms of transfer should be favourable.[391] The reference to "mutually agreed terms" implies that such transfers be the subject of negotiations, *inter alia*, to satisfy the needs of developing countries, but also to ensure adequate protection of relevant intellectual property rights.[392] Where intellectual property rights exist, Parties should explore the use of economic incentives (see Article 13 (Integrating Environment and Development)) to encourage appropriate transfers.[393] There are, however, many relevant and useful technologies already in the public domain, and therefore free for Parties to directly transfer.

ARTICLE 42

SHARING BENEFITS OF BIOTECHNOLOGY

Parties shall provide for the fair and equitable sharing of benefits arising out of biotechnologies based upon genetic resources with States providing access to such genetic resources on mutually agreed terms.

Article 42 is largely based on Article 15(7) of the Convention on Biological Diversity, the first legally binding international instrument to require the "fair and equitable" sharing of benefits arising out of biotechnologies. It is premised on the notion that genetic resources form part of the natural resources over which States have sovereign rights. The present provision is stronger than the Convention on Biological Diversity in requiring a specific result, whereas that Convention asks Contracting Parties to take measures *which aim* at fair and equitable sharing.

"Benefits," in this context, might include: research and development results, commercial or other benefits (eg. royalties) derived from utilising the genetic resources provided, access and transfer of technology using such resources,[394] participation in biotechnological research activities based on the genetic resources,[395] and priority access to the results and benefits arising from biotechnological use of the genetic resources.[396]

The present provision anticipates a negotiation between provider and recipient which will precede every transfer of genetic resources, both direct and indirect. Although many, if not most,

---

391 See Article 16(2) of the Convention on Biological Diversity (1992) and Paragraph 34.4 of Agenda 21 (1992). See also Article 46(1)(c) (International Financial Resources) of the Draft Covenant.

392 See generally the Uruguay Round TRIPs Agreement (1993).

393 Examples of such tools include tax relief to encourage exports, reformed foreign investments rules, and compensation mechanisms. See also Article 34.18 of Agenda 21 (1992).

394 See Article 16(3) of the Convention on Biological Diversity (1992).

395 See Article 19(1) of the Convention on Biological Diversity (1992).

396 See Article 19(2) of the Convention on Biological Diversity (1992).

transactions will be between private entities, the responsibility falls upon the governments to ensure the results are "fair and equitable." Thus, a regulatory framework reflecting this objective will be helpful in guiding private parties' contractual arrangements. This regulatory framework should also encourage contractual parties to clarify the potential short and long-term benefits of the transaction, how the benefits will be distributed, and who owns the samples collected. This framework would not be sufficient if it only required that the terms be mutually agreed, since the bargaining power of the parties to the transaction may be very different, especially since most transfers are between developing countries rich in genetic resources and industrialized countries. Accordingly, the requirements of fairness and equity are imposed. By allowing the providing State to share in the benefits, the conservation and sustainable use of these genetic resources, and their associated ecosystems, will be encouraged.

The particular circumstances surrounding each transaction will determine whether those qualifications are met. Of significance will be the value and amount of the particular genetic resource provided, and the value of the biotechnology. The true yield resulting from commercial exploitation may not be readily apparent before the transaction takes place, so it may be appropriate to insert a proviso in the agreement allowing for subsequent adjustment. One way in which Parties can comply with their obligations to transfer international financial resources (Article 46 (International Financial Resources)) is through building the capacity of developing country Parties to accurately assess the value of their genetic resources, in addition to allowing their use to be sustainable.

ARTICLE 43

INFORMATION AND KNOWLEDGE

1. **Parties shall facilitate the exchange of publicly available information relevant to the conservation and sustainable use of natural resources, taking into account the special needs of developing countries.**

2. **Parties shall require that access to indigenous knowledge be subject to the prior informed consent of the concerned communities and to specific regulations recognizing their rights to, and the appropriate economic value of, such knowledge.**

Article 43 deals with one of the most effective tools in achieving sustainable development: the international exchange of information necessary to rectify the information gap between industrialized and developing countries. Intra-national provision of information is addressed in Article 12(3) (Persons). The requirement that environmental information be exchanged between States is found in several treaties[397] and is prominent in Agenda 21.[398] The information exchanged will, in most cases, be that to which individuals have access to under Article 12(3).

---

[397] See e.g., Article 10 of the Convention on the Prevention of Marine Pollution from Land-Based Sources (1974); Article 200 of the UNCLOS (1982); Article 8 of the LRTAP Convention (1979); Article 10 of

The wording in Paragraph 1 is deliberately general and is related to the obligation pertaining to cooperation between Parties.[399] It is also crucial to individuals from other States who wish to exercise their right to equal access to proceedings relating to the environment (Article 12(4) (Persons) and Article 53 (Recourse Under Domestic Law and Non-Discrimination)).[400] Further, such information is essential in order to address global environmental problems at the international level, as a common concern (Article 3 (Common Concern of Humanity)). The terms set forth in this provision are not intended to determine the interpretation of those related provisions, although there may be some overlap.

The scope of shared information should be broad so as to include potentially damaging processes including pollution. Guidance may be had from Article 17(2) of the Convention on Biological Diversity (1992), which states that:

> [s]uch exchange of information shall include exchange of results of technical, scientific and socio-economic research, as well as information on training and surveying programmes, specialized knowledge, indigenous and traditional knowledge ... It shall also, where feasible, include repatriation of information.

The 1992 Convention for the Protection of the Marine Environment of the Northeast Atlantic specifies that shared information includes what is available in written, visual, aural or data-base form.[401]

The obligation in paragraph 1 is not one of result (i.e., that a specific quantity of information be transferred), but instead requires that information exchange be facilitated.[402] "Facilitate" in this context means that the obstacles to the exchange of information in the public domain will be removed, whether the information stems from public or private sources. The means to comply with this requirement are left to the discretion of the Parties concerned. It may be done bilaterally or through competent international organizations.[403] States may wish to explore the possibility of

---

the Kuwait Regional Convention (1978); Article 13 of the Wider Caribbean Region Marine Environment Convention (1983); Articles 7 and 15 of the Amazonian Cooperation Treaty (1978); Articles 4(1)(h) and 7(2)(b) of the Climate Change Convention (1992).

398 See especially Chapter 34 of Agenda 21 (1992).

399 These include Article 15 (Prevention and Response to Accidents), Article 25(2) (Waste), Part VII (Transboundary Issues), in particular, with respect to shared natural resources, Article 40(2)(b) (Scientific and Technical Cooperation), Article 41 (Development and Transfer of Technology) and Article 44 (Education, Training and Public Awareness).

400 See also OECD Council Recommendations C(74)224 (Annex) and C(77)28 (Article 8(a)) on this point. See also, Article 9 of the ECE Industrial Accidents Convention (1992).

401 Article 9(2) of the North-East Atlantic Convention (1992).

402 This is the wording of Article 17 of the Biodiversity Convention (1992).

403 E.g., as provided for in Article 200 of UNCLOS (1982).

establishing networks in the form of clearing-houses, as recommended by Agenda 21.[404] The qualification that the information be derived from publicly available sources does not bar States from voluntarily transmitting confidential information, although in those cases the receiving States should respect the confidentiality.[405] Effective implementation of this provision will require the transmittal of the information in an understandable form, non-technical where appropriate. Finally, the clause requiring consideration of the special needs of developing countries implies some preferential treatment.[406]

Paragraph 2 is based on the premise that indigenous peoples have a proprietary or quasi-proprietary right to their knowledge.[407] It echoes the thrust of Article 8(j) of the Convention on Biological Diversity (1992), but without the qualification that the entitlement to an equitable sharing of benefits arising from the utilization of such knowledge is subject to national legislation. Indigenous knowledge has tended to be exploited by outsiders without due respect for the communities imparting the knowledge. This provision seeks to provide greater control by indigenous peoples of their traditional knowledge, using the technique of requiring their prior informed consent as a condition for access to it.[408] This provision also requires Parties to regulate by law this access and to accord legal recognition to the rights of indigenous peoples to their knowledge. Finally, the paragraph calls for according appropriate economic value to such knowledge, which provides greater precision than the terminology in the Convention on Biological Diversity, which speaks of "equitable sharing of benefits arising from the utilization of such knowledge ..."[409]

ARTICLE 44

EDUCATION, TRAINING AND PUBLIC AWARENESS

1. **Parties shall disseminate environmental knowledge by providing to their public and, in particular, to indigenous peoples and local communities, information, educational materials, and opportunities for environmental training and education.**

---

404 Paragraph 34.15 *et seq.* of Agenda 21 (1992).

405 As required, for example, by Article 4 of the Vienna Convention on the Ozone Layer (1985).

406 E.g., where a Party decides to impose a levy to cover the expense of the exchange of information, in the case of a recipient developing country this charge may be reduced.

407 See e.g., Principle 22 of the Rio Declaration (1992) and Paragraph 26.4 of Agenda 21 (1992). The rights of indigenous peoples in general are also accorded considerable emphasis in Chapter VI, section D of the Cairo Conference Programme of Action (1994).

408 This is similar to the requirement in Article 8(j) of the Convention on Biological Diversity (1992).

409 Article 8(j) of the Convention on Biological Diversity (1992).

2. Parties shall co-operate with each other, and where appropriate with competent international and national organizations, to promote environmental education, training, capacity-building, and public awareness.

Article 44 seeks to enhance public knowledge of environmental matters, recognising that often individuals contribute effectively to environmental conservation efforts. Public knowledge also can enhance support for government action in the environmental field. Moreover, effective individual participation in decision-making processes (Article 12(3) (Persons)) is predicated upon adequate environmental knowledge. Finally, this provision seeks to give effect to the basic right of children to be educated in a manner which develops their respect for the natural environment.[410] Similar provisions are common in environmental treaties[411] and detailed recommendations are made in Chapter 36 of Agenda 21. Both national and international efforts to increase this knowledge are contemplated here.

Paragraph 1 places on each Party the primary obligation to increase the environmental knowledge of its nationals, because each Party possesses the means to harness and disseminate it, whether directly or through private entities. Efforts should be aimed at the public at large, but also at indigenous peoples and local communities. This latter point recognizes the special roles these groups have in the achievement of sustainable development.[412]

Paragraph 1 lists three categories of environmental knowledge to be disseminated. The first, information, connotes all information relating to the environment which is publicly available. Dissemination can be through electronic, print or broadcast media, and should be in a non-technical accessible format. The second, educational materials, includes information packaged in a manner which can be most effectively assimilated by the public. Dissemination can be easily achieved through primary and secondary schools, although adult educational venues should also be encouraged. The final item, opportunities for environmental training and education, is necessary for the former two to be effective. In most cases, Parties will have to allocate sufficient resources to existing educational infrastructure.

---

410 Article 29(1)(e) of the Convention on the Rights of the Child (1989).

411 E.g., Article 27 of the World Heritage Convention (1972); Article 11 of the 1982 Protocol Concerning Mediterranean Specially Protected Areas to the Barcelona Convention; and Article 6 of the Climate Change Convention (1992). See also Principle 19 of the Stockholm Declaration (1972); Principle 15 of the World Charter for Nature (1982); and Article 16(d) of the ECE Bergen Ministerial Declaration on Sustainable Development (1990). Article 19 of the Desertification Convention (1994) (capacity-building, education and public awareness); and Article 3(3) of the Aarhus Convention (1998) requires that each party promote environmental education and environmental awareness among the public, especially on how to obtain access to information, to participate in decision-making and to obtain access to justice in environmental matters.

412 See Chapter 26 of Agenda 21 (1992).

Paragraph 2 calls on States to cooperate with a view to enhancing environmental knowledge throughout the world.[413] Discretion is left to each Party to determine the most effective manner of cooperation, whether directly or through competent international or national organizations.[414]

Paragraph 2 also requires States to promote capacity-building, especially needed in developing countries, for which bilateral or multilateral assistance may be appropriate. Agenda 21 devotes an entire chapter to this theme in relation to enhancing the capacity of developing countries.[415] It calls on each country to undertake a review of its capacity and capacity-building requirements in relation to its national sustainable development strategies and on the Secretary-General of the UN to submit a report to the General Assembly on technical cooperation programmes for sustainable development and on what is needed to strengthen this cooperation.[416] Agenda 21 also recommends the following: full use of international and non-governmental organizations in the planning and facilitating of capacity-building strategies[417] and in actual technical cooperation;[418] requests for technical cooperation to be in the framework of long-term sector or sub-sector needs;[419] establishment of mechanisms within recipients, donors, UN organizations, and non-governmental organizations to review international technical cooperation;[420] and harmonization of the delivery of assistance at the regional level through consultative and review mechanisms.[421]

---

413 See e.g., Article 202(a) of UNCLOS (1982); Article 13(b) of the Convention on Biological Diversity (1992); and Article 6 of the Climate Change Convention (1992).

414 See Article 6 of the Declaration of Environmental Policies and Procedures Relating to Economic Development (1990), where the major development banks commit themselves to "prepare, publish and disseminate documentation and audio-visual material providing guidance on the environmental dimension of economic development activities".

415 Chapter 37 of Agenda 21 (1992). See also Principle 12 of the Stockholm Declaration (1972) and Article 7 of the WCED Legal Principles (1986). Since capacity-building is necessary for developing countries to fulfil their obligations under this Draft Covenant, this requirement is a practical implication of the global environment being a Common Concern of Humanity (Article 3). In this regard, it is related to virtually all provisions of this Covenant, particularly Article 40 (Scientific and Technical Cooperation), Article 41 (Development and Transfer of Technology), and Article 43 (Information and Knowledge). Of crucial significance is also Article 46 (International Financial Resources). Indeed, the Climate Change Convention (1992) and Convention on Biological Diversity (1992) condition the compliance of developing countries with the fulfilment of the obligations of developed country parties to transfer financial resources.

416 Paragraph 37.4 of Agenda 21 (1992).

417 Paragraph 37.5 of Agenda 21 (1992).

418 Paragraphs 37.8 - 37.10 of Agenda 21 (1992).

419 Paragraph 37.6 of Agenda 21 (1992).

420 Paragraph 37.7 of Agenda 21 (1992).

421 Paragraph 37.11 of Agenda 21 (1992).

ARTICLE 45

NATIONAL FINANCIAL RESOURCES

1. **Parties undertake to provide, in accordance with their capabilities, financial support and incentives for those national activities aimed at achieving the objectives of this Covenant.**

2. **Parties shall pursue innovative ways of generating new public and private financial resources for sustainable development, including the use of economic instruments, regulatory fees and taxes, and reallocation of resources at present committed to military purposes.**

Article 45 complements those that provide for general and specific obligations to protect the environment and in particular to adopt rules and standards in this regard. Many of these actions require significant financial resources to ensure their full effectiveness. In contrast to Article 46 (International Financial Resources), the emphasis in this provision is on harnessing financial resources on the national level in accordance with national capabilities to achieve the objectives of the Draft Covenant.

Paragraph 1 sets out a general obligation to undertake to provide such resources. The provision is qualified in terms of individual capabilities, since it is apparent that many countries, particularly developing countries, have limited resources available to implement the Draft Covenant.[422] The precise amounts will vary from country to country, but the preparation of national action plans (Article 35 (National Action Plans)) will likely assist in estimating the funds required. As such, the obligation is one of "best efforts," which is intended to increase in quantity as Parties increase their level of economic development. Even without external financial assistance, all Parties can take significant strides towards meeting this obligation by allocating their current expenditures more wisely: either more cost-effectively or on higher priority problem areas. The reference to "incentive" should be understood broadly so that in additional to financial incentives it encompasses all regulatory activity which induces voluntary pursuit of an objective. This is in recognition of the important role private financing can play in the achievement of sustainable development, so long as it is properly channelled.[423] Examples include eco-labelling[424] or granting a local community ac-

---

422 See e.g., Act No. LXXXII of 1992 creating a Central Environment Fund (Hungary).

423 This Article is supported in general by Principle 17 of the World Charter for Nature (1982), which calls for the provision of "[f]unds, programmes and administrative structures necessary to achieve the objective of the conservation of nature", and by Agenda 21 (1992), which calls for States to financially support environmental programmes (Paragraphs 34.22, 34.23 and 34.29 on Financing and Cost Evaluation). On a country-specific basis, Paragraph 36.7 of Agenda 21 provides specific strategies for financing such endeavours in relation to environmental education, training and public awareness. In addition, Paragraph 37.9 calls upon the assistance of financial institutions in this process.

424 E.g., EC Council Regulation EEC/880/92 on a Community Eco-label Award Scheme (1992).

cess to a protected area for specific purposes so long as this does not disrupt the goals of the protected area. Other examples might be more indirect, such as land tenure reform or technical in-kind assistance to communities. This provision also encourages Parties to remove "perverse incentives" that defeat the objective of the Draft Covenant.[425]

Paragraph 2 sets forth specific applications of the general goal laid out in Paragraph 1. "Fees and taxes" are singled out for special emphasis,[426] although all types of "economic instruments" should be considered.[427] In so doing, however, considerations of equity suggest that these instruments should be aimed at those who consume the environmental resource in question, such as non-subsistence consumers, business and industry. In many cases the implementation of this Article will require legislation or other legal instruments.[428] Since budgetary considerations are closely linked with overall governmental policy-making, they should include the reallocation of certain resources, as suggested.[429]

ARTICLE 46

INTERNATIONAL FINANCIAL RESOURCES

1. **Parties shall co-operate in establishing, maintaining, and strengthening ways and means of providing new and additional financial resources, particularly to developing countries for:**

   (a) **environmentally sound development programs and projects;**

   (b) **measures directed towards solving major environmental problems of global concern, and for the implementation measures of this Covenant where they would entail special or abnormal burdens, owing, in particular, to the lack of sufficient financial resources, expertise or technical capacity; and**

   (c) **making available, under favorable conditions, the transfer of environmentally sound technologies.**

2. **Parties, taking into account their respective capabilities and specific national and regional developmental priorities, objectives and circumstances, shall endeavor to augment their aid programs to reach the United Nations Gen-**

---

425 E.g., grants for non-beneficial land-clearance and agricultural and fisheries subsidies.

426 See e.g., Law on Natural Resource Taxes (Latvia) and Law on Pollution Tax (Lithuania).

427 E.g., tradeable pollution allowances (e.g. as provided for under the US Clean Air Act, as amended).

428 See also Article 13(2)(b) (Integrating Environment and Development).

429 See Paragraph 33.16(e) of Agenda 21 (1992).

eral Assembly target of 0.7% of Gross National Product for Official Development Assistance or such other agreed figure as may be established.

3. Parties shall consider ways and means of providing relief to debtor developing countries, including by way of cancellations, rescheduling or conversion of debts to investments, provided that such relief is limited to enable the debtor developing countries to further their sustainable development.

4. A Party that provides financial resources to a State for activities that may result in a significant adverse impact on the environment shall, in cooperation with the recipient State, ensure that an environmental impact is conducted. The resources provided shall include those necessary for the recipient State to carry out such assessment.

Article 46 reflects a recent trend in international environmental treaties to make provision for a flow of financial resources from industrialised countries to developing countries with a view to enabling them to fulfil their treaty obligations.[430]

Paragraph 1 does not specify the modalities for providing resources, leaving this for the Parties to decide in the course of their cooperation. However, certain trends are discernable, and as such the mechanisms should: (a) be transparent; (b) be democratic in nature and create an equitable balance between developing and developed countries; (c) provide access and disbursement to all developing countries without any conditionality; and (d) provide funding of activities according to the priorities and needs of developing countries and taking into account Agenda 21.[431] These resources are called "new and additional" because they should be separate from, and in addition to, the regular aid budgets of industrialized countries. Several proposals have been put forth for the provision of international financial resources for the purposes enumerated in this provision, such as the creation of a fund based on import levies.[432]

---

430 See e.g., Articles 20 and 21 of the Desertification Convention (1994), Article 5 of the Montreal Protocol (1987), Article 4(3) of the Climate Change Convention (1992), Article 20 of the Biological Diversity (1992). In addition, note the role of the Global Environmental Facility in this regard. See also Chapter 33 of Agenda 21 (1992) and Principle 10 of the Forest Principles (1992). It has been noted by some commentators from developing countries that without such assistance, these agreements will remain largely unimplemented by developing countries (and under some treaties, e.g., Climate Change and Biological Diversity, implementation in developing countries is contingent upon industrialized countries' fulfilment of their obligations relating to financial resources and technology transfer). Article 21 of the International Tropical Timber Agreement creates the Ball Partnership Fund based on contributions from donor members, 50 % of income earned and other private and public sources. Its purpose is "to assist producing members to make the investments necessary to achieve the objective of the Agreement."

431 See Paragraph 12 of the Kuala Lumpur Declaration (1992) and Paragraph 33.14(a)(iii) of Agenda 21.

432 See e.g., the suggestion to create a "Solidarity Fund", put forth by the outgoing EU Ambassador to the GATT, Ambassador Tran Van-Trinh. Also, Paragraph 33.14 of Agenda 21 (1992) identifies, *inter alia*,

Subparagraph (a) should be read in conjunction with Article 8 (Right to Development) and Article 13 (Integrating Environment and Development). Subparagraph (b) is directed towards environmental matters of global concern, but this provision is broader than the UNCED treaties in not limiting the transfer of financial resources to meeting the "agreed incremental costs."[433] Any agreed mechanism should be based on information received from the Depositary regarding each Party's experience (Article 71(2)) and should be regularly reviewed by the Review Conference (Article 63). Subparagraph (c) should be read in conjunction with Article 41 (Development and Transfer of Technology), so that any condition for the transfer of technology is mutually agreed. This provision leaves it to the discretion of each State as to how to deal with the intellectual property aspects of this provision (e.g., as may apply under the Uruguay Round TRIPs Agreement (1989), but clearly the financial mechanism can be structured so as to purchase licences, patents, etc. It should be emphasized that this provision is not intended to defeat such rights.[434]

Paragraph 2 primarily concerns ordinary overseas development assistance levels, to be distinguished from "new and additional resources" referred to in Paragraph 1. It affirms the political commitment made in Paragraph 33.13 of Agenda 21 (1992) and elsewhere to endeavour to have such levels reach 0.7% of gross national product.[435] The wording of the provision suggests application to all Parties, not only industrialized ones, and accordingly other Parties, such as newly industrialized countries, should contribute appropriate amounts of resources to overseas development assistance.

Paragraph 3 requires Parties to consider means of lowering the international debt of developing countries, based on the recognition that this crippling burden prevents some countries from

---

the International Development Association, regional and sub-regional development banks, the Global Environment Facility, and private financing through non-governmental entities as possible vehicles for maximizing the availability of new and additional resources.

433 See Article 10 of the 1987 Montreal Protocol, Article 11 of the Climate Change Convention (1992), and Article 20 of the Convention on Biological Diversity (1992). Article 20 of the Desertification Convention (1994) is similar: It requires developed States Parties to (a) mobilize substantial financial resources, including grants and concessional loans, in order to support the implementation of programs to combat desertification and mitigate the effects of drought; (b) promote the mobilization of adequate, timely and predictable financial resources, including new and additional funding from the Global Environment Facility of the agreed incremental costs of those activities concerning desertification that relate to its four focal area, in conformity with the relevant provisions of the instrument establishing the GEF." This concept has been criticized for being difficult to apply in practice, necessitating arbitrariness.

434 See also Article 16(2) of the Convention on Biological Diversity (1992), Article 4(5) of the Climate Change Convention (1992) and Article 5 of the Montreal Protocol (1987).

435 See Paragraph 33.13 and the Tokyo Declaration on Financing Global Environment and Development (1992).

developing sustainably.[436] The appropriateness and precise modalities of such measures are left to the discretion of the Parties, except that any relief must be applied to sustainable development activities. One practical application of this provision would be to implement "debt-for-nature swaps."[437] A second alternative is for creditors to provide debt relief to the poorest heavily indebted countries, as provided for under the December 1991 Agreement of the Paris Club.

Paragraph 4 flows from the requirements of Article 37 (Environmental Impact Assessment), requiring donor Parties to conduct an EIA with respect to activities arising out of their development assistance.[438] The use of the term "State" indicates that this provision applies regardless of whether the recipient State is party to the Draft Covenant. As a guideline, the donor Party should, in cooperation with the recipient State, make best efforts to comply where appropriate with the provisions of Article 37.[439] In order to allow the recipient State to effectively participate in the EIA process, it might be necessary for the donor Party to provide needed technical assistance and human resources.

The rationale for this requirement is based on the international duty of all States to protect the environment as a common concern (Article 3 (Common Concern of Humanity)), which in this instance means that their developmental assistance is not used in environmentally hazardous ways.[440]

PART IX. RESPONSIBILITY AND LIABILITY

An effective system of remedies for environmental harm resulting from the breach of provisions of the Draft Covenant and other international environmental law is essential to environmental protection and sustainable development. Part IX details the duties owed by Parties when such harm

---

436 *Cf.* Article 20 of the Desertification Convention (1994) and Paragraph 33.14(e) of Agenda 21 (1992). See also UNGA Declaration on International Economic Cooperation in Particular the Revitalizing of Economic Growth and Development of the Developing Countries (1990).

437 See e.g., Article 20(2)(d) of the Desertification Convention (1994) and Paragraph 33.16(a) of Agenda 21 (1992).

438 See e.g., *Natural Resources Defense Council, Inc. v. Nuclear Regulatory Commission (NRC)* (1981) (although the issue has not been fully settled in the United States); OECD Council Recommendation C(85)104 on Environmental Assessment of Development Assistance Projects (1985), OECD Council Recommendation on Measures Required to Facilitate the Environmental Assessment of Development Assistance Projects and Programmes (1986), and OECD Development Assistance Committee Guidelines on Environment and Aid (1992). Although the wording of this provision is *prima facie* directed at transfers of funds by States, read in conjunction with Article 11(5)(States), it suggests that State members of international development banks should seek to have these institutions also conduct EIAs, which currently is the common practice.

439 See also Article 37 of the Lomé IV Convention (1989) and World Bank Operational Directive 4.00, Annex A: Environmental Impact Assessment (1989).

440 See also Article 37(5) (Environmental Impact Assessment).

has occurred, whether within or outside their territory or jurisdiction, both to other Parties and in relation to individuals. This Part is based on the general international law doctrines of State responsibility and liability, and draws inspiration from the ILC's work. It also takes into account national and international experience with liability regimes in environmental law. Because regional economic integration organizations may not have sufficient legal personality to be "responsible" or "liable" under international law, this Part is primarily directed to State Parties to the Draft Covenant.[441]

This Part responds to the call contained in Principle 22 of the Stockholm Declaration on the Human Environment for States to "develop further the international law regarding liability and compensation for the victims of pollution and other environmental damage caused by activities within the jurisdiction or control of such States to areas beyond their jurisdiction." Numerous international instruments have reiterated the Stockholm statement.[442]

The provisions of Part IX require the provision of remedies for environmental harm on both the civil and inter-State levels. Some instruments favour a civil liability regime alone,[443] holding liable the "polluter" or the "operator or owner of a facility,"[444] whereas others are based purely on State responsibility.[445] Each on its own has been demonstrated to be of limited effectiveness. In the case of State responsibility, the inadequacies are due to the (a) the traditional view that only those States with standing can bring actions and, even if standing is no barrier, an affected State may choose not to provide its diplomatic protection; (b) States do not have standing to bring actions for the protection of areas beyond national jurisdiction; and (c) the innocent victim may be left uncompensated in cases where the State causing the harm has met its due diligence obligations. In contrast, civil liability may be inadequate when (a) the operator is insolvent or else unable to make full reparation for the harm caused and (b) when it is inequitable to place the entire burden of reparation on a private entity because the State permitted the activity to take place.

---

441 *Cf.* Article 35(1) of the Statute of the International Court of Justice (1945).

442 For example, in the field of marine pollution, see Article 20 of the South Pacific Convention (1986); Article 14 of the Wider Caribbean Marine Environment Convention (1983); Article 15 of the West and Central African Marine Environment Convention (1981). See also Principle 13 of the Rio Declaration (1992).

443 *Cf.* Article 11 of the South-East Pacific Marine Environment Convention (1981). Other Conventions combine civil liability with international responsibility. See Article XIII of the Kuwait Regional Convention (1978); Article XIII of the Jeddah Convention on the Marine Environment (1982). The Basel Protocol on Liability and Compensation for Damage Resulting from the Transboundary Movement of Hazardous Wastes and their Disposal (1999); Articles 6 and 7, Liability for Carriage of Noxious Elements by Sea (1996).

444 E.g., Article 3 of the Paris Nuclear Liability Convention (1960); Article II of the Vienna Nuclear Liability Convention (1963); and Article III of the Oil Pollution Civil Liability Convention (1969).

445 This is the general presumption in international law behind most environmental treaties which do not create specific civil liability regimes. See also Article 12 of the Barcelona Convention (1976) and Articles 139(2) and 235(1) of UNCLOS (1982).

As such, the intention of this Part is to offer a combination of civil and inter-State remedies, the latter including remedies based on both international responsibility and international liability.[446]

There are two general reasons for including a regime of State responsibility and liability additional to the civil liability regime: (a) a State may have breached its obligations to prevent harm causing it to be responsible or liable, as the case may be, for this breach; and (b) it may be impossible to identify the private operator or the amount of the damage may be too great for the operator to bear and the State of origin should bear subsidiary liability.

The purpose of this Part is to set forth basic rules; Parties are encouraged to further develop these rules and tailor them to specific contexts.

ARTICLE 47

STATE RESPONSIBILITY

Each State Party is responsible under international law for the breach of its obligations under this Covenant or of other rules of international law concerning the environment.

Article 47 sets forth the well-established rule that a State is responsible under international law for the breach of its international obligations. The Article is intended to cover not only the operational obligations contained in the Draft Covenant, but also those in other environmental treaties as well as in general international law. "Responsibility" in the legal sense is to be distinguished from its meaning in the moral or normative sense. Here it is based on the general rule of international law that States are legally accountable for breaching their international obligations.[447] This case is distinguishable from cases of State liability, dealt with in Article 48 (State Liability).

International law determines the consequences for each State once it is found to be responsible. The ILC has indicated that the breach of an obligation gives rise to two consequent obliga-

446 See, generally, Paris Nuclear Liability Convention (1960) and the Vienna Nuclear Liability Convention (1963). See the Basel Protocol on Liability and Compensation for Damage Resulting from the Transboundary Movement of Hazardous Wastes and their Disposal (1999) which provides for strict liability shifting from the exporter to importer as well as liability of any person for intentional, reckless or negligent acts or for non-compliance with the provisions implementing the Convention. State responsibility is also foreseen for failing to comply with the obligations of the Protocol.

447 This is referred to as a "primary obligation" of international law. Article 1 of the ILC Draft Articles on State Responsibility (1980) reads, "Every internationally wrongful act of a State entails the international responsibility of that State." An "internationally wrongful act" is defined in Article 3 as occurring when "(a) conduct consisting of an action or omission is attributable to the State under international law; and (b) that conduct constitutes a breach of an international obligation of that State."

tions: to cease any continuing breaches and to make reparation.[448] Reparation includes restitution to the *status quo ante*, which is the preferred remedy in cases of environmental harm, compensation, satisfaction, and assurances and guarantees of non-repetition (see also Article 49 (Cessation and Compensation)).[449] These remedies are applicable to cases of actual and potential transboundary harm to the environment, including harm to the global commons.

ARTICLE 48

STATE LIABILITY

Each State Party is liable for significant harm to the environment of other States or of areas beyond the limits of national jurisdiction, as well as for injury to persons resulting therefrom, caused by acts or omissions of its organs or by activities under its jurisdiction or control.

Article 48 provides that State Parties are liable for significant transboundary harm to the environment, including for harm to the environment *per se*[450] and injury to persons resulting from such harm.[451] It is distinguishable from Article 47 (State Responsibility) in that it includes cases where there has been harm resulting from an activity which is not a breach of an international obligation. In other words, this Article will be triggered in cases of accidental harm, where there is no breach of a Party's due diligence obligations. In so doing, this Article addresses situations

---

448 In the *Chorzów Factory (Indemnity)* case, the Permanent Court of Justice declared:

> The essential principle contained in the actual notion of an illegal act – a principles which seems to be established by international law and practice and in particular by decisions of arbitral tribunals – is that reparation must, as far as possible, wipe out all the consequences of the illegal act and reestablish the situation which would, in all probability, have existed if that act had not been committed. Restitution in kind, or, if this is not possible, payment of a sum corresponding to the value which a restitution in kind would bear; the award, if need be, of damages for loss sustained which would not be covered by restitution in kind or payment in place of it – such are the principles which should serve to determine the amount of compensation due for an act contrary to international law.

449 See Articles 7, 8, 10, and 10 bis provisionally adopted as Part II of the ILC Draft Articles on State Responsibility.

450 This is reflected in the Article 3 of the 1992 London Protocol to the Oil Pollution Civil Liability Convention and Article 2(7) of the Council of Europe Civil Liability Convention (1993).

451 "Persons" include harm to people and property. Many precedents exist for international liability for such harm: e.g., Article IV(1) of the Space Objects Liability Convention (1972), Article 1(2) of the Oil Pollution Civil Liability Convention (1969), Article 3 of the Paris Nuclear Liability Convention (1960), Article I(k) of the Vienna Nuclear Liability Convention (1963), and Article 2(7) of the Council of Europe Civil Liability Convention (1993). See also *Trail Smelter* case, on which damages were awarded for injury to people and property.

where harm might occur but the activity is considered acceptable on account of its benefits or the low probability that it will cause serious harm.[452]

The rationale for imposing liability, even for accidental harm, is derived from the general obligation set forth in Article 11(1)(b) (States), and arises once the physical fact of significant transboundary harm exists. Thus, this Article does not provide remedies for cases of potential harm.

The threshold for liability being triggered is that the harm be "significant." This has become the accepted standard in international law, based on the view that the victim must tolerate harm less than "significant," as the inevitable consequence of normal use of elements of the environment.[453]

"Harm to the environment" should be understood as encompassing (a) impairment of the environment, provided that compensation for impairment of the environment shall be limited to the cost of measures of reinstatement actually undertaken or to be undertaken and (b) the cost of reasonable measures to prevent or minimize harm.[454] This latter aspect should not be understood to encompass potential harm, which is covered by Article 50 (Consequences of Failure to Prevent Harm), but addresses the measures undertaken after the harm has occurred. "Injury to persons" in this provision encompasses (a) various forms of harm resulting in legal injury; (b) loss of or damage to property, loss of profit, or impairment of rights; and (c) the cost of reasonable measures to prevent or minimize harm.

The scope of this provision is broad, including the activities of Parties and those of private entities under their jurisdiction, in recognition that many ultrahazardous activities will be privately controlled. In placing liability on the Party itself for the actions of private entities, this provision implements the principle that where a State permits the pursuit of dangerous activities because of the general benefits derived from these activities, it, and not the innocent victims, should bear the loss in cases of transboundary harm.[455]

The nexus between "harm to the environment" and "injury to individuals resulting therefrom" recognizes that an injury to the environment can coincide with an injury to a private legal interest,

---

452 *Cf.* Article 11 of the WCED Legal Principles (1986).

453 See the *Trail Smelter* case, where the arbitral tribunal ruled that responsibility/liability is only at stake, "when the case is of serious consequence and the injury is established by clear and convincing evidence". See also *Lac Lanoux* case, which speaks of a "risque abnormal dans les relations de voisinage". On the use of "significant", see e.g., Article 5 of the Nordic Convention (1974), Article 5 of the LRTAP Convention (1979), Article 3 of the Espoo Convention (1991).

454 *Cf.* Article 2 of the Council of Europe Civil Liability Convention (1993).

455 This provision does not preclude Parties from recovering their losses from the private entities concerned. One means of doing so is to require operators to carry indemnification and compensation insurance.

although the converse is not always true. This Article is based on the premise that States have an interest in pursuing claims for injury to their nationals as well as to the environment *per se*.

ARTICLE 49

CESSATION, RESTITUTION AND COMPENSATION

1. **Each State Party shall cease activities causing significant harm to the environment and shall, as far as practicable, re-establish the situation that would have existed if the harm had not occurred. Where that is not possible, the State Party of the origin of the harm shall provide compensation or other remedy for the harm. In particular, Parties shall co-operate to develop and improve means to remedy the harm, including measures for rehabilitation, restoration or reinstatement of habitats of particular conservation concern.**

2. **Where a State Party suffers such harm caused in part by its own negligence or that of persons under its jurisdiction or control, the extent of any redress or the level of any compensation due may be reduced to the extent that the harm is caused by negligence of that Party or persons under its jurisdiction or control.**

Article 49, setting forth inter-State remedies, describes the duties of a Party when transboundary environmental harm occurs. It imposes an obligation on all Parties to cooperate in developing remedial measures, including rehabilitation, restoration or reinstatement of particular habitats. It also contains the well-recognized tort concept that the negligence of one who suffers harm will reduce or extinguish a claim for redress or compensation.

Paragraph 1, obliges a Party to cease activities causing significant harm to the environment and to remedy harm that has occurred. This is without regard to whether the harm resulted from an intentional activity, negligence, or an inadvertent accident and whether the harm is caused within the Party's territory or without. The duty to cease harmful conduct is intended to apply in cases where harm to the environment is of a continuing nature, and includes long-term as well as cumulative harm. The duty to cease causing harm is generally recognized in international law,[456] and was included with little opposition in the ILC Draft Articles on State Responsibility.[457] Cessation is future oriented, aimed at preventing further harm from occurring,[458] particularly in cases of cumulative environmental harm caused by a series of acts.

---

456 See e.g., *Trail Smelter* case.

457 A basis for the requirement to cease the injuring activities is found in the *Trail Smelter* case. See also Article 21(2) of the WCED Legal Principles (1986).

458 In contrast, the function of reparation is to "wipe out all the consequences" of the past infringing conduct. *Cf.* Article 6 of ILC Draft Articles on State Responsibility.

When cessation comes after harm has already occurred,[459] Paragraph 1 requires application of the principle of restitution in kind (*restitutio in integrum*), i.e., re-establishment of the situation that existed prior to the harm.[460] In this context, restitution in kind means replacement of harmed components of the environment with equivalent components ("*in natura*"). This concept best meets the idea of reparation and of protection of the environment; thus it is more appropriate than monetary compensation.[461] Restitution in kind is also included in Paragraph 1 as the model for future development of the law. The ILC also supports restitution in kind.[462]

In some cases, harm to the environment is irreversible or cannot be repaired in kind, e.g., severe oil tanker accidents and oil pollution of the seabed. In these instances, monetary compensation will likely constitute the appropriate form of reparation. This compensation will include the costs of all reasonable measures of reinstatement actually undertaken or to be undertaken, as well as costs for reasonable measures to prevent or minimize harm. Unlike certain other treaties,[463] this Article does not contain a limitation on the amount of compensation that may be due for the harm caused. The phrase "other remedy for such harm" indicates that in addition to financial losses, an injured State might suffer non-monetary harm, thereby being entitled to remedies other than compensation. For example, in the case of environmental harm constituting an "international crime,"[464] personal responsibility, satisfaction, and punitive sanctions might be appropriate.

The second sentence of Paragraph 1 calls for Parties to develop and improve methods to remedy environmental harm, in recognition that further development of the law is needed. A particular focus should be on restoring the environment, particularly protected areas or fragile ecosystems ("habitats of particular conservation concern"), after environmental harm has occurred. Remediation may include "any reasonable measures aiming to reinstate or restore damaged or destroyed components of the environment, or to introduce, where reasonable, the equivalent of these components into the environment."[465]

---

459 To give effect to this remedy before the harm has occurred, State Parties might further develop their system of injunctive relief to prevent harm.

460 Article 7 of the ILC Draft Articles on State Responsibility.

461 It is supported by the ECE Task Force Guidelines on Responsibility and Liability Regarding Transboundary Water Pollution and by the Council of Europe Civil Liability Convention (1993). See also Article 21 of the WCED Legal Principles (1986).

462 See Article 8 of the Draft Articles on State Responsibility.

463 E.g., Article V(1) of the Oil Pollution Civil Liability (1969).

464 See Article 19(3)(d) of ILC Draft Articles on State Responsibility (1980) and Articles 22(2)(d) and 26 the ILC Draft Code of Crimes Against Peace and Security of Mankind (1991).

465 See also Article 2(8) of the Council of Europe Convention Civil Liability Convention (1993), defining "measures of reinstatement".

Paragraph 2 reiterates the well recognized principle that the extent of compensation due is reduced to the extent the harm has been caused by negligence of the injured party.[466] This provision contains the essential elements of paragraph 2 of Article 6 bis of the ILC Draft Articles on State Responsibility.

ARTICLE 50

CONSEQUENCES OF FAILURE TO PREVENT HARM

Each State Party may be held responsible for significant harm to the environment resulting from its failure to carry out the obligations of prevention contained in this Covenant, in respect to its activities or those of its nationals.

Article 50 provides for responsibility in cases where State Parties have not fulfilled their obligations of prevention, highlighting the importance of this principle in the protection of the environment.[467] It includes breach of the express requirements of prevention (e.g. Article 15 (Prevention of and Response to Emergencies) and Article 23 (Prevention of Harm)) as well as those which are implied by all the substantive provisions of the Draft Covenant.[468] It is well recognized in international law that such responsibility exists,[469] and is linked to every State's due diligence obligations. This implies that where activities might cause potential harm but are considered tolerable, the highest standards must continue to be applied, including best available technology standards. If not responsibility, and not liability under Article 48, will be triggered. One possible method for State Parties to give effect to the obligation of prevention is to have an effective regime of injunctive relief available to prevent environmental harm.

ARTICLE 51

EXEMPTIONS

The State Party of origin of the harm shall not be responsible or liable if the harm,

(a) is directly due to an act of armed conflict or a hostile activity where the requirements under Article 32 of this Covenant are met, except an armed

---

[466] See e.g., Article III(3) of the Oil Pollution Civil Liability Convention (1969); Article IV(2) of the Vienna Nuclear Liability Convention (1963); and Article 9 of the Council of Europe Civil Liability Convention (1993).

[467] This is expressed in Article 6 (Prevention).

[468] *Cf.* Article 6 (Prevention).

[469] E.g., *Velasquez Rodriguez* case (1988), where the Court held that Honduras was responsible for preventing the breach of Article 1(1) of the Inter-American Human Rights Convention by virtue of the term "ensure" in that provision. See also the *Corfu Channel* case where the ICJ held Albania responsible for damage caused to British warship which it was presumed to know about.

conflict initiated by the State Party of origin in violation of international law;

(b) is directly due to a natural phenomenon of an exceptional and inevitable character; or

(c) is caused wholly by an act or omission of a third party.

This provision expresses well-recognized exemptions from responsibility or liability in general international law of *force majeure*, civil war, hostilities, insurrection and harm intentionally caused by a third person. Precedents exist in numerous environmental protection conventions.[470] The one departure from precedent is to qualify the exemption for armed conflict by requiring compliance with the provisions of Article 32 (Military and Hostile Activities), thereby establishing responsibility and liability for breaches of that provision which cause environmental harm.

ARTICLE 52

CIVIL REMEDIES

1. Parties shall ensure the availability of effective civil remedies that provide for cessation of harmful activities as well as for compensation to victims of environmental harm irrespective of the nationality or the domicile of the victims.

2. Parties that do not provide such remedies shall ensure that compensation is paid for the damage caused by their acts or omissions or by activities of persons under their jurisdiction or control.

3. In cases of significant environmental harm, if an effective remedy is not provided in accordance with paragraph 1, the State Party of nationality of the victim shall espouse the victim's claim by presenting it to the State Party of origin of the harm. The State Party of origin shall not require the exhaustion of local remedies as a pre-condition for presentation of such claim.

Article 52 requires Parties to ensure effective civil remedies for victims of environmental harm. In this Article, "Parties" is used instead of "State Parties" because of the legal possibility that regional economic integration organizations may have the authority to enact a regime of civil remedies.

---

470 See especially Article IV of the Vienna Nuclear Liability Convention (1963), Article III of the Oil Pollution Civil Liability Convention (1969), the Seabed Liability Convention (1977), and the Council of Europe Civil Liability Convention (1993).

Paragraph 1 responds to Principles 10[471] and 13[472] of the Rio Declaration. The remedies must provide for cessation of harmful activities as well as for compensation and must be available without discrimination on the basis of nationality or domicile. This is to be contrasted with the similar language appearing in Article 33(c) (Transboundary Environmental Effects) which requires non-discrimination in access to procedures prior to the occurrence of harm. The second sentence provides that Parties must ensure that compensation is actually paid for damage caused either by activities of the Party or by private actors, both by citizens or non-citizens, whatever procedure is instituted for presenting a claim.

The title "Civil Remedies" emphasizes that the scope of this Article is broader than liability, including both substantive law (e.g. tort law) and the establishment of procedures for hearing claims of environmental harm. The call to ensure civil remedies is based on the recognition that protection of the environment, especially from ecological damage, needs further development in most legal systems. The same is true of the concept of strict liability for hazardous activities or substances.[473] There are also complex, often unresolved, problems of channelling liability in cases of chronic pollution and where there are cumulative impacts, and of the role of insurance and liability funds.[474] Article 52(1) requires national law-makers and executive organs in all Parties to establish an effective regime of civil remedies to protect victims of environmental harm. "Cessation" indicates that the protection should be preventive as well as compensatory.

The reference to making effective remedies available "irrespective of the nationality or the domicile of the victims" is an incorporation of the recognized international law principle of non-discrimination.[475] It imposes a duty on Parties to develop substantive and procedural law to provide effective remedies for victims of transboundary harm as well as for those injured locally. It is related to the following Article, which reinforces the procedural aspects of the duty, requiring each Party to ensure that whatever remedies are available currently or will be developed in the future, equal access is afforded to residents and non-residents of the State. In so doing, this provision encourages the development of international minimum standards in this regard.

---

[471] "Effective access to judicial and administrative proceedings, including redress and remedy, shall be provided."

[472] "States shall develop national law regarding liability and compensation for the victims of pollution and other environmental damage."

[473] Although the concept is known in some jurisdictions: see e.g., *Rylands v. Fletcher* (1868).

[474] For an international regime creating a liability fund, see the case of marine oil pollution (i.e., Fund Convention (1971), TOVALOP (1969) and CRISTAL (1971)). For an example of a national fund for environmental liability, see Superfund Act (USA).

[475] The principle was adopted in the OECD Council Recommendation Concerning Transboundary Pollution (1974) and reiterated in later instruments. See also Article 13 of the WCED Legal Principles (1986), ECE Task Force Guidelines on Responsibility and Liability Regarding Transboundary Water Pollution, and ECE Code of Conduct on Accidental Pollution of Inland Waters (1990).

Paragraph 2 requires Parties to ensure that compensation be paid, whether or not the Party has developed or incorporated effective preventive or remedial measures. Although not stated explicitly, the compensation afforded must meet standards of general international law. The duty to ensure that compensation is paid means that a Party must take the necessary measures to see that private parties provide compensation in cases where they have caused harm, or else must provide compensation themselves.[476]

Paragraph 3 concerns those instances where the private victim cannot pursue a claim for compensation against a private entity or the State causing the harm. National courts may refuse to hear the claim on the basis of lack of jurisdiction or competence, especially where the action is filed against the State itself. Even if the claim is directed against a private party, issues such as the national *ordre public* can result in the case being dismissed. An action against a foreign polluter brought in the victim's courts can similarly fail because of a "local action" rule,[477] because of lack of jurisdiction or due to application of the "act of state" doctrine precluding national courts from judging the governmental actions of another State.

This provision requires that the Party of nationality of the victim espouse the claim by presenting it to the State where the harm originated. Under existing norms making espousal discretionary, States have been reluctant to pursue claims. As a result, the Guidelines of the ECE Task Force on Responsibility and Liability Regarding Transboundary Water Pollution have requested the States of victims "to bear in mind the necessity to protect their nationals against transboundary water pollution ... and to make use of the right of diplomatic protection." The elimination of a requirement of exhaustion of local remedies finds precedent in Article XI of the Space Objects Liability Convention (1972).[478]

ARTICLE 52 BIS

OFFENSES

1. **Parties shall establish, as appropriate, criminal or administrative offenses for violations of environmental law or for activities that cause or are likely to cause serious harm to the environment.**

---

476 See e.g., Brussels Supplementary Nuclear Energy Convention (1963) which establishes subsidiary State liability. Note that the Basel Protocol on Civil Liability (1999) requires that remedies include compensation for measures of reinstatement actually undertaken or to be undertaken.

477 E.g., application of this rule prevented American victims from suing in the United States the Smelter in Trail, British Columbia, thus giving rise to the well-known inter-State arbitration between Canada and the United States.

478 "Presentation of a claim to a launching State for compensation for damage under this Convention shall not require the prior exhaustion of any local remedies which may be available to a claimant State or to natural or juridical persons it represents."

2. Parties shall establish sanctions for such offenses that take into account the seriousness of the offenses and may include fines, confiscation, suspension or cancellation of permits or other benefits, imprisonment, and the obligation to reinstate the environment.

The function of criminal law is to protect the most important values of society, by creating and enforcing penalties, including those involving deprivation of liberty. Administrative procedures also serve to enforce national laws, including those implementing treaty obligations. Increasingly, multilateral environmental agreements are requiring states to create criminal or administrative offenses in national law against those who pollute and perform other acts damaging to the environment.[479] Some international agreements specify that the offenses must be criminal in nature.[480] Other agreements call for administrative actions and penalties.[481] This Covenant does not specify whether the offenses created should be criminal or administrative, leaving it to the discretion of the Party, but it requires effective sanctions in either case.

A few international agreements are devoted entirely to the use of criminal law for environmental protection, although it is recognized that prevention of the impairment of the environment must be achieved, primarily through other measures. The Convention on the Protection of the Environmental through Criminal Law (Strasbourg, 4 Nov. 1998, EmuT 998:82) notes that imposing criminal or administrative sanctions on legal persons as well as natural persons can play an effective role in the prevention of environmental violations. The treaty specifies certain offenses for criminalization when committed intentionally or negligently and when they cause lasting deterioration, death or serious injury to any person or create a significant risk of doing so or that produce or are likely to produce substantial damage to protected monuments, other protected objects, property, animals or plants. These are: (1) discharge of pollutants; (2) unlawful movement of hazardous wastes; (3) unlawfully operating a dangerous facility; and (4) unlawful activities concerned with radioactive substances. States also shall create criminal or administrative offenses for negligent or intentional acts that violate domestic laws even when they do not produce harmful consequences.

The Agreement on Co-operative Enforcement Operations Directed at Illegal Trade in Wild Fauna and Flora (Lusaka, 8 Sept. 1994), does not create new criminal offenses, but calls on the State Parties to cooperate in investigating and prosecuting cases of illegal trade in wild fauna and flora. It establishes a regional Task Force for Co-operative Enforcement Operations with legal personality to investigate violations pertaining to illegal trade and to present evidence about such violations, to gather information and maintain databases and to provide available information related to the return to the country of original export of confiscated wild fauna and flora.

---

479 CITES, Montreal Protocol? UNCLOS ? Article 19, Straddling Stocks Agreement (1997).

480 Bamako, MARPOL.

481 Straddling Stocks, Article 19(1)(e).

More generally, a resolution adopted by the UN Economic and Social Council[482] insists on the importance of environmental criminal law and, *inter alia*, recommends that states seriously consider enacting legislation prohibiting and sanctioning the export of products that have been banned from domestic use, as well as the production and import of specific dangerous materials, unless sufficient precautionary measures can be taken in respect of their use, treatment or disposal in their countries. It also recommends giving support to the idea of imposing criminal or non-criminal fines or other measures on corporations.

Paragraph 1 of Article 52 bis similarly requires that Parties to the Covenant establish criminal or administrative offenses, as appropriate, in the field of environmental protection.[483] There are two categories of offenses. First, those that involve a violation of an international treaty or domestic law, even if no damage or harm is caused or can be proven, for instance, the dumping of some polluting substances into the water. Many legal systems already provide that the breach of a statutory environmental duty, even without measurable harm, can result in criminal or administrative proceedings, sanctions or remedies. Second, activities that cause or are likely to cause serious harm to the environment may be made offenses, even if no specific breach of international or domestic regulations are shown.

Paragraph 2 requires that the sanctions established be related to the seriousness of the offenses and it provides a non-exclusive list of possible alternatives.[484] Penal sanctions can range from fines for petty offenses to imprisonment for more serious offenses. Administrative procedures include injunctions, fines, and refusal, suspension, revocation, or modification of permits. Other sanctions may include a denial of government contracts or blacklisting of harmful products. Lending institutions may refuse loans or other benefits to projects failing to meet environmental standards or those scheduled for establishment in areas not attaining quality objectives. It may be required that offenders reinstate the environment.[485] The European Convention on Criminal provides that sanctioning measures shall include the confiscation of instrumentalities and proceeds or property equal in value to such proceeds in regard to criminal offenses.

---

482 Based on a recommendation of the Commission on Crime Prevention and Criminal Justice, Third Session, Vienna, 26 April - 6 May 1994, reprinted in 24 EPL 286 (1994).

483 Such offenses do not at present form part of international criminal law.

484 See e.g., Article 19(2) of the Straddling Stocks Agreement ("... Sanctions applicable in respect of violations shall be adequate in severity to be effective in securing compliance and to discourage violations wherever they occur and shall deprive offenders of the benefits accruing from their illegal activities. Measures applicable in respect of masters and other officers of fishing vessels shall include provisions which may permit, *inter alia*, refusal, withdrawal or suspension of authorizations to serve as masters or officers on such vessels.").

485 Articles 6, 8. European Criminal Law Convention also requires sanctions which take into account the serious nature of the offenses. "The sanctions available shall include imprisonment and pecuniary sanctions and may include reinstatement of the environment."

ARTICLE 53

RECOURSE UNDER DOMESTIC LAW AND NON-DISCRIMINATION

1. **Each State Party of origin shall ensure that any person in another State Party who is adversely affected by transboundary environmental harm has the right of access to administrative and judicial procedures equal to that afforded nationals or residents of the State Party of origin in cases of domestic environmental harm.**

2. **Each State Party shall ensure that adversely affected persons have a right of recourse for violations of environmental regulations by that Party or any person or entity associated with that Party.**

Article 53, like the previous provision, is based on the well-recognized principle of non-discrimination.

Paragraph 1 obliges the State Party of origin to grant to a potential or *de facto* injured person a right of access to any administrative or judicial procedures equal to that of nationals or residents.[486] The requirement that the procedures afford effective, non-discriminatory remedies is governed by Article 48 (State Liability). Regarding administrative procedures, including environmental impact assessments, recent conventions and directives enhance non-discriminatory public participation. For example, the Convention on Civil Liability for Damage Resulting from Activities Dangerous to the Environment (1993) provides in Article 14(1) that "[a]ny person shall, at his request and without his having to prove an interest, have access to information relating to the environment held by public authorities." Access to information, as a preventive measure, could help reduce the filing of lawsuits by foreign persons, and is guaranteed by Articles 15 and 16 of that Convention. "Person" includes physical and legal persons.

---

[486] *Cf.* Article 3 of the Nordic Convention (1974) states:

> Any person who is affected or may be affected by a nuisance caused by environmentally harmful activities in another Contracting State shall have the right to bring before the appropriate Court of Administrative Authority of that State the question of the permissibility of such activities, including the question of measures to prevent damage, and to appeal against the decision of the Court or the Administrative Authority to the same extent and on the same terms as a legal entity of the State in which the activities are being carried out.
>
> The provisions of the first paragraph of this Article shall be equally applicable in the case of proceedings concerning compensation for damage caused by environmentally harmful activities. The question of compensation shall not be judged by rules which are less favourable to the injured party than the rules of compensation of the State in which the activities are being carried out.

Similar provisions are contained in the ECE Code of Conduct on Accidental Pollution of Transboundary Inland Waters (1990).

Paragraph 2 ensures that victims can proceed against the State or its entities, as well as against private parties where actual or potential harm is involved or there have been violations of environmental regulations. This provision takes into account that a State enterprise may directly cause the harm by its activities or indirectly by issuing licenses to or by failing to control a private activity under its ambit. While there may be complications to implement this provision where domestic law does not allow judicial control over government actions,[487] this provision is a necessary means to ensure that governments as well as private parties are held accountable for violations of environmental regulations.

ARTICLE 54

IMMUNITY FROM JURISDICTION

Parties may not claim sovereign immunity in respect of proceedings instituted under this Covenant.

This provision prevents a State against which proceedings have been instituted from claiming immunity from jurisdiction, and in so doing, guarantees judicial resolution of actions brought against State organs.

Although international law in this area is not fully settled, there is wide recognition of a "tort exception" to sovereign immunity,[488] as well as a generally accepted principle that a State can waive jurisdictional immunity. Article 54 reiterates a formulation found in various civil liability agreements.[489]

The need for this provision is based on the policy of ensuring that all environmental litigation is fully dealt with on its merits, so as to ensure that a remedy is provided. It has been developed because of the reluctance of States to bring claims against each other and because inter-State litigation is impeded by a lack of consent to submit to the jurisdiction of the ICJ or an arbitral tribunal. Thus, it is desirable to allow individuals to bring actions and enforce judgments against States in national courts. In most cases, such actions will be brought in the State of origin, but there may be occasions when the action is brought in the State of the victim. In this case, Article 53 (Recourse

---

487 But see also Article 54 (Immunity from Jurisdiction) of the Draft Covenant.

488 See e.g., Article 12 of the ILC Draft Articles on the Jurisdictional Immunities of States and their Personal Property.

489 E.g., Article 13(e) of the Paris Nuclear Liability Convention (1960) provides, "[i]f an action is brought against a Contracting Party under this Convention, such Contracting Party may not, ... invoke any jurisdictional immunities before the court competent in accordance with this Article." Similar provisions can be found in Article X(3) of the Vienna Nuclear Liability Convention (1963) and Article X(3) of the Brussels Convention on the Liability of Operators of Nuclear Ships (1962).

Under Domestic Law and Non-discrimination) will also apply to prevent that State from invoking immunity from jurisdiction in the State of the victim, as well as from invoking it in its own courts where enforcement of the resulting judgment is sought.

ARTICLE 55

ENVIRONMENTAL HARM IN AREAS BEYOND NATIONAL JURISDICTION

The provisions of Articles 47 to 54 may be invoked by any affected person for harm to the environment of areas beyond national jurisdiction.

A general obligation not to cause potential or actual harm to the environment of areas beyond the limits of national jurisdiction is found in Article 11(1) (States). Article 55 fills a gap in current law in providing protection for the global commons by allowing private actions to enforce the Article 11 duty. The importance of the global commons, and the growing "Tragedy of the Commons" justifies this approach.[490]

"Affected person" should be read broadly. It includes any person or entity harmed or whose interests are affected in areas beyond national jurisdiction. By analogy to trusteeship rights, interest groups concerned with particular elements in the global commons, such as those for the protection of marine mammals or Antarctica, can be considered "affected." Although duties towards the commons are viewed as obligations *erga omnes* (see Article 3 (Common Concern of Humanity)), the scope of this Article does not mean that no standing rules apply. Rather, this provision contemplates that the "affected person" must have suffered an injury to a legally-protected interest in order to bring a claim for appropriate remedies against harm to the environment and against the breach of any obligation relating to the commons.

PART X. APPLICATION AND COMPLIANCE

This Part seeks to ensure that the Covenant is implemented in an effective manner and to place it within its broader international context. Regarding the former, the Covenant contains provisions for reporting, as well as compliance and dispute-settlement mechanisms. The provision on compliance mechanisms is particularly innovative. This Part addresses how the Covenant fits into the already existing framework of international law on environment and development. The general and non-exclusive nature of the Covenant is evident by the expressed and implicit references to other treaties, as is its law-making and framework nature.

490 *Cf.* Article 58 (Areas Beyond National Jurisdiction) of the Draft Covenant.

ARTICLE 56

OTHER TREATIES

Parties shall endeavor to become and remain party to treaties relating to the subject matter of this Covenant and shall implement them.

Article 56 acknowledges the dynamic nature of the environment and legal rules concerned with it. The Draft Covenant addresses subjects already governed by many international treaties. Such treaties will undoubtedly continue to proliferate in the coming decades. The Draft Covenant does not seek to replace these treaties, but rather to build an integrated legal framework of minimum standards which underpins existing law. Thus, Article 56 encourages Parties to adhere to other related treaties. The term "endeavour to" requires States to make a good faith effort to adhere and remain party to such treaties.

Complexities may occur where existing treaty law is not fully consistent with the contents of the Draft Covenant. To the extent that all parties to the prior treaty are also parties to the Covenant, the Covenant could be viewed as a successor treaty according to Article 59 of the Vienna Convention on the Law of Treaties (1969) and the earlier treaty suspended or terminated insofar as it is incompatible with the Covenant.[491] In cases of lesser potential conflict, the provisions of the earlier treaties should be considered in light of their object and purpose and read broadly to be reconciled with the Draft Covenant obligations to the fullest extent possible. Future treaties should be drafted in conformity with the obligations contained in the Draft Covenant.[492]

The second aspect of Article 56 is the obligation to implement other treaties, a specific application of *pacta sunt servanda*, a fundamental principle of international law. The duty is not qualified by the words "endeavour to", but is a strict duty to carry out in good faith obligations that are assumed under treaties relating to the subject matter of the Draft Covenant. The latter phrase should be read broadly.[493]

---

[491] It may also be possible to view the Draft Covenant as an agreement to modify an earlier multilateral agreement pursuant to Article 41 of the Vienna Convention on the Law of Treaties (1969).

[492] *Cf.* Article 22 of the Convention on Biological Diversity (1992); Article 237 of UNCLOS (1982). See also Article 8 of the Desertification Convention which calls for coordination of activities carried out under various conventions.

[493] See Article 34 of the Straddling Stocks Agreement (1995): "States Parties shall fulfil in good faith the obligations assumed under this Agreement and shall exercise the rights recognized in this Agreement in a manner which would not constitute an abuse of right."

ARTICLE 57

MORE STRINGENT MEASURES

1. The provisions of this Covenant shall not affect the right of Parties individually or jointly to adopt and implement more stringent measures than those required under this Covenant.

2. The provisions of this Covenant shall not prejudice any stricter obligation which Parties have entered into or may enter into under existing or future treaties.

Article 57 is related to the previous provision, reflecting the likelihood that States will continue to set individual and international environmental standards on matters governed by the Draft Covenant. Paragraph 1 sets forth the general proposition that such action can be more stringent than that required under the Draft Covenant, while Paragraph 2 affirms that stricter obligations arising from other treaties, whether past or future, are not to be prejudiced by anything in the Draft Covenant.

The Draft Covenant is thus intended to be a minimum set of obligations, upon which Parties can elaborate additional more stringent requirements at national or international levels. In particular, the Draft Covenant acknowledges that the diversity of environmental and developmental conditions around the world is vast and in many cases these differences will require more detailed and strict obligations than can be elaborated in this present document. Such differing standards may result from the need to create local or regionally specific regulation on account of particular ecosystems, pollution threats, or socio-economic factors.[494] As such, higher standards are admissible under the Draft Covenant, although lower ones are not.

Any such higher standards must be for *bona fide* environmental purposes. Recalling Article 30(1)(c) (Trade and Environment) of the Draft Covenant, these provisions should not be for economic protection.[495]

---

494 Regional regulation, which may be stricter than what is provided under a global convention, is contemplated by Article VIII of the London Convention (1972), Article 197 of UNCLOS (1982), and Article 11 of the Basel Convention (1989). Article XIV (1) of CITES (1973) explicitly allows for individual States to take stricter measures.

495 *Cf.* Article 130(t) of the EC Treaty (1957), as amended, which allows individual Member States to introduce more stringent protective measures than those outlined in the Treaty, so long as the other provisions of the Treaty are also complied with. See also EC secondary legislation; EC Council Directive EEC/440/75 on Quality of Surface Water; EC Council Directive EEC/360/84 on Air Pollution from Industrial Plants and EC Council Directive EEC/278/86 on the Protection of the Soil.

ARTICLE 58

AREAS BEYOND THE LIMITS OF NATIONAL JURISDICTION

In areas beyond the limits of national jurisdiction, Parties shall observe the provisions of the present Covenant to the full extent of their competence.

Article 58 gives effect to the fundamental principles expressed in the Draft Covenant that States are required to protect and preserve the environment of areas beyond national jurisdiction (Article 11(1)(b) (States))[496] and that the global environment is a common concern of humanity (Article 3). It operates in addition to the provisions in Part VII (Transboundary Issues). Areas beyond national jurisdiction, otherwise known as the global commons, include the high seas, the deep seabed, and outer space.

Many provisions of international law already provide protection to these areas. The most comprehensive relate to the marine environment, as codified by Parts VII (Section 2) and XII of UNCLOS (1982). Even prior to its adoption, several international agreements regulated the taking of marine resources[497] and pollution[498] of the high seas. The norms governing outer space are not as detailed, although elements of a precautionary regime exist.[499]

The reference to "the full extent of their competence" affirms that under general international law Parties have jurisdiction over and are responsible for state activities as well as those of their nationals[500] and vessels flying their flags.[501]

---

496 See also Principle 21 of the Stockholm Declaration (1972); Helsinki Final Act (1975) (Basket 5 on Environment); Principles 3, 21(d) and 21(e) of the World Charter for Nature (1982); and Principle 2 of the Rio Declaration (1992).

497 E.g., Whaling Convention (1946), Atlantic Tunas Convention (1966). See also FAO High Seas Fishing Agreement (1993). *Cf. Behring Sea Fur Seals* arbitration; *Fisheries Jurisdiction* case.

498 There are international rules and standards based on various sources of pollution: e.g., on dumping of waste, the London Convention (1972) and North-East Atlantic Pollution Convention (1990); on pollution from vessels: MARPOL Convention (1973) and its 1978 London Protocol, SOLAS Convention (1974); on oil pollution: Intervention Convention (1969), Oil Pollution Civil Liability Convention (1969) and Fund Convention (1971); for radioactive pollution from nuclear tests, Nuclear Test Ban Treaty (1963) (*Cf.* the *Nuclear Tests* case).

499 See Article 9 of the Outer Space Treaty (1967); Article 2 of the Space Objects Liability Convention (1972); Article VI Space Objects Registration Convention (1975); and Article 7 of the Moon Treaty (1979).

500 But this is only in certain cases, particularly in relation to criminal law.

501 *Cf.* Article 4(b) of the Convention on Biological Diversity (1992). Also note the requirement under Article 32(5) (Military and other Hostile Activities) that all military personnel, aircraft, vessels and installations are also subject to rules of environmental protection.

ARTICLE 59

RELATIONS WITH NON-PARTIES

Parties shall encourage non-Parties to act in a manner that is consistent with the objective of this Covenant.

Article 59 is premised on the view that the traditional concept of reciprocity in treaty-making is inappropriate to the attainment of sustainable development. The obligations contained in the Draft Covenant are intended to reflect the dynamic, indivisible and interdependent nature of the global environment. The international community as a whole is intended to benefit from the implementation of the Draft Covenant, not only those party to it.

Article 59 does not purport to impose duties on third States, in accordance with Article 34 of the Vienna Convention on the Law of Treaties (1969),[502] except to the extent that the Draft Covenant is declaratory of customary international law; third States are free to indicate their assent to the obligations contained herein without necessarily becoming parties. The Draft Covenant also does not grant non-parties particular benefits from Parties, except to the extent that they may receive such benefits in the course of a Party complying with its obligations under the Draft Covenant. For example, a Party is not required to provide additional development assistance to non-parties, but should it choose to provide such assistance, it will be required to conduct an environmental impact assessment (Article 46 (International Financial Resources)). At the same time, the Draft Covenant seeks to create a minimum set of standards to be applied universally by the Parties. As such, this provision can operate to prevent non-parties from gaining any significant competitive advantage over States bound by it. Other environmental treaties contain similar provisions.[503]

---

502 Note that the Draft Covenant does not purport to be an exceptions to this rule, as is Article 2(6) of the UN Charter (1945).

503 See e.g., Article X of CITES (1973), Article 7 of the Basel Convention (1989), and Article 4 of the 1987 Montreal Protocol. Article 17 of the Straddling Stocks Agreement (1995) goes further. A state which is not a member of a sub-regional or regional fisheries management organization or is not a participant in one and which does not otherwise agree to apply the conservation and management measures established by such organization or arrangement, is not discharged from the obligation to cooperate, in accordance with the Convention and this Agreement, in the conservation and management of the relevant straddling fish stocks and highly migratory fish stocks. Such state shall not authorize vessels flying its flag to engage in fishing operations for the straddling fish stocks or highly migratory fish stocks which are subject to the conservation and management measures established by such organization or arrangement.

ARTICLE 60

REPORTING

1. **Parties undertake to submit periodic reports on the measures they have adopted, progress made, and difficulties encountered in implementing their obligations under this Covenant.**

2. **All reports shall be submitted to the Secretary-General of the United Nations.**

Article 60 requires each Party to submit regular national reports on its experience in implementing the Draft Covenant. This is intended to assist each Party to identify those areas where more measures need to be taken and in measuring each Party's compliance with the Draft Covenant, related to the non-compliance procedure established under the Draft Covenant (Article 61 (Compliance and Dispute Avoidance)). A subsidiary aim of the provision is to put into operation the obligation to exchange information, a key to effective environmental protection.[504] It will also assist Parties in deciding upon their international transfers of financial resources (Article 46 (International Financial Resources)). For these reasons, national reporting has become a standard feature of modern international environmental agreements.[505]

Paragraph 1 does not determine the precise periodicity of these reports which should be set by the Depositary (Article 71) in consultation with other Parties. It may be subject to decisions taken at the Review Conference (Article 63). The content of the reports might be based on the national action plans to be drawn up by every Party (Article 35 (National Action Plans)) as well as on reports required under any other environmental treaty. Reports should include the texts or summaries of all measures adopted, including international agreements, legislation, regulations, decrees, programmes, action plans, and any other measures a Party considers relevant. The reports also should include an estimate of the effects of the enumerated measures. "Progress made and difficulties encountered" includes the factual situation (i.e., state of the environment, particularly as observed when implementing Article 39 (Monitoring of Environmental Quality)) as well as an analysis of the efficacy of the legal measures taken in response. Bearing in mind differences of capacity, Parties should, as far as possible, agree on common methodologies and formats, to allow

---

504 See Article 43 (Information and Knowledge) of the Draft Covenant. Article 71(2)(a) (Depositary) requires the Depositary to disseminate these reports, preferably to all parties, and it is contemplated that the reports referred to in Article 71(2)(b) will be based on the national reports.

505 See e.g., Article 8 of the LRTAP Convention (1979); Article 5 of the Vienna Convention on the Ozone Layer (1985); Article 7 of the 1987 Montreal Protocol: Article 17 of the 1991 Madrid Protocol to the Antarctic Treaty; Article 29 of the World Heritage Convention (1972); Article 26 of the Convention on Biological Diversity (1992), Article 12 of Climate Change Convention (1992). Article 9 of the Danube Convention (1994).

the making of useful comparisons. This could perhaps be discussed during Review Conferences (Article 63).

Paragraph 2, designates the Secretary General of the United Nations to receive these reports. The Draft Covenant does not specify any follow-up action by ECOSOC, although it may be appropriate to consider submitting the reports to the Commission on Sustainable Development.

ARTICLE 61

COMPLIANCE AND DISPUTE AVOIDANCE

In the framework of environmental treaties to which they are party or by other means, Parties shall maintain or promote the establishment of procedures and institutional mechanisms, including enquiry and fact-finding, to assist and encourage States to comply fully with their obligations and to avoid environmental disputes. Such procedures and mechanisms should improve and strengthen reporting requirements, and be simple, transparent, and non-confrontational.

Article 61 encourages Parties to devise mechanisms for compliance and dispute avoidance within the framework of their environmental treaty obligations. "Environmental treaties" encompasses all international obligations relating to environmental and developmental matters, including the Draft Covenant.

The first element, compliance, refers to mechanisms to enhance compliance rather than to traditional dispute settlement regimes exclusively.[506] This is based on the view that the traditional concept of reciprocity in treaty relations is inadequate to achieve the objective of the Draft Covenant. Other, non-reciprocal fields of international law, such as human rights and the protection of Antarctica, have long used compliance mechanisms to enhance implementation of treaty obligations and prevent disputes.[507] These mechanisms avoid the need for recourse to remedies available under express dispute resolution regimes or under general international law.[508] The Draft Covenant seeks to promote this trend, echoing Agenda 21.[509]

---

[506] E.g., Montreal Protocol (1987); Climate Change Convention (1992); 1985 Helsinki Protocol on the Reduction of Sulphur Emissions to the LRTAP Convention; and 1991 Geneva Protocol concerning the Control of Emissions of Volatile Organic Compounds to the LRTAP Convention. This is based, in part, on the experience of international human rights law.

[507] E.g., the establishment of an inspection procedure whose reports are widely available under 1991 Madrid Protocol on Environmental Protection to the Antarctic Treaty; Article 14 provides an additional means for facilitating compliance.

[508] See e.g., Article 60 of the Vienna Convention on the Law of Treaties (1969).

[509] See Paragraphs 39.8 - 39.10.

The second element, dispute avoidance, relates closely to the use of compliance mechanisms and represents a progressive development of international law although some dispute avoidance mechanisms exist.[510] Meeting this obligation will not entail amending applicable treaties, since the measures contemplated here are largely informal and can be integrated into the institutional frameworks of those instruments.

Regarding the first element, compliance mechanisms may be effective in supervising achievement of the objective of sustainable development, as well as in avoiding disputes. A non-confrontational mechanism or "constructive dialogue"[511] can be useful to assess the adequacy of measures taken by Parties to implement environmental treaties, and can offer suggested means to improve, especially in cases of inadequacies due to lack of national capacity. The use of such a mechanism is particularly appropriate in the context of modern international environmental law which relies on the principle of common but differentiated responsibilities and where obligations are often progressive or interrelated.[512] With such obligations, it may be difficult to determine whether an act is in compliance. A compliance mechanism may assess performance and make recommendations in a non-adversarial context, before an inter-State dispute arises.

In general, it should not be necessary to amend existing environmental treaties in order to meet this obligation, since Conferences of the Parties established by most environmental treaties tend to have sufficiently broad mandates to accommodate this requirement. Indeed, the international regime set up in order to protect the ozone layer can be considered in this regard as a model, but the Montreal Protocol (1987) did not itself establish a compliance mechanism.[513] It was created later.

---

510 See Article 28 of the Straddling Stocks Agreement (1995) ("States shall cooperate in order to prevent disputes: To this end, States shall agree on efficient and expeditious decision-making procedures within sub-regional and regional fisheries management organizations and arrangements and shall strengthen existing decision-making procedures as necessary."); and Article 17 of the Watercourses Convention (1997) (States shall enter into consultations and, if necessary, negotiations with a view to arriving at an equitable resolution of potential disputes. Negotiations shall be conducted on the basis that each state must in good faith pay reasonable regard to the rights and legitimate interests of the other State.)

511 E.g., the review process of the UN Human Rights Committee.

512 Convention on Biological Diversity (1992) and Climate Change Convention (1992).

513 The only mention of such a mechanism appears in Article 8 of the 1987 Montreal Protocol, which reads:

> The Parties, at their first meeting, shall consider and approve procedures and institutional mechanisms for determining non-compliance with the provisions of this Protocol and for the treatment of Parties found to be in non-compliance.
>
> In this case, the mechanism was established by a decision of the parties (UNEP/OzL.Pro.4/15, 25 November 1993). The compliance mechanism established under the Montreal Protocol can be triggered by one party against another, the Secretariat to the relevant treaty, and by a party in respect of itself.

Compliance mechanisms are linked to requirements relating to exchanges and dissemination of information.[514] In particular, emphasis is placed on national reporting of measures taken to implement treaty obligations, which in the case of the Draft Covenant is required under Article 60 (Reporting). In this regard, NGO's often have access to important environmental information and it is to be hoped that they can participate when compliance mechanisms evolve into greater use.

The provision outlines three requisite characteristics of compliance mechanisms: that they be simple, transparent, and non-confrontational. These are sought in the regime established under the Montreal Protocol (1987). One positive factor in that agreement is that decisions on how to respond to non-compliance are left to the main institutional body, the Meeting of the Parties.

It is apparent that to be effective, compliance mechanisms should coordinate with other treaty bodies, such as its secretariat and financial mechanism, as well as with relevant international organizations. The particular action available once the compliance mechanism has been activated might vary on the basis of specific subject-matter and should be devised within the context of each environmental treaty. In the case of the Draft Covenant, matters may proceed to the attention of the Review Conference (Article 63).

The rationale for dispute avoidance, the second element of this provision, is that it is generally agreed that it is not possible to quantify monetarily some types of environmental damage or to achieve full restoration to the *status quo ante* in all cases of breach of an international obligation.[515] Thus, it is better to prevent such damage from occurring than to seek formal dispute resolution after the fact. Article 61, accordingly, would have Parties act before a situation escalates into a formal dispute. Some examples of this might include provision of financial resources, technical assistance, or transfer of technology. The relevant provisions of the Draft Covenant covering these matters should continue to apply in cases of non-compliance. In order to identify when circumstances warrant such action, mechanisms and procedures should be developed for regular information exchange.[516] Coordination and cooperation with relevant international organizations should enhance the ability to avoid disputes. Finally, disputes may be resolvable in national courts and decisions there made enforceable in the jurisdictions of other Parties.[517]

---

514 See e.g., Article VI of the FAO High Seas Fishing Agreement (1993), which specifies in detail what information is to be exchanged. See also Articles 15 (Prevention and Response to Emergencies), 33 (Transboundary Environmental Effects), 34 (Transboundary Natural Resources), 39 (Monitoring of Environmental Quality), and 43 (Information and Knowledge).

515 See e.g., *Chorzów Factory* case (Jurisdiction). See also *Chorzów Factory* case (*Indemnity*).

516 See e.g., Article VII of the US-Canada Air Quality Agreement (1991)) as well for as early notification and consultation (See paragraph 39.10 of Agenda 21 (1992)). Environmental impact assessments (see Article 37) and measures to mitigate the environmental risks posed by approved activities should also be undertake (see e.g., Article V of the US-Canada Air Quality Agreement (1991).

517 See e.g., Oil Pollution Civil Liability Convention (1969); Canada-US Agreement on Fisheries Enforcement (1990).

Institutional arrangements can facilitate dispute avoidance. The 1991 ECE Convention on Environmental Impact Assessment in a Transboundary Context establishes an inquiry commission which can be triggered by any party in the event that agreement cannot be reached on whether it is likely that a significant transboundary environmental impact will occur.[518] The experience of the European Commission as a forum to resolve matters, avoiding their submission to the European Court of Justice, has been positive. The implementation committees established in connection with compliance procedures under other instruments also can be effective in this context,[519] as can the technical bodies established under some environmental treaties.[520] Similarly, the verification procedures established under some treaties to investigate alleged non-compliance, whether through a secretariat[521] or through specialized arrangements,[522] can facilitate negotiations aimed at preventing matters from escalating into a formal dispute. Finally, the jurisdiction of the International Court of Justice to hand down non-binding advisory opinions can be invoked in certain cases to provide guidance to States.[523]

ARTICLE 62

SETTLEMENT OF DISPUTES

1. Parties shall settle disputes concerning the interpretation or application of this Covenant by peaceful means, such as by negotiation, enquiry, mediation, conciliation, arbitration, judicial settlement, resort to regional agencies or arrangements, or by any other peaceful means of their own choice.

2. If parties to a dispute do not reach agreement on a solution or on a dispute settlement arrangement within one year following the notification by one party to another that a dispute exists, the dispute shall, at the request of one of the parties, be submitted to either an arbitral tribunal, including the Permanent Court of Arbitration, or to judicial settlement, including by the In-

518 Article 3(7) and Appendix IV.

519 See e.g., the committees established under the 1987 Montreal Protocol; Articles 10 and 11 of the 1991 Madrid Protocol; Article 8 of the 1985 Helsinki Protocol on the Reduction of Sulphur Emissions to the LRTAP Convention; Article VIII of the US-Canada Air Quality Agreement (1991).

520 E.g., Article 25 of the Convention on Biological Diversity (1992) creates a Subsidiary Body on Scientific, Technical and Technological Advice.

521 E.g., as provided for in Article 19 of the Bamako Convention (1991).

522 E.g., as those established under the Verification Annex to the Chemical Weapons Convention (1993).

523 See Article 96 of the UN Charter (1945) and Chapter 4 of the Statute of the International Court of Justice (1945) for the conditions under which the Court has such jurisdiction and the procedure to be followed.

ternational Court of Justice and the International Tribunal for the Law of the Sea as appropriate.

Article 62 establishes a non-exhaustive list of venues available to Parties seeking to peacefully settle disputes concerning the interpretation or application of the Draft Covenant.[524] In contrast to Article 61, this provision applies once a formal dispute exists. It allows parties to a dispute the flexibility to pursue peaceful means of their choice. The flexibility provided in the Draft Covenant is intended to encourage settlement. Given the non-reciprocal nature of the Draft Covenant, it is preferable that Parties seek redress under these mechanisms rather than exercising any entitlement under general international law to repudiate the treaty.[525]

Paragraph 1 follows closely the language of other global environmental treaties.[526] An innovation is the suggestion that the good offices of regional agencies or arrangements be employed, particularly those established under regional environmental treaties, because they may be able to achieve a satisfactory settlement where the disputants are from the same region. Given the desire to solve environmental disputes quickly and effectively, parties should explore the "alternative" dispute resolution mechanisms before resorting to judicial settlement.

Where the subject-matter of the dispute is regulated under another environmental treaty, the obligation under the Draft Covenant is discharged if the dispute settlement mechanism under the other treaty is invoked. However, recourse to such a body should occur only if the principles upon which the present Covenant is based can be integrated into that framework.

The provision applies when three conditions are satisfied. The first is that a dispute exist. This term should be interpreted broadly, in accordance with the *dicta* of the International Court of Justice that a dispute is "a disagreement on a point of law or fact, a conflict of legal views or of interests between two persons."[527] Secondly, the dispute is between Parties, regarding either an act by another Party or by any institution which may be created under the Draft Covenant.[528] This provision does not apply to controversies among or involving non-State actors, unless taken up by Parties.[529] Thirdly, at least insofar as arbitral or judicial settlement is sought, the dispute must be

---

524 This is in conformity with the obligation set forth in Article 2(3) of the UN Charter (1945), which is declaratory of customary international law.

525 See Article 60 of the Vienna Convention on the Law of Treaties (1969) on the doctrine of material breach.

526 See e.g., Article 20 of the Basel Convention (1989); Article 14 of the Climate Change Convention (1992); Article XXV of the Antarctic Marine Living Resources (1980) Convention.

527 See e.g., *Southwest Africa (preliminary Objections)* case; *Mavrommatis Palestine Concessions (Jurisdiction)* case; *Cameroons* case; *Peace Treaties* case; *Nuclear Tests* case; *Headquarters* case.

528 See, *ICAO Council* case.

529 See *Mavrommatis Palestine Concessions (Jurisdiction)*, (*Greece v. United Kingdom*).

one which the States involved have standing to pursue, by virtue of having a legal interest in the matter. General principles of international law can assist on the matter of standing. The International Law Commission has taken a broad view of the matter, stating that an injured State in the context of a multilateral treaty is one whose right is infringed by an internationally wrongful act "... if it is established that the right has been expressly stipulated in that treaty for the protection of the collective interests of the States parties thereto."[530] The consequence of the environment being a "common concern of humanity" (Article 3) is that all Parties have an interest in its protection.

Paragraph 2 is intended to ensure that disputes are settled if at least one of the parties to the dispute so desires. It provides that if efforts at resolution fail after one year, any party may submit the dispute to arbitral or judicial settlement. The purpose is to require a binding ruling by an impartial body. As the Draft Covenant is not intended to amend existing environmental treaties, it will be left to the parties to determine the modalities of the venue. The duty of all Parties to cooperate in good faith requires that once notification of any such intention is received by the other parties, they shall negotiate on the acceptable venue. The mechanisms listed in this provision are illustrative only, and parties are free to devise other binding arrangements between themselves, including recourse to national judicial bodies. All parties to the dispute must treat as binding any ruling of such a body.

ARTICLE 63

REVIEW CONFERENCE

After the entry into force of this Covenant, the Secretary General of the United Nations shall convene every five years a conference of Parties to it in order to review its implementation. The United Nations, its specialized agencies and the International Atomic Energy Agency, as well as any State or regional economic integration organization not party to this Covenant may be represented at the Review Conference as observers. The International Union for Conservation of Nature and Natural Resources and the International Council of Scientific Unions may also be represented as observers. Any non-governmental organization accredited to the UN Economic and Social Council and qualified in matters covered by this Covenant, may be represented at a session of the Review Conference as an observer in accordance with the rules of procedure the Review Conference may adopt.

Article 63 provides a framework, in the form of regular meetings, by which the implementation of the Draft Covenant can be reviewed by Parties to it. Meetings on the particulars of implementation can be useful because many of the obligations set forth in the Draft Covenant are ones of result, without specifying means. In addition, unforeseeable changes in the international commu-

[530] Article 5(2)(f) of the ILC Draft Articles on State Responsibility.

nity or the global environment may necessitate adjustments to the Draft Covenant. The Draft Covenant covers matters which are addressed in a number of other international instruments and significant aspects of their implementation may require consideration within the framework of the Draft Covenant. Finally, review conferences are intended to be occasions when detailed multilateral discussion can take place on all matters requiring States to cooperate with each other.

The functions of the review conference have been omitted deliberately from the text, in the expectation that the Parties themselves will tailor this process to their needs. A conference might decide to invoke the formal amendment procedure outlined in Article 64 (Amendment). In other circumstances, less formal modifications may be discussed. Another conference might adopt an agreed interpretation of a set of provisions. This is particularly important for the Draft Covenant which is intended to evolve over a long period of time. Finally, review conferences may follow up or act on the recommendations made under any compliance mechanism set up (see Article 61).

Experience with the review conference may lead Parties to decide that a more elaborate international institutional arrangement is necessary to support the implementation of the Draft Covenant. Initially, however, Article VIII of ENMOD, which provides for an initial review conference to be convened with a possibility of future meetings, if parties agree, was considered a suitable model for the Draft Covenant. The importance of the matters regulated by this Draft Covenant suggested an alteration from this formula so that review conferences occur on a regular basis; five years should suffice to ensure consistency without redundancy.

Article 63 makes provision for bodies which may participate in the review conference as observers. The provision follows the language of equivalent provisions in existing global environmental treaties,[531] save in four respects.

First, express mention is made of the entitlement of any regional economic integration organization (REIO) that is not party to participate as an observer. It is possible that an REIO, which intends to become a Party, has not completed all the necessary procedures by the time the first or even subsequent review conferences take place.[532] There is no policy reason for treating such organizations differently from States who are not yet parties. Secondly, an automatic entitlement to participate as observers is accorded the IUCN and the ICSU: this reflects the close relationship of IUCN to the development of the Draft Covenant, and recognizes that both IUCN and ICSU have potential to contribute to the implementation of the Draft Covenant, on account of their wide-ranging expertise. Thirdly, in addition to applying the usual criterion that NGO observers must be qualified in matters covered by the Draft Covenant, NGOs must also be accredited with ECOSOC. The ECOSOC list of observers is long, but it is still limited and will keep the number of NGOs entitled to participate to a manageable number. Finally, many precedents specify that NGOs may

---

531 E.g., Article 7(6) of the Climate Change Convention (1992).

532 E.g., this occurred recently for the European Union at the first meeting of the Parties to the Basel Convention (1989).

be allowed to participate "unless at least one third of the Parties present object." This point is left to be addressed by the rules of procedure of the review conference. Parties retain the discretion on how to agree rules of procedure, but it is customary for them to be adopted by consensus.[533]

PART XI. FINAL CLAUSES

Since the Draft Covenant is intended to become a binding global treaty, it must contain a set of technical rules governing issues such as becoming a Party, entry into force, amendments etc. Part XI sets forth these rules, mostly standard clauses based on well-established precedents in international environmental law.

ARTICLE 64

AMENDMENT

1. **Any Party may propose amendments to this Covenant. The text of any such proposed amendment shall be submitted to the Secretary-General of the United Nations who shall transmit it, within six months, to all the Parties.**

2. **At the request of one-third of the Parties, the Secretary-General of the United Nations shall call a special conference to consider the proposed amendment. The Parties shall make every effort to reach agreement on any proposed amendment by consensus. If all efforts at reaching a consensus have been exhausted, and no agreement reached, the amendment shall as a last resort be adopted by a two-thirds majority vote of the Parties to this Covenant who are present and voting at the special conference. The adopted amendment shall be communicated by the Secretary-General of the United Nations, who shall circulate it to all Parties for ratification, acceptance or approval. For purposes of this Article present and voting means Parties present and casting an affirmative or negative vote.**

3. **Instruments of ratification, acceptance or approval in respect of an amendment shall be deposited with the Secretary-General of the United Nations. An amendment shall enter into force for those States accepting it on the ninetieth day after the date of receipt by the Secretary-General of the United Nations of an instrument of ratification, acceptance or approval by at least two-thirds of the Parties. An amendment shall enter into force for any other Party on the ninetieth day following the date on which that Party deposits its**

[533] E.g., Article 23 of the Convention on Biological Diversity (1992) and Article 15 Basel Convention (1989).

instrument of ratification, acceptance or approval of the said amendment with the Secretary-General of the United Nations.

The present Article diverges from the precedents only in that its second paragraph provides for a special conference convened to consider proposed amendments if one third of the parties so request. This is to be contrasted with the general provision in other treaties for amendments to be adopted "at a meeting of the Conference on the Parties."[534] The need to provide expressly for the holding of a special conference follows from the fact that the present Covenant envisages a Review Conference only once every five years (Article 63), whilst the precedents provide for meetings of their parties at regular intervals, often once a year.[535] The procedure for the adoption of amendments is a standard one in accordance with other environmental treaties. The provisions of the Vienna Convention on the Law of Treaties (1969) apply to the case of those States which do not adhere to an amendment which has entered into force,[536] as it does to the case of becoming party to the Covenant after an amendment is in force.[537]

ARTICLE 65

SIGNATURE

1. **This Covenant shall be open for signature at _______________ by all States and any regional economic integration organization from ____________ until _______________.**

2. **For purposes of this Covenant, regional economic integration organization means an organization constituted by sovereign States of a given region, to which its member States have transferred competence in respect of matters governed by this Covenant and which has been duly authorized, in accordance with its internal procedures, to sign, ratify, accept, approve or accede to it.**

The length of time for the Draft Covenant to be open for signature and whether the Covenant should be open for signature at more than one location have been left blank in Paragraph 1 because they are political issues to be decided by the negotiating States. According to the normal practice in

---

534 E.g., Article 15 of the Climate Change Convention (1992); Article 29 of the Convention on Biological Diversity (1992); Article 17 of the Basel Convention (1989) and Article 9 of the Vienna Convention on the Ozone Layer (1985).

535 E.g., Article 15 of the Climate Change Convention (1992), Article 29 of the Convention on Biological Diversity (1992), Article 17 of the Basel Convention (1989), Article 9 of the Vienna Convention on the Ozone Layer (1985), Article 313 of UNCLOS (1982).

536 See Article 40(4) of the Vienna Convention on the Law of Treaties (1969).

537 See Article 40(5) of the Vienna Convention on the Law of Treaties (1969).

other environmental treaties, signature is not an expression of consent to be bound.[538] Subsequent to signature but prior to ratification, acceptance or approval, States and REIOs are required to refrain from acts which would defeat the object and purpose of the Covenant.[539]

The definition in Paragraph 2 of "regional economic integration organizations" echoes the language of other environmental treaties.[540] The key phrase in the definition is "to which its member States have transferred competence". This distinguishes a REIO from other international organizations. The most prominent example to date of an REIO is the European Union.

ARTICLE 66

RATIFICATION, ACCEPTANCE OR APPROVAL

1. **This Covenant shall be subject to ratification, acceptance or approval by States and by regional economic integration organizations. Instruments of ratification, acceptance, or approval, shall be deposited with the Secretary-General of the United Nations.**

2. **Any regional economic integration organization which becomes party to this Covenant without any of its member States being party shall be bound by all the obligations under this Covenant. In the case of such organizations, one or more of whose member States is party to this Covenant, the organization and its member States shall decide on their respective responsibilities for the performance of their obligations under this Covenant. In such cases, the organization and the member States shall not be entitled to exercise rights under this Covenant concurrently.**

3. **In their instruments of ratification, acceptance or approval, regional economic integration organizations shall declare the extent of their competence with respect to the matters governed by this Covenant. These organizations shall also inform the Depositary of any relevant modification in the extent of their competence.**

The normal practice in environmental treaties[541] is to require an expression of consent to be bound in the form of ratification, acceptance or approval (Paragraph 1).[542] It is now commonplace for such provisions in environmental treaties to specify the way in which the treaty's obligations

---

[538] Article 12 of the Vienna Convention on the Law of Treaties (1969) lays out specific conditions for signature to be binding.

[539] See Article 18 of the Vienna Convention on the Law of Treaties (1969).

[540] E.g., Article 1(6) of the Vienna Convention on the Ozone Layer (1985).

[541] Article 22 Basel Convention; Article 13 of the Vienna Convention on the Protection of the Ozone

bind REIOs and their member states. For example, such provisions have allowed the European Communities to become party to numerous environmental treaties. The provisions of Paragraph 2 ensure that, between them, a REIO and its member States will observe every obligation, recognising that if a particular obligation is met by the one it need not be met by the other. Paragraph 3 requires REIOs to declare at the time of ratification, rather than at signature as required in certain treaties,[543] the extent of their competence with regard to the Draft Covenant.

ARTICLE 67

ACCESSION

1. **This Covenant shall be open for accession by States and by regional economic integration organizations from the date on which this Covenant is closed for signature. The instruments of accession shall be deposited with the Secretary-General of the United Nations.**

2. **In their instruments of accession, regional economic integration organizations shall declare the extent of their competence with respect to the matters governed by this Covenant. These organizations shall also inform the Secretary-General of the United Nations of any relevant modification in the extent of their competence.**

Provision for accession[544] is necessary if, as in the present Covenant, it is decided to lay down a period of finite duration for signature. The language follows the precedents closely.[545]

ARTICLE 68

ENTRY INTO FORCE

1. **This Covenant shall enter into force on the ninetieth day after the deposit of the twenty-first instrument of ratification, acceptance, approval, or accession.**

Layer; Article 34 of the Convention on Biological Diversity (1992) and Article 22 of the Climate Change Convention (1992).

542 This is provided for under Article 14 of the Vienna Convention on the Law of Treaties (1969).

543 E.g., Annex IX, Article 2, of UNCLOS (1982).

544 This is permitted under Article 15 of the Vienna Convention on the Law of Treaties (1969).

545 E.g., Article 22 of the Climate Change Convention (1992); Article 14 of the Vienna Convention on the Ozone Layer (1985); Article 23 of the Basel Convention (1989) and Article 35 of the Convention on Biological Diversity (1992).

2. For each State or regional economic integration organization that ratifies, accepts, or approves, this Covenant or accedes thereto after the deposit of the twenty-first instrument of ratification, acceptance, approval, or accession, this Covenant shall enter into force on the ninetieth day after the date of deposit by such State or regional economic integration organization of its instrument of ratification, acceptance, approval, or accession.

3. For the purposes of paragraph 1 above, any instrument deposited by a regional economic integration organization shall not be counted as additional to those deposited by member States of such organization.

This text follows the precedents save with regard to the number of Parties required to trigger entry into force. The precedents vary considerably in this regard: UNCLOS (1982) requires sixty,[546] the Vienna Convention on the Ozone Layer (1985) twenty,[547] the Basel Convention (1989) twenty,[548] the Climate Change Convention (1992) fifty,[549] the Convention on Biological Diversity thirty,[550] and the 1987 Montreal Protocol eleven (subject to certain qualifications).[551] The number 21 was selected in this instance to enable an early entry into force while at the same time ensuring that the Covenant will become operational only when a significant number of States join. As usual, the instrument of an REIO shall not, for this purpose, be counted as additional to any deposited by its members.

ARTICLE 69

RESERVATIONS

No reservations may be made to this Covenant.

Under Article 19 of the Vienna Convention on the Law of Treaties, a State may enter a reservation unless "the reservation is prohibited by the treaty." Environmental agreements normally preclude no reservation.[552] In a few instances, parties may register exceptions with regard to tech-

---

546 Article 308(1).

547 Article 17(1).

548 Article 25(1).

549 Article 23(1).

550 Article 36(1).

551 Article 16(1).

552 See e.g., Article 24 of the Climate Change Convention (1992); Article 18 of the Vienna Convention on the Ozone Layer (1985), Article 18 of the 1987 Montreal Protocol; Article 26(1) of the Basel Convention (1989).

nical details contained in annexes.[553] The obligations contained in the Draft Covenant form an integrated and balanced whole, and are of such importance that reservations to any provisions would detract from the Draft Covenant's object and purpose.

ARTICLE 70

WITHDRAWALS

1. **At any time after two years from the date on which this Covenant has entered into force for a Party, that Party may withdraw from this Covenant by giving written notification to the Secretary-General of the United Nations.**

2. **Any such withdrawal shall take place upon expiry of one year after the date of its receipt by the Secretary-General of the United Nations, or on such later date as may be specified in the notification of the withdrawal.**

This provision follows the standard format for such clauses. The only variation among the precedents concerns the length of time one must be party to a treaty before being permitted to withdraw from it.[554] The Draft Covenant will not terminate merely because, as a result of withdrawals, the number of parties falls below twenty-one.[555]

ARTICLE 71

DEPOSITARY

1. **The Secretary-General of the United Nations shall be the Depositary of this Covenant.**

2. **In addition to his functions as Depositary, the Secretary-General shall:**

   (a) **establish a schedule for the submission, consideration, and dissemination of the periodic reports submitted under Article 60;**

---

[553] For example, the listing of individual endangered species provided under Article XXIII of the CITES (1973).

[554] E.g., Article 38 of the Convention on Biological Diversity (1992) requires 2 years; ; Article 25 under the Climate Change Convention (1992) 3 years; Article 27 under the Basel Convention (1989) 3 years; Article 19 under the Vienna Convention on the Ozone Layer (1985) 4 years; Article 17 under the LRTAP Convention (1979) and its protocols, 5 years. Some environmental treaties do not lay down any necessary qualifying period for withdrawal, such as Article 317 of UNCLOS (1982) and Article XXIV of CITES (1973).

[555] See Article 55 of the Vienna Convention on the Law of Treaties (1969).

(b) report to all Parties, as well as to competent international organizations, on issues of a general nature that have arisen with respect to the implementation of this Covenant; and

(c) convene necessary conferences of Parties in accordance with this Covenant.

The designation of depositary is generally decided during the negotiating process. The formulation of Paragraph 1 allows the negotiating States to follow the practice for many global environmental treaties in nominating the UN Secretary-General or a State as Depositary.[556] The requirements of depositaries set out in the Vienna Convention on the Law of Treaties apply.[557] Paragraph 2 sets forth three other functions of the Secretary-General.[558] The first is to give effect to the requirement under Article 60 (Reporting) of the Draft Covenant that Parties file periodic reports on the implementation of the Covenant. A schedule for the submission of such reports should be established after full consultation with the Parties. It may be necessary to allow some flexibility to developing countries which may not have the capacity to prepare frequent reports. Discretion on dissemination of the reports is vested in the Depositary, although it is to be hoped that the reports will gain the widest possible circulation. The second function arises out the provision for consideration of the periodic reports. It requires the Depositary to make known issues of a general nature which arise out of the implementation of the Draft Covenant. These are issues, or a pattern of issues, which relate to a number of Parties. These reports are to go to all Parties and to competent international organizations, although dissemination to others is not prohibited. Competent international organizations can include other UN bodies, such as the Commission on Sustainable Development, as well as regional or bilateral environmental bodies or the secretariats of other international environmental conventions. The substance of the reports may form the basis of the agenda of a Review Conference (see Article 60), although Parties are free to raise at these Conferences issues not addressed by the Secretary-General. Parties are also entitled to resolve any difficulties informally or through any compliance mechanism which is established (see Article 62 (Settlement of Disputes)). The third function expressed in this provision is to convene the conferences of parties contemplated by the Covenant, namely the Review Conferences and conferences to consider amendments (Article 63 (Review Conference)).

---

556 See e.g., Article 19 of the Climate Change Convention (1992); Article 41 of the Convention on Biological Diversity (1992); Article 28 of the Basel Convention (1989); Article 319 of the UNCLOS (1982); and Article 20 of the Vienna Convention on the Ozone Layer (1985).

557 Article 77(1) of the Vienna Convention on the Law of Treaties (1969).

558 Article 77(1) of the Vienna Convention on the Law of Treaties (1969) permits the accordance of specifically-tailored functions to the depositary.

TABLE OF AUTHORITIES*

I. Treaties**

Treaty Concerning the Regulation of the Salmon Fishery in the Rhine River Basin, 30 June 1885 (EMuT 885:48) ["Rhine Fishing Convention (1885)"]

Convention for the Protection of Birds Useful to Agriculture, Paris, 19 March 1902 (30 Martens (2d) 686; 102 BFSP 969) (EMuT 902:22) ["Paris Birds Convention (1902)"]

Treaty between the United States and Great Britain Respecting Boundary Waters Between the United States and Canada, Washington, 11 January 1909 (4 AJIL (Suppl.) 239) ["Boundary Waters Treaty (1909)"]

Geneva Protocol for the Prohibition of the Use in War of Asphyxiating, Poisonous or Other Gases, and of Bacteriological Methods of Warfare, 17 June 1925 (UKTS 27 (1930), Cmnd 5280) (EMuT 925:45) ["Geneva Gas Protocol (1925)"]

Convention Relative to the Preservation of Fauna and Flora in their Natural State, London, 8 November 1933 (UKTS 27 (1930), Cmnd 5280) (EMuT 933:83) ["Convention on Preservation of Fauna and Flora (1933)"]

Convention on Nature Protection and Wildlife Preservation in the Western Hemisphere (Washington), 12 October 1940 (161 UNTS 193) (EMuT 940:76) ["Western Hemisphere Convention (1940)"]

Charter of the United Nations, San Francisco, 1945 (1 UNTS xvi) (EMuT 945:47) ["UN Charter (1945)"]

Statute of the International Court of Justice, San Francisco, 26 June 1945 (UKTS 67 (1946), Cmnd 7015; USTS 993)

International Convention for the Regulation of Whaling, Washington, 2 December 1946 (161 UNTS 72) (EMuT 946:89) ["Whaling Convention (1946)"]

General Agreement on Tariffs and Trade, 1947 (55 UNTS 187) (EMuT 947:82) ["GATT (1947)"]

Convention on the Prevention and Punishment of the Crime of Genocide, New York, 9 December 1948 (78 UNTS 277)

International Convention for the Protection of Birds, Paris, 18 October 1950 (638 UNTS 186) (EMuT 950:77) ["Birds Convention (1950)"]

Convention for the Protection of Human Rights and Fundamental Freedoms, Rome, 4 November 1950 (213 UNTS 221) (EMuT 950:82) ["European Human Rights Convention (1950)"]; and Protocol I, Paris, 18 May 1954

International Convention for the Prevention of Pollution of the Sea by Oil, London, 12 May 1954 (327 UNTS 3) (EMuT 954:36) ["OILPOL Convention (1954)"]

---

* The short forms used in the text of the Commentary are indicated in square brackets along side the relevant entry.

** EMuT = International Environmental Law – Multilateral Treaties, Kluwer Law International (UK).

Hague Convention on the Protection of Cultural Property In the Event Armed Conflict, 14 May 1954 (249 UNTS 240) ["Hague Cultural Property Convention (1954)"]

Interim Convention on the Conservation of North Pacific Fur Seals, Washington, 9 February 1957 (314 UNTS 105 (as amended by subsequent protocols in 15 UST 316, TIAS 5558; 20 UST 2292, TIAS 6774; 27 UST 3371, TIAS 8368; and 32 UST 5881, TIAS 10020)) ["North Pacific Seals Convention (1957)"]

Treaty Establishing the European Economic Community, Rome, 25 March 1957 (298 UNTS 11) (EMuT 957:23) ["EC Treaty as amended"]; as amended by the Single European Act, Luxembourg, 17 February 1986, and the Hague, 28 February 1986 (UKTS 31 (1989), Cmnd 9758) (EMuT 986:16); and the Maastricht Treaty on European Union, Maastricht, 7 February 1992 (OJ No C191, 29.07.1992) (EMuT 992:11)

Convention on Fishing and Conservation of the Living Resources of the High Seas, Geneva, 29 April 1958 (559 UNTS 285) (EMuT 958:31) ["High Seas Living Resources Convention (1958)"]

Convention on the High Seas, Geneva, 29 April 1958 (450 UNTS 82) (EMuT 958:33) ["High Seas Convention (1958)"]

Antarctic Treaty, Washington, 1 December 1959 (402 UNTS 71) ["Antarctic Treaty (1959)"]; and Protocol on Environmental Protection, Madrid, 4 October 1991 (reprinted in 30 ILM 1461 (1991)) (EMuT 959:91) ["Madrid Protocol (1991)"]

The Indus Waters Treaty, Karachi, 19 September 1960, 1962 UNTS 126

Convention on Third Party Liability in the Field of Nuclear Energy, Paris, 29 July 1960 (956 UNTS 251 (as amended by 1964 Protocol (UNTS 69 (1968), Cmnd 3755) and 1982 Protocol (UKTS 6 (1989), Cmnd 659)) (EMuT 960:57) ["Paris Nuclear Liability Convention (1960)"]

Convention on the Liability of Operators of Nuclear Ships, Brussels, 25 May 1962 (IAEA Legal Series No. 4 (1966)) (EMuT 962:40)

Act on Navigation and Economic Cooperation Between States of the Niger Basin, Niamey, 1963 (EMuT 963:80)

Brussels Supplementary Convention to the Paris Convention on Third Party Liability in the Field of Nuclear Energy, Brussels, 31 January 1963 (1041 UNTS 358); as amended by 1964 Protocol (UKTS 44 (1975), Cmnd. 5948) (EMuT 963:10) ["Brussels Supplementary Nuclear Energy Convention (1963)"]

Convention on Civil Liability for Nuclear Damage, Vienna, 21 May 1963 (1063 UNTS 265) (EMuT 963:40) ["Vienna Nuclear Liability Convention (1963)"]

Treaty Banning Nuclear Weapon Tests in the Atmosphere, in Outer Space and Under Water, Moscow, 5 August 1963 (480 UNTS 43) (EMuT 963:59) ["Nuclear Test Ban Treaty (1963)"]

Agreement Concerning the Use of Water Resources in Frontier Waters, 17 July 1964 (552 UNTS 188)

Agreement Concerning the River Niger Commission and the Navigation and Transport on the River Niger, Niamey, 25 November 1964 (587 UNTS 19) (EMuT 964:87) ["River Niger Agreement (1964)"]

International Convention for the Conservation of Atlantic Tunas, Rio de Janeiro, 14 May 1966 (673 UNTS 63) (EMuT 966:38) ["Atlantic Tunas Convention (1966)"]

International Covenant on Civil and Political Rights, UNGA Res 2200 (XXI) (Annex), 16 December 1966 (999 UNTS 171) (EMuT 966:93) ["Covenant on Civil and Political Rights (1966)"]

International Covenant on Economic, Social and Cultural Rights, UNGA Res 2200 (XXI) (Annex), 16 December 1966 (993 UNTS 3) (EMuT 966:94) ["Covenant on Economic, Social and Cultural Rights (1966)"]

Treaty on Principles Governing the Activities of states in the Exploration and Use of Outer Space, Including the Moon and Other Celestial Bodies, 27 January 1967 (610 UNTS 205) (EMuT 967:07) ["Outer Space Treaty (1967)"]

African Convention on the Conservation of Nature and Natural Resources, Algiers, 15 September 1968 (1001 UNTS 4) (EMuT 968:68) ["African Convention (1968)"]

European Agreement on the Restriction of the Use of Certain Detergents in Washing and Cleaning Products, Strasbourg, 16 September 1968 (788 UNTS 181) (EMuT 968:69) ["European Detergent Agreement (1968)"]; as amended Protocol, Strasbourg, 25 October 1983 (EMuT 968:69/A) (UKTS 75 (1984), Cmnd 9369)

Convention on Jurisdiction and Enforcement of Judgements in Civil and Commercial Matters, Brussels, 27 September 1968 (OJ L 304/77 1978; UKTS 10 (1988), Cmnd 306) (EMuT 968:75)

Vienna Convention on the Law of Treaties, Vienna, 23 May 1969 (1155 UNTS 331) (EMuT 969:39)

American Convention on Human Rights, San Jose, 22 November 1969 (reprinted in 9 ILM 673) ["American Convention on Human Rights (1969)"]; and Additional Protocol in the Area of Economic, Social and Cultural Rights, San Salvador, 17 November 1988 (OASTS 69; reprinted in 28 ILM 156 (1989))

Convention on Civil Liability for Oil Pollution Damage, Brussels, 29 November 1969 (973 UNTS 3) (EMuT 969:88 and 969:88/A-C) ["Oil Pollution Civil Liability Convention (1969)"]; see also Protocol, London, 19 November 1976 (UKTS 26 (1981)); and Protocol, London, 27 November 1992 (IMO Doc. LEG/CONF. 9/15, 2 December 1992)

Convention on the Intervention on the High Seas in Cases of Oil Pollution Damage, Brussels, 29 November 1969 (973 UNTS 3) (EMuT 969:89) ["Intervention Convention (1969)"]; see also Protocol, London, 2 November 1973 (UKTS 27 (1983), Cmnd 8924) (EMuT 973:83)

Convention on Wetlands of International Importance Especially as Waterfowl Habitat, Ramsar, 2 February 1971 (996 UNTS 245) (EMuT 971:09 and 971:09/A) ["Ramsar Convention (1971)"]; as amended, Paris, 3 December 1982 (Misc 1 (1984) Cmnd 9113; reprinted in 22 ILM 698 (1983))

Convention Relating to Civil Liability in the Field of Maritime Carriage of Nuclear Material, Brussels, 17 December 1971 (974 UNTS 255; 1143 UNTS 341) (EMuT 971:93)

Convention on the Establishment of an International Fund for Compensation for Oil Pollution Damage, Brussels, 18 December 1971 (1110 UNTS 58); see also [1976 Protocol] London Protocol of 25 May 1984 (IMO Doc LEG/CONF. 6/67), and Protocol of 27 November 1992 (IMO Doc LEG/CONF. 9/16)) (EMuT 971:94 and 971:94/A-C) ["Fund Convention (1971)"]

Convention for the Prevention of Marine Pollution by Dumping from Ships and Aircraft, Oslo, 15 February 1972 (UK Misc. No. 21 (1972), Cmnd. 4984); as amended by Protocol (1983) (UKTS 59 (1989)) and amendment to Annexes I and II (1985) (EMuT 972:12 and 972:12/A, B) ["Oslo Marine Pollution Convention (1972)"]

Convention on International Liability for Damage Caused by Space Objects, Geneva, 29 March 1972 (961 UNTS 187) (EMuT 972:24) ["Space Objects Liability Convention (1972)"]

Convention on the Prohibition of the Development, Production and Stockpiling of Biological Weapons, London/Moscow/Washington, 10 April 1972 (1015 UNTS 163) (EMuT 972:28) ["Biological Weapons Convention (1972)"]

Convention for the Conservation of Antarctic Seals, London, 1 June 1972 (29 UST 441; UKTS 45 (1978), Cmnd 7209) (EMuT 972:41) ["Antarctic Seals Convention (1972)"]

Convention for the Protection of the World Cultural and Natural Heritage, Paris, 16 November 1972 (1037 UNTS 151) (EMuT 972:86) ["World Heritage Convention (1972)"]

Convention on the Prevention of Marine Pollution By Dumping of Wastes and Other Matter, London, 19 December 1972 (1046 UNTS 120) (EMuT 972:96) ["London Convention (1972)"]

Convention on International Trade in Endangered Species of Wild Flora and Fauna, Washington, 3 March 1973 (993 UNTS 243) (EMuT 973:18) ["CITES (1973)"]

International Convention on the Prevention Pollution from Ships, London, 2 November 1973 (UN.Leg. Series ST/LEG/SER.B/18, 461; IMCO 74.01; as amended by Protocol, London, 17 February 1978 (reprinted in 17 ILM 546 (1978)) (EMuT 973:84 and 973:84/A) ["MARPOL Convention (1973)"]

Agreement on the Conservation of Polar Bears, Oslo, 15 November 1973 (27 UST 3918; reprinted in 13 ILM 13 (1974)) (EMuT 973:85) ["Polar Bears Agreement (1973)"]

Nordic Convention on the Protection of the Environment, Stockholm, 19 February 1974 (1092 UNTS 279) ["Nordic Convention (1974)"]

Convention on the Protection of the Marine Environment of the Baltic Sea Area, Helsinki, 22 March 1974 (reprinted in 13 ILM 546 (1974)) (EMuT 974:23) ["Baltic Sea Convention (1974)"]

Convention for the Prevention of Marine Pollution from Land-Based Sources, Paris, 4 June 1974 (UKTS 64 (1978), Cmnd. 7251) (EMuT 974:43) ["Paris Marine Pollution Convention (1974)"]

International Convention for the Safety of Life at Sea, London, 1 November 1974 (1184 UNTS 3) (EMuT 974:81) ["SOLAS Convention (1974)"] as amended 1998

Convention on Registration of Objects Launched into Outer Space, New York, 14 January 1975 (1023 UNTS 15) (EMuT 974:83) ["Space Objects Registration Convention (1975)"]

Convention for the Protection of the Mediterranean Sea Against Pollution, Barcelona, 16 February 1976 (1102 UNTS NI-16908; reprinted in 15 ILM 285 (1976)) (EMuT 976:13, 976:13/C and 976:13/D) ["Barcelona Convention (1976)"]; see also Protocol for the Protection of the Mediterranean Sea Against Pollution from Land-Based Sources, Athens, 17 May 1980 (reprinted in 19 ILM 869); and Protocol Concerning Mediterranean Specially Protected Areas, Geneva, 3 April 1982 (UNEP Doc) UNTS Reg. No. 24079

Convention on the Conservation of Nature in the South Pacific, Apia, 12 June 1976 (EMuT 976:45) ["Apia Convention on South Pacific Nature (1976)"]

Agreement for the Protection of the Rhine Against Chemical Pollution, Bonn, 3 December 1976 (1124 UNTS 375) (EMuT 976:89) ["Rhine Chemical Convention (1976)"]

Convention on the Prohibition of Military or Other Use of Environment Modification Techniques, Geneva, 10 December 1976 (1108 UNTS 151) (EMuT 977:37) ["ENMOD Convention (1976)"]

Convention on Civil Liability for Oil Pollution Damage Resulting from Exploration for and Exploitation of Seabed Mineral Resources, London, 1 May 1977 (UK Misc No 8 (1977), Cmnd 6791) (EMuT 977:33) ["Seabed Liability Convention (1977)"]

Protocol I Additional to the Geneva Conventions of 12 August 1949 Relating to the Victims of International Armed Conflicts, 8 June 1977 (ICRC, *Protocols Additional to the Geneva Conventions of 12 August 1949,* Geneva, 1977; 1125 UNTS 3) (EMuT 977:43) ["Additional Protocol I (1977)"]

Protocol II Additional to the Geneva Conventions of 12 August 1949 Relating to the Protection of Non-International Armed Conflicts (12 December 1977) (ICRC, *Protocols Additional to the Geneva Conventions of 12 August 1949*, Geneva (1977), pp. 89-101; 1125 UNTS 609) (EMuT 977:44) ["Additional Protocol II (1977)"]

Great Lakes Water Quality Agreement, 1978, UST 1383, TIAS 9257, as amended 16 October 1983, TIAS 10798, and 18 November 1987, CTS 1987, No. 32

Regional Convention for Co-operation in the Protection of the Marine Environment From Pollution, Kuwait, 24 April 1978 (1140 UNTS 133) (EMuT 978:31) ["Kuwait Regional Convention (1978)"]

Treaty for Amazonian Cooperation, Brasilia, 3 July 1978 (reprinted in 17 ILM 1045 (1978)) (EMuT 978:49) ["Amazonian Cooperation Treaty (1978)"]

Convention on the Conservation of European Wildlife and Natural Habitats, Berne, 19 September 1979 (UKTS 56 (1982), Cmnd 8738) (EMuT 979:70) ["Berne Convention on European Wildlife (1979)]

Geneva Convention on Long-Range Transboundary Air Pollution, 13 November 1979 (UN Doc ECE/HLM.1/R.1; UKTS 57 (1983), Cmnd 9034) (EMuT 979:84 and 979:84/A) ["LRTAP Convention (1979)"]; see also Protocol on a Programme for Monitoring and Evaluation of the Long-Range Transmission of Air Pollutants in Europe (EMEP), (reprinted in 24 ILM 485 (1985)), Geneva, 28 September 1984; Protocol on the Reduction of Sulphur Emissions or their Transboundary Fluxes by at least 30 Per Cent, Helsinki, 8 July 1985 (UN Doc. ECE/EB.AIR/12), renegotiated protocol adopted in 1994 (EMuT 979:84/B); Protocol on Control of Emissions of Nitrogen Oxides or their Transboundary Fluxes (reprinted in 27 ILM 698 (1988)), Sophia, 31 October 1988 (EMuT 979:84/C); Protocol Concerning the Control of Emissions of Volatile Organic Compounds or their Transboundary Fluxes, Geneva, 18 November 1991 (UNECE, Environmental Conventions, 1992; UN Doc ECE/EB.AIR/30) (EMuT 979:84/D)

Agreement Governing the Activities of States on the Moon and Other Celestial Bodies, 5 December 1979 (UN Gen Ass Resn 34/68, GAOR, 34th Sess, Supp 46, p. 77; UN Doc (A/34/46)) (EMuT 979:92) ["Moon Treaty (1979)"]

Convention on the Elimination of All Forms of Discrimination Against Women, New York (UNGA Resolution 34/180, GAOR, 34th Sess, Supp 46, p. 193; UKTS 2 (1989), Cmnd 643)

Agreement between Spain and Portugal on Cooperation in Matters Affecting the Safety of Nuclear Installations in the Vicinity of the Frontier, Lisbon, 31 March 1980

Convention on the Conservation of Antarctic Marine Living Resources, Canberra, 20 May 1980 (UKTS 48 (1982), Cmnd 8714; reprinted in 19 ILM 837 (1980)) (EMuT 980:39) ["Antarctic Marine Living Resources Convention (1980)"]

Convention on the Conservation of Migratory Species of Wild Animals, Bonn, 23 June 1979 (Cmnd 7888; reprinted in 19 ILM 11 (1980)) (EMuT 979:55) ["Convention on Migratory Species (1980)"]

Convention on Prohibitions on the Use of Certain Conventional Weapons Which May be Deemed to be Excessively Injurious or to Have Indiscriminate Effects, Geneva, 10 October 1980 (UN Doc A/CONF. 95/15 and Corr 1-5; UK Misc. 23 (1981), Cmnd. 8370) ["Inhumane Weapons Convention (1980)"]

Convention for Cooperation in the Protection and Development of the Marine and Coastal Environment of the West and Central African Region, Abidjan, 23 March 1981 (UN Doc UNEP/IG.22/7; reprinted in 20 ILM 746 (1981)) (EMuT 981:23) ["West and Central African Marine Environment Convention (1981)"]

African Charter on Human Rights and People's Rights, Banjul, 20 June 1981 (OAU Doc CAB/LEG/67/3/Rev 5; reprinted in 21 ILM 52 (1982)) ["African Charter on Human Rights (1981)"]

Agreement on Regional Cooperation in Combating Pollution of the Southeast Pacific by Hydrocarbons or Other Harmful Substances in Cases of Emergency, Lima, 12 November 1981 (ND (Loose-leaf), Doc. J. 18) (EMuT 981:85) ["South-East Pacific Hydrocarbons Agreement (1981)"]

Convention for the Protection of the Marine Environment and Coastal Areas of the South-East Pacific, Lima, 12 November 1981 (UN Doc UNEP-CPPS/IG. 32/4) (EMuT 981:84) ["South-East Pacific Marine Environment Convention (1981)"]

Regional Convention for the Conservation of the Red Sea and the Gulf of Aden Environment, Jeddah, 14 February 1982,(9 ELP 56 (1982)) and Protocol for Concerning Regional Co-operation in Combating Pollution by Oil and Other Harmful Substances in Cases of Emergency (UNEP Doc; 9 EPL 56 (1992)) (EMuT 982:13 and 982:14) ["Jeddah Convention on the Marine Environment (1982)"]

UN Convention on the Law of the Sea, Montego Bay, 10 December 1982 (UN Doc A/CONF 62/122 (with corrigenda); Misc 11 (1983), Cmnd 8941) (EMuT 982:92) ["UNCLOS (1982)"]

Mexico-United States of America: Agreement to Cooperate in the Solution of Environmental Problems in the Border Area, September 1983 (reprinted in 22 ILM 1025 (1983)) ["US-Mexico Border Environment Agreement (1983)"], Annexes, January 1987 (reprinted in 26 ILM 16 (1987))

Agreement for Co-operation in Dealing with Pollution of the North Sea By Oil and Other Harmful Substances, Bonn, 13 September 1983 (UK Misc. 26 (1983), Cmnd. 9104) (EMuT 983:68) ["North-Sea Oil Pollution Agreement (1983)"]

Convention for the Protection and Development of the Marine Environment of the Wider Caribbean Region, Cartagena de Indias, 24 March 1983 (UKTS 38 (1988), Cmnd. 399; reprinted in 22 ILM 221 (1983)) (EMuT 983:23, 983:24 and 983:23/B) ["Wider Caribbean Marine Environment

Convention (1983)"]; Protocol Concerning Co-operation in Combating Oil Spills in the Wider Caribbean Region (UKTS 38 (1988), Cmnd. 399; reprinted in 22 ILM 221 (1983)); and Protocol Concerning Specially Protected Areas and Wildlife, Kingston, 18 January 1990 (EMuT 990:85)

Convention on the Protection of the Ozone Layer, Vienna, 22 March 1985 (UNEP Doc IG.53/5; UKTS 1 (1990), Cmnd 910) (EMuT 985:22, 985:22/A and 985:22/B) ["Vienna Convention on the Ozone Layer (1985)"]; and Protocol on Substances that Deplete the Ozone Layer, Montreal, 16 September 1987 (UKTS 19 (1990), Cmnd 977) ["Montreal Protocol (1987)"], as amended by Adjustment and Amendment to the Montreal Protocol on Substances that Deplete the Ozone Layer, London (reprinted in 30 ILM 537 (1991)), and Copenhagen (reprinted in 32 ILM 874 (1992))

Convention for the Protection, Management and Development of the Marine and Coastal Environment of the Eastern African Region, Nairobi, 21 June 1985 (UNEP Doc; EMuT 985:46) ["Eastern African Marine Environment Convention (1985)"]; Protocol Concerning Protected Areas and Wild Fauna and Flora in the Eastern African Region (EMuT 985:47); and Protocol Concerning Co-operation in Combating Marine Pollution in Cases of Emergency in the Eastern African Region (ND (Loose-leaf) Doc. J. 26) (EMuT 985:48)

ASEAN Agreement on the Conservation of Nature and Natural Resources, Kuala Lumpur, 9 July 1985 (15 EPL 64) (EMuT 985:51) ["ASEAN Agreement (1985)"]

Mexico-United States: Agreement for cooperation on Environmental Programs and Transboundary Problems, Annex III, and Hazardous Wastes and Hazardous Substances, 12 November 1986 (reprinted in 26 ILM 25 (1987))

Convention on the Law of Treaties between States and International Organizations or between International Organizations, Vienna, 21 March 1986 (UN Doc. A/CONF. 129/15) (EMuT 986:22)

Convention on Assistance in Case of a Nuclear Accident or Radiological Emergency, Vienna, 26 September 1986 (IAEA Doc. GC(SPL.1)/2, Annex II; IAEA INFCIRC 336; reprinted in 25 ILM 1370 (1986)) (EMuT 986:72) ["Nuclear Assistance Convention (1986)"]

Convention on Early Notification of a Nuclear Accident, Vienna, 26 September 1986 (IAEA Doc. GC(SPL.1)/2, Annex II; IAEA INFCIRC 335; reprinted in 25 ILM 1370 (1986)) (EMuT 986:71) ["Nuclear Notification Convention (1986)"]

Convention for the Protection of the Natural Resources and Environment of the South Pacific Region, Noumea, 24 November 1986 (reprinted in 26 ILM 38 (1987)) (EMuT 986:87) ["South Pacific Convention (1986)"]; see also Protocol for the Prevention of Pollution of the South Pacific Region by Dumping, Noumea, 25 November 1986 (EMuT 986:87/A); and Protocol Concerning Co-operation in Combating Pollution Emergencies in the South Pacific Region (reprinted in 26 ILM 58 (1987)) (EMuT 986:87/B)

Convention on the Regulation of Antarctic Mineral Resource Activities, Wellington, 2 June 1988 (UK. Misc 6 (1989) Cmnd 634; reprinted in 27 ILM 859 (1988)) ["Antarctic Minerals Convention (1988)"]

Convention on the Transboundary Movements of Hazardous Wastes and Their Disposal, Basel, 22 March 1989 (reprinted in 28 ILM 657 (1989)) (EMuT 989:22) ["Basel Convention (1989)"]

International Convention on Salvage, London, 28 April 1989 (IMO/LEG/CONF.7/27 (1989)) (EMuT 989:32) ["Salvage Convention (1989)"]

ILO Convention No. 169 Concerning Indigenous and Tribal Peoples in Independent Countries, 27 June 1989 (72 ILO Off. Bull. 59 (1989); reprinted in 28 ILM 1382 (1989)) (EMuT 989:48) ["ILO Indigenous Peoples Convention (1989)"]

Convention on Civil Liability for Damage Caused During Carriage of Dangerous Goods by Road, Rail and Inland Navigation Vessels, 10 October 1989 (ECE Doc. ECE/Trans/79) ["ECE CRTD Convention (1989)"]

Convention on the Rights of the Child, 20 November 1989 (GA Res 44/34 (Annex), 4 December 1989; reprinted in 28 ILM 1457 (1989))

Convention for the Prohibition of Fishing With Long Driftnets in the South Pacific, Wellington, 24 November 1989 (reprinted in 29 ILM 1449 (1990)) (EMuT 989:87) ["South Pacific Driftnets Convention (1989)"]

Fourth ACP-EEC Lomé Convention, 15 December 1989 (ETS 96 (1990), Cmnd 1364; reprinted in 29 ILM 738 (1990)) (EMuT 989:93) ["Lomé IV Convention (1989)"]

Canada-US Agreement on Fisheries Enforcement, 1990 (reprinted in 30 ILM 418 (1991))

Accord of Co-operation for the Protection of the Coasts and Waters of the North-East Atlantic Against Pollution Due to Hydrocarbons or Other Harmful Substances, Lisbon, 17 October 1990 (reprinted in 30 ILM 1227 (1991)) (EMuT 990:79) ["North-East Atlantic Pollution Convention (1990)"] [Agreement on Co-operation for Combating Protection in the North-East Atlantic]

International Convention on Oil Pollution Preparedness, Response and Co-operation, London, 30 November 1990 (reprinted in 30 ILM 735 (1991)) (EMuT 990:88) ["Oil Pollution Preparedness Convention (1990)"]

Convention on the Ban of the Import into Africa and the Control of Transboundary Movement and Management of Hazardous Wastes Within Africa, Bamako, 29 January 1991 (reprinted in 30 ILM 775 (1991)) (EMuT 991:08) ["Bamako Convention (1991)"]

Convention on Environmental Impact Assessment in a Transboundary Context, Espoo, 25 February 1991 (UNECE, Environmental Conventions 1992; reprinted in 30 ILM 802 (1991)) (EMuT 991:15) ["Espoo Convention (1991)"]

Agreement between the Government of the United States of America and the Government of Canada on Air Quality, Ottawa, 13 March 1991 (reprinted in 30 ILM 676 (1991)) ["US-Canada Air Quality Agreement (1991)"]

Convention on the Protection and Use of Transboundary Watercourses and International Lakes, Helsinki, 17 March 1992 (UN Doc E/ECE/1268) (EMuT 992:20) ["ECE Transboundary Watercourses Convention (1992)"]

Convention on the Transboundary Effects of Industrial Accidents, Helsinki, 17 March 1992 (UN Doc E/ECE/1268) (EMuT 992:22) ["ECE Industrial Accidents Convention (1992)"]

Convention on the Protection of the Marine Environment of the Baltic Sea Area, Helsinki, 9 April 1992 (OJ No. L 73, 16.3.1994 p. 20) (EMuT 992:28) ["Baltic Sea Convention 1992"]

UN Framework Convention on Climate Change, New York, 9 May 1992 (UN Doc A/CONF.151/26 (Vol. I); reprinted in 31 ILM 849 (1992)) (EMuT 992:35) ["Climate Change Convention (1992)"]

Convention on Biological Diversity, Rio de Janeiro, 5 June 1992 (reprinted in 31 ILM 822 (1992)) (EMuT 992:42) ["Convention on Biological Diversity (1992)"]

Convention on the Protection of the Marine Environment of the North-East Atlantic, Paris, 22 September 1992 (IMO Doc. LDC 15/INF.11; reprinted in 32 ILM 1069 (1993)) (EMuT 992:71) ["North-East Atlantic Convention (1992)"]

North American Free Trade Agreement, 17 December 1992 (reprinted in 32 ILM 289 and 605 (1993)) (EMuT 992:93) ["NAFTA (1992)"]

FAO Agreement to Promote Compliance with International Conservation and Management Measures By Fishing Vessels on the High Seas (1993) ["FAO High Seas Fishing Agreement (1993)"]

Convention on the Prohibition of the Development, Production, and Stockpiling and Use of Chemical Weapons and On Their Destruction, 13 January 1993 (reprinted in 32 ILM 804 (1993)) (EMuT 993:04) ["Chemical Weapons Convention (1993)"]

Convention on Civil Liability for Damage Resulting from Activities Dangerous to the Environment, Lugano, 21 June 1993 (reprinted in 32 ILM 1228 (1993)) (EMuT 993:19) ["Council of Europe Civil Liability Convention (1993)"]

Agreement Establishing the World Trade Organization, Marrakesh, 15 April 1994 (reprinted in 33 ILM 1144) ["WTO Agreement (1994)"]

Uruguay Round: Agreement on Trade-Related Aspects of Intellectual Property Rights, 15 December 1993 (reprinted in 33 ILM 81 (1994)) ["Uruguay Round TRIPS Agreement (1993)"]

UN Convention to Combat Desertification in Those Countries Experiencing Serious Drought and/or Desertification, Particularly in Africa, 17 June 1994 (reprinted in 33 ILM 1328 (1994)) (EMuT 994:76) ["Desertification Convention (1994)"]

Convention on the Protection of the Alps, 7 Nov. 1991, 31 I.L.M. 767 (EMuT 991:83)

International Tropical Timber Agreement, 26 January 1994 (EMuT 994:07)

Convention on Cooperation for the Protection and Sustainable Use of the Danube River (Sofia, 29 June 1994) (EMuT 994:49)

Agreement for the Implementation of the Provisions of the United Nations Convention on the Law of the Sea relating to the Conservation and Management of Straddling Fish Stocks and Highly Migratory Fish Stocks (New York, 4 Aug. 1995) (EMuT 982:92/B)

Convention to Ban the Importation into Forum Island Countries of Hazardous Wastes and Radioactive Wastes and to Control the Transboundary Movement and Management of Hazardous Wastes within the South Pacific (16 Sept. 1995) (EMuT 995:69)

African Nuclear-Weapon Free Zone Treaty (11 April 1996) (EMuT 996:28)

International Convention on Liability and Compensation for Damage in Connection with the Carriage of Hazardous and Noxious Substances by Sea (3 May 1996) (EMuT 996:34)

Comprehensive Nuclear Test Ban Treaty (24 Sept. 1996) (EMuT 996:71)

Declaration on the Establishment of the Arctic Council, Ottawa, September 19, 1996, 35 I.L.M. 1382 (1996).

Convention on the Law of the Non-Navigational Uses of International Watercourses (New York, 21 May 1997) (EMuT 997:38)

Convention on the Prohibition of the Use, Stockpiling, Production and Transfer of Anti-Personnel Mines and on their Destruction (Oslo, 18 September 1997) (EMuT 997:70)

Kyoto Protocol to the United Nations Framework Convention on Climate Change (11 Dec. 1997), 37 I.L.M. 22 (1998) (EMuT 992:35/A)

Convention on Access to Information, Public Participation in Decision-Making and Access to Justice in Environmental Matters (Aarhus, 25 June 1998) (EMuT 998:48)

II. United Nations Resolutions

UN General Assembly Resolution 1803 (1962) on Permanent Sovereignty over Natural Resources

UN General Assembly Resolution 217A (III): Universal Declaration of Human Rights

UN General Assembly Resolution 2542 (1970): Declaration on Social Progress and Development

UN General Assembly Resolution 2625 (1970): Declaration on Principles of International Law Concerning Friendly Relations and Co-operation Among States in Accordance with the Charter of the United Nations, ["Declaration on Principles of International Law (1970)"]

UN General Assembly Resolution 2995 (1972) on Co-operation between States in the Field of the Environment

UN General Assembly Resolution 2996 (1972) on International Responsibility of States in Regard to the Environment

UN General Assembly Resolution 2997 (1972) on Institutional and Financial Arrangements for International Environmental Co-operation

UN General Assembly Resolution 3281 (1974): Charter of Economic Rights and Duties of States

UN General Assembly Resolution 37/199 Alternate Approaches and Ways and Means within the United Nations system for Improving the Effective Enjoyment of Human Rights and Fundamental Freedoms

UN General Assembly Resolution 37/7 on a World Charter for Nature (IPE/SD* 82-1-28; ESoL** 982:8005) ["World Charter for Nature"]

UN General Assembly Resolution 41/128: Declaration on the right to development

---

* IPE/SD = International Protection of the Environment/Conservation in Sustainable Development, Oceana Publications Inc. (NY/USA).

** ESoL = International Environmental Soft Law, Kluwer Law International (UK).

UN General Assembly Resolution 42/186 on Environment Perspective to the Year 2000 and Beyond (IPE/SD 87-12-11; ESoL 987:9235)

UN General Assembly Resolution 43/53 on Protection of the Global Climate for Present and Future Generations of Mankind (IPE/SD 88-12-06; ESoL 987:9235)

UN General Assembly Resolution 44/207 on Protection of Global Climate for Present and Future Generations of Mankind (IPE/SD 89-12-22)

UN General Assembly Resolution 44/225 on Large-Scale Pelagic Driftnet Fishing and its Impacts on the Living Marine Resources of the World's Oceans and Seas

UN General Assembly Resolution 44/228 on the United Nations Conference on Environment and Development (IPE/SD 89-12-22)

UN General Assembly Resolution 45/212 on Protection of Global Climate for Present and Future Generations of Mankind

UN General Assembly Resolution 45/94 on the Need to Ensure a Healthy Environment for the Well-Being of Individuals

UN Security Council Resolution 687/1991 Concerning the Restoration of Peace and Security in Iraq and Kuwait

UN General Assembly Resolution 46/169 on the Protection of Global Climate for Present and Future Generations of Mankind

UN General Assembly Resolution 47/37 Protection of the Environment in times of Armed Conflict

UN General Assembly Resolution 49/50 United Nations Decade of International Law

III. Other International Documents

Helsinki Rules on the Uses of the Waters of International Rivers, International Law Association, 20 August 1966 (52 ILA 484 (1967); 11 IPE 5506)

Final Act on the United Nations International Conference on Human Rights at Teheran, 13 May 1968 ((UN Doc. A/CONF. 32/41, UN pub. E/68/XIV/2)

Tanker Owners Voluntary Agreement on Oil Pollution Damage, 29 November 1969 (reprinted in 9 ILM 45); see also 1987 Supplement ["TOVALOP (1969)"]

Contract Regarding an Interim Supplement to Tanker Liability for Oil Pollution, 14 January 1971 (reprinted in 10 ILM 137) ["CRISTAL (1971)"]

OECD Recommendation on Guiding Principles Concerning International Economic Aspects of Environmental Policies, 26 May 1972 (OECD C(72) 128)

European Soil Charter Council of Europe (Resolution (72) 19, 30 May 1972) (ESoL 972:4105)

Stockholm Action Plan for the Human Environment (UN Doc. A/CONF.48/14 at 2-65 and Corr. 1 (1972)) ["Stockholm Plan of Action"]

Stockholm Declaration on the Human Environment, 16 June 1972 (UN Doc. A/CONF.48/14/Rev. 1 (UN Pub. E.73, II.A.14) (1973)) (ESoL 972:4505) ["Stockholm Declaration"]

OECD Council Recommendation on the Implementation of the Polluter-Pays Principle (OECD C(74) 223)) (ESoL 974:8525)

OECD Council Recommendation Concerning Transboundary Pollution (Recommendation C(74) 224; reprinted in 14 ILM 234 (1975))

OECD Council Recommendation on a Comprehensive Waste Management Policy (OECD C(76)155 (Final))

Conference on Security and Co-operation in Europe: Helsinki Final Act (reprinted in 14 ILM 1292 (1975)) ["Helsinki Final Act (1975)"]

OECD Council Recommendation on Implementation of a Regime of Equal Right of Access and Non-Discrimination in Relation to Transfrontier Pollution (OECD C(77)28 (Final)) (ESoL 977:3705)

UNEP Draft Principles of Conduct in the Field of the Environment for the Guidance of States in the Conservation and Harmonious Utilization of Natural Resources Shared by Two or More States, 19 May 1978 (UNEP/1G 12/2 (1978); reprinted in 17 ILM 1097 (1978)) (ESoL 978:1005)

ILC Draft Articles on State Responsibility (Part 1), 1980 Y.B. ILC, Vol. II (Part 2) p. 30 (for Article provisionally adopted in Part II, see ILC Reports to the UN General Assembly for subsequent years)

FAO Soil Charter, 1981 (21 FAO Conf/Res 8/81; reprinted in 50 FAO SB 79)

ILA Rules on International Law applicable to Transfrontier Pollution, Montreal, 4 Sept. 1982, 60 ILA 158 (1983)

London Dumping Consultative Meeting Resolution LDC.21.(9) on Dumping of Radioactive Wastes at Sea, London, 1985 (IMO Doc. LDC 9/12, Annex 4 (1985)) (IPE/SD 85-09-27)

OECD Council Recommendation on Environmental Assessment of Development Assistance Projects and Programmes, Rec. C(85)104, 1985 (IPE/SD 85-06-20)

Montreal Guidelines for the Protection of the Marine Environment Against Pollution from Land-Based Sources (Decision 13/18/11 of the Governing Council of UNEP, 24 May 1985) (IPE/SD 85-05-24; ESoL 985:3905)) ["Montreal Guidelines"]

FAO Code of Conduct on the Distribution and Use of Pesticides, FAO Conference Resolution 10/85, 28 November 1985

OECD Council Recommendation on Measures Required to Facilitate the Environmental Assessment of Development Assistance Projects and Programmes (OECD C.(85)104, 1985) (IPE X/C/23-10-86)

OECD Council Decision/Recommendation on Exports of Hazardous Wastes from the OECD Area, 5 June 1986 (C(86)64 (Final)) ["OECD Decision on Hazardous Wastes (1986)"]

OECD Guidelines for Multinational Enterprises, annexed to the Declaration of June 21, 1976 on International Investment and Multinational Enterprises, as amended in 1979 and 1984. OECD, The Guidelines For Multinational Enterprises 11 (1986)

ILC Draft Articles on the Jurisdictional Immunities of States and Their Property, 1986 (reprinted in 26 ILM 625 (1987))

Report of the Experts Group on Environmental Law of the World Commission on Environment and Development, reprinted as Munro, R.D. and Lammers, J.G. (eds) (1987). LEGAL PRINCIPLES AND RECOMMENDATIONS FOR ENVIRONMENTAL PROTECTION AND SUSTAINABLE DEVELOPMENT, Graham & Trotman, London ["WCED Legal Principles (1986)"]

Seoul Rules on International Groundwaters, International Law Association, Report of the Sixty-Second Conference, 1987

UNEP Cairo Guidelines and Principles for the Environmentally Sound Management of Hazardous Wastes (UNEP Governing Council Decision 14/30 (1987)) (IPE/SD 87-06-19; ESoL 987:4405) ["Cairo Guidelines on Hazardous Wastes"]

UNEP Goals and Principles of Environmental Impact Assessment (Decision 14/25 of the Governing Council of UNEP, of 17 June 1987) (IPE/SD 87-06-19)

Report of the World Commission on Environment and Development, 4 August 1987 (UN Doc. A/42/427) ["WCED Brundtland Report (1987)"]; reprinted as World Commission on Environment and Development (1987). OUR COMMON FUTURE, Oxford University Press, Oxford.

United Nations ECOSOC, Draft Code of Conduct on Transnational Corporations. 1 February 1988 (UN Doc. E/1988/39/Add.1 (1988))

Goa Guidelines on Intergenerational Equity (1988), reprinted in E. Brown Weiss, *In Fairness to Future Generations* (1989)

Bellagio Draft Treaty on Transboundary Groundwaters, reprinted in 29 *Natural Resources Journal* (1989)

OSCOM Decision 89/1 on the Reduction and Cessation of Dumping Industrial Wastes at Sea, 14 June 1989

World Bank Operational Directive 4.00 Annex A: Environmental Impact Assessment

European Charter on Environment and Health (1989), 7 December 1989, First European Conference on Environment and Health, Frankfurt, Germany, reproduced in Burhenne, W.E. and Jahnke M., *International Environmental Soft Law (1993)* (IPE/SD 89-12-07; ESoL 989:9105)

Langkawi Declaration on the Environment (Heads of Government of the Commonwealth), reprinted in (1990) 5 *American University Journal of International Law and Policy*, 589 (IPE/SD 89-10-21; ESoL 989:7805)

ECE Code of Conduct on Accidental Pollution of Transboundary Inland Waters, ECE decision C(45) (E/ECE/1225 (1990)) (ESoL 990:4105)

UN General Assembly Declaration on International Economic Cooperation in Particular the Revitalizing of Economic Growth and Development of the Developing Countries, 1990 (Resolution S-18/3 (1990)) (IPE/SD 90-05-01)

ECE Bergen Ministerial Declaration on Sustainable Development, 5 May 1990 (ESoL 990:3705), Joint Agenda for Action adopted by the UN Economic Commission for Europe on 11 May 1990 (IPE/SD 90-05-16; ESoL 990:3605)

ECE Task Force Guidelines on Responsibility and Liability Regarding Transboundary Water Pollution, 1990

IAEA Code of Practice on the International Transboundary Movement of Radioactive Waste (IAEA GC (XXXIV) 920, 27 June 1990) (IPE/SD 90-09-21)

Business Charter for Sustainable Development 1991, reprinted in 21 EPL (1992) 35

ILC Draft Code of Crimes Against Peace and Security of Mankind, 1991 ILC Rep. (UN Doc. A/46/10)

OECD Council Recommendation on Integrated Pollution Prevention and Control (OECD C(90)164/Final/Appendix, 1991)

Beijing Ministerial Declaration on Environment and Development, 19 June 1991, UN Doc. A/CONF.151/PC/85

OECD Development Assistance Committee Guidelines on Environment and Aid, 1992

Kuala Lumpur Declaration on Environment and Development, Second Ministerial Conference of Developing Countries on Environment and Development, 26-29 April 1992, reprinted in 22 EPL (1992) 266 (IPE/SD 92-04-29)

Tokyo Declaration on Financing Global Environment and Development, reprinted in 22 EPL (1992) 265

Understandings in the Final Declaration of the Second Review Conference of the Parties to ENMOD (UN Doc. ENMOD/CONF.II/11)

Statement of Principles for a Global Consensus on the Management, Conservation and Sustainable Development of All Types of Forests, Rio de Janeiro, 14 June 1992 (A/CONF.151/26 (Vol. I)) (ESoL 992:4435) ["Forests Principles"]

Agenda 21, Rio de Janeiro, 14 June 1992 (UN Doc. A/CONF.151/26 (1992), also reprinted as Robinson, N. (ed) (1993). AGENDA 21: EARTH'S ACTION PLAN, IUCN EPLP No. 27, Oceana Publications, NEW York/London/Rome. (ESoL 992:4505 through 992:4905)

Rio de Janeiro Declaration on Environment and Development, 14 June 1992 (UN Doc. A/CONF.151/5) (ESoL 992:4405) ["Rio Declaration"]

Helsinki Summit Declaration of the Conference on Security and Cooperation in Europe, 10 July 1992

Council of Europe Recommendation 92(8) on Soil Protection, 8 May 1992

Programme for the Development and Periodic Review of Environmental Law (UNEP/GC. 17/5, 2 Feb. 1993) ["Montevideo Programme"]

U.N. World Conference on Human Rights: Vienna Declaration and Programme of Action (reprinted in 32 ILM 1661 (1993)) ["Vienna Declaration (1993)"]

International Maritime Organization Resolution no. 774(18), Guidelines for Preventing the Introduction of Unwanted Aquatic Organisms and Pathogens from Ships' Ballast Water and Sediment Discharges, 4 November 1993 (A 18/Res.774 (26 November 1993)) (IPE/SD 93-11-04)

Declaration of Human Duties, Trieste, 27 November 1993 (IPE/SD 93-11-27)

ILC Draft Articles on the Law of the Non-Navigational Uses of International Watercourses (1994 ILC Rep. p. 197 *et seq.* (1994)) (IPE/SD 94-12-09) ["ILC Draft Articles on International Watercourses (1994)"]

ILC Resolution on Confined Transboundary Groundwater (1994 ILC Rep p. 197)

International Conference on Population and Development, Annex Programme of Action of the International Conference on Population and Development, Cairo, 13 September 1994 (A.CONF.171/13) ["Cairo Conference Programme of Action"]

ICRC Guidelines for Military Manuals and Instructions on the Protection of the Environment in Times of Armed Conflict (UN Doc. A/49/323) (IPE/SD 94-08-19) ["ICRC Guidelines for Military Manuals (1994)"]

ILC Draft Articles on Liability for Injurious Consequences Arising from Acts Not Prohibited by International Law. Report of the ILC on the work of its forty-sixth session (UN Doc. GAOR Supp. No. 10 (A/49/19)), p. 367 *et seq.* (for Articles provisionally adopted so far). ["ILC Draft Articles on Liability 1994"]

1994 Code of Practice on the Introductions and Transfers of Marine Organism, Report of the ICES Advisory Committee on the Marine Environment, ICES Cooperative Research Report No. 204 (IPE/SD 94-09-30)

Dissemination of the Principles of the Rio Declaration on Environment and Development, 19 December 1994 (IPE/SD 94-12-19)

Final Act of the UN Conference on Stranddling Fish Stocks and Highly Migratory Fish Stocks, 4 August 1995 (IPE/SD 95-08-04)

Guidelines on Access to Environmental Information and Public Participation in Environmental Decision-Making, 25 October 1995 (ESoL 995:8005)

Code of Conduct for the Import and Release of Exotic Biological Control Agents, Endorsed by the 2nd Session of the FAO Conference, 1 November 1995 (IPE/SD 95-11-01)

Code of Conduct for Responsible Fisheries (FAO), 1 November 1995 (ESol 995:8205)

Guidelines on Implementation of the International Safety Management (ISM) Code by Administrations: adopted by the 19th Session of the IMO Assembly, London, 23 November 1995 (IPE/SD 95-11-23)

Resolutions on Indigenous Populations, 21 December 1995 (IPE/SD 95-12-21)

Resolution on the Right to Development, 22 December 1995 (IPE/SD 95-12-22)

Negotiations in the World Trade Organisation (WTO) on Trade and the Environment – Resolution adopted by the European Parliament, Strasbourg, 24 May 1996 (IPE/SD 96-05-24)

Non-Governmental Organisations – Consultative Relationship with the UN: Resolution adopted by the UN Economic and Social Council, 25 July 1996 (IPE/SD 96-07-25)

Common Fisheries Policy after the year 2000. Resolution adopted by the European Parliament, 6 November 1997 (IPE/SD 97-11-06)

Access to Information, Public Participation in Decision-making and Access to Justice in Environmental Matters – Resolution, 4th Ministerial Conference "Environment for Europe", Århus, Denmark, 25 June 1998 (IPE/SD 98-06-25)

Resolution of the 53rd UN-General Assembly World Solar Programme 1996-2005, 16 October 1998 (IPE/SD 98-10-16)

Resolution of the 53rd UN-General Assembly Right to Development, 12 December 1998 (IPE/SD 98-12-12)

Dispute Avoidance and Dispute Settlement in International Environmental Law – Conclusions by the International Group of Experts of the United Nations Environment Programme, 19 January 1999 (IPE/SD 99-01-19)

The Rome Declaration on the Implementation of the Code of Conduct for Responsible Fisheries, Adopted by the FAO Ministerial Meeting, 11 March 1999 (IPE/SD 99-03-11)

Tokyo '99 Declaration on Global Commons, 5 May 1999 (IPE/SD 99-06-05)

Guidelines for Reviewing Laws and Institutions to Promote the Conservation and Wise Use of Wetlands (RAMSAR), 18 May 1999 (ESoL 999:3805)

IV. Legislation

A. National Constitutions

Constitution of Brazil, 1988

Political Constitution of Chile, 1980

Constitution of China, 1982

Constitution of Colombia, 1991

Constitution of Ecuador, 1984

Constitution of Guatemala, 1985

Constitution of Hungary, 1949, amended 1972, 1983, 1989

Constitution of India, 1949, amended 1984, 1985

Constitution of the Islamic Republic of Iran, 1980

Constitution of the Republic of Korea, 1988

Constitution of Namibia, 1990

Constitution of Papua New Guinea, 1984

Constitution of the Philippines, 1986

Constitution of Vanuatu, 1980

B. National Legislation

Federal Endangered Species Protection Act, 21 December 1992 (Act. No. 194/1992) (Australia)

Agricultural Land Tenure Act, as amended, 1993 (Bulgaria)

Act Respecting Environmental Rights in Ontario, 1994 (Canada)

Law on the Prevention of Environmental Impact, No. 11/1990, 13 July 1990 (BO No. 92,19900723, p. 2616) (Canary Islands)

Ley 99 Crecion del Ministerio del Medio Ambiente, 22 December 1993 (Colombia)

Decree 179 of 2 February 1993 (Cuba)

Act on the Environment, 5 December 1991 (Czech Republic)

General Regulation of Pesticides and Related Products of Agricultural Use, Decree 939 of 12 July 1993 (Ecuador)

Law on the Environment, Law No. 4, 1994 (Egypt)

Law on the Protection of Nature, No. 76-629, 10 July 1976 (JO 19760713 Rect.JO 19761128) (France)

Act on the Conservation of Natural Areas and of Wild Flora and Fauna, 1989 (France)

Decree for the Implementation of Article 2 of the Act of 10 July 1976 Concerning Nature Protection, No. 77-1141, 12 October 1977 (France)

Act on the Prevention of Harmful Effects on the Environment Caused by Air Pollution, Noise, Vibration and Similar Phenomena (Federal Emission Control Act - BImSchG), 14 May 1990 (Germany)

Environmental Liability Act, 10 December 1990 (BGBl. I. 2634) (Germany)

Packaging Regulation, 19910612, 12 June 1991 (BGBl. IS. 1410); as amended by 19931026 (BGBl. IS. 1782) (Germany)

Basic Law on the Protection of the Environment, No. 1650/1986, 10 October 1986 (GG 160/A/1986); amended by No. 1788/1988, 14 June 1988 (GG 131/A/1988) (Greece)

General Law on the Environment, Decree 104-93 of 8 June 1993 (Honduras)

Act. No. LXXXII of 1992 creating a Central Environment Fund, Order of the Minster of Environmental Protection and Regional Policy No. 20/1993 (IV.23) KTM (Hungary)

Basic Environmental Policy Act, Law No. 4257, 1 August 1990 (Korea)

Law on Natural Resource Taxes, 1990 (Latvia)

Law on Pollution Tax, 1991 (Lithuania)

Resource Management Act 1991, No. 69, 22 July 1991 (New Zealand)

The Pollution Control Act, Act No.6 of 13 March 1981 Concerning Protection Against Pollution and Concerning Waste (Norway)

National Integrated Protected Areas System Act, 27.7.1992, No.7586/1992, Official Gazette 20.7.1992 No.29 (Philippines)

Environment Protection Act (1969:387) (Sweden)

Environmental Protection Act, 1990 c.43 (c. 43/1990), 1 November 1990 (United Kingdom)

Clean Air Act, 42 USCA, §§ 7401, *et seq.* (USA)

Comprehensive Environmental Response, Compensation and Liability Act of 1980, 42 USCA § 9601 *et seq.* ["Superfund Act"] (USA)

Federal Water Pollution Act as amended by the Clean Water Act of 1977, 33 USCA §§ 1251 *et seq.* (USA)

Endangered Species Act, 16 USCA, § 1531 *et seq.* (USA)

National Environmental Policy Act, 42 USCA § 4321, *et seq.* Implementing Regulations 40 CFR § 1508.27 (1992) (USA)

Toxic Substances Control Act, 15 USCA, §§ 2601 *et seq.* (USA)

California Environmental Quality Assessment Act (California Health and Safety Code) § 25570 *et seq.* (West 1995) (USA)

New Jersey Environmental Cleanup Responsibility Rules Act (New Jersey Admin. Code tit. 7, § 7 (26 B)) (USA)

C. European Union Regulations and Directives

EC Council Directive 75/440/EEC on the Quality Required of Surface Water Intended for the Abstraction of Drinking Water in the Member States, 16 June 1975 (OJ L 194 (25/07/75), p. 26); amended by 79/886/EEC (OJ L 271 (29/10/79), p. 44), 91/692/EEC (OJ L 377 (31/12/91), p. 59)

EC Council Directive 76/464/EEC on Pollution Caused by Certain Dangerous Substances Discharged Into the Aquatic Environment of the Communities, 4 May 1976 (OJ L 129 (18/05/76), p. 23)

EC Council Directive 79/117/EEC on the Conservation of Wild Birds, 2 April 1979 (OJ L 103 (25/04/79), p. 1); as amended 29/07/97 Dir. 97/49/EC (OJ L 223 (13/08/97), p. 9)

EC Council Directive on Air Quality Limit Values and Guide Values for Sulphur Dioxide and Suspended Particulates, 15 July 1980 (OJ L 229, (30/07/80))

EC Council Directive 82/884/EEC on a Limit Value for Lead in the Air, 3 December 1982 (OJ L 378 (31/12/82), p. 15)

EC Council Directive 83/129/EEC Concerning the Importation of Skins of Certain Seal Pups, 28 March 1983 (OJ L 19 (9/2/83); Extended by 85/444/EEC (OJ L 259 (01/10/85), p. 70) and 89/370/EEC (OJ L 163 (14/06/89), p. 37)

EC Council Directive 84/360/EEC on the Combating of Air Pollution from Industrial Plants, 28 June 1984 (OJ L 188 (16/07/84), p. 20); amended by 91/692/EEC (OJ L 377 (31/12/91), p. 48)

EC Council Directive 85/337/EEC on the Assessment of the Effects of Certain Public and Private Projects on the Environment, 27 June 1985 (OJ L 175 (05/07/85), p. 40)

EC Council Directive 86/278/EEC on the Protection of the Environment, and in Particular of the Soil, When Sewage Sludge is Used in Agriculture, 12 June 1986 (OJ L 181, (04/07/86), p. 6. Amended by 91/692/EEC (OJ L 377 (31/12/91), p. 48)

EC Council Directive 90/219/EEC on the Contained Use of Genetically Modified Micro-organisms, 23 April 1990 (OJ L 117, (08/05/90), p. 1)

EC Council Directive 90/220/EEC on the Deliberate Release into the Environment of Genetically Modified Organisms, 23 April 1990 (OJ L 117, (08/05/90), p. 15)

EC Council Directive 90/313/EEC on Freedom of Access to Information on the Environment, 7 June 1990 (OJ L 158 (23/06/90), p. 56)

EC Council Directive 92/43/EEC on the Conservation of Natural Habitats and of Wild Flora and Fauna, 21 May 1992 (OJ L 206 (22/07/92), p. 7)

EC Council Regulation 92/880/EEC on a Community Eco-label Award Scheme, 23 March 1992 (OJ L 99 (11/04/92), p. 1)

EC Council Regulation 93/259/EEC on the Supervision and Control of Shipments of Waste Within, Into and Out of the European Community (OJ L 30 (06/02/93), p. 1)

V. Cases & Decisions

Appeal Relating to the Jurisdiction of the ICAO Council (India v. Pakistan), *ICJ Rep.* (1972) 46, ["ICAO Council Case"]

Australian Conservation Foundation v. Commonwealth of Australia (1980), 54 ALJR 176 (Australia)

Bangalore Medical Trust v. B.S. Muddappa, AIR 1991 SC 1902 (India)

Barcelona Traction, Light and Power Co. (Belgium v. Spain), *ICJ Rep.* (1970) 3, ["Barcelona Traction Case"]

Cameroons (Cameroons v. United Kingdom), *ICJ Rep.* (1963) 3

Canada - Measures Affecting Exports of Unprocessed Herring and Salmon, 22 March 1988, BISD/35S/98 (GATT Panel)

Chorzów Factory (Germany v. Poland) (Indemnity; Jurisdicition), *PCIJ*, Ser. A, no. 9 (1927)

Chorzów Factory (Germany v. Poland) (Merits) *PCIJ*, Ser. A, no. 17 (1928)

Corfu Channel (United Kingdom v. Albania), *ICJ Rep.* (1949) 4

Damodhar Rao, T. v. Municipal Corporation of Hyderabad, AIR 1987 AP 171 (India)

Delimitation of the Maritime Boundary in the Gulf of Maine Area (Canada v. United States of America), *ICJ Rep.* (1984) 246, ["Gulf of Maine"]

EC Commission v. Belgium, C-2/90 [1992] CMLR 365 (European Court of Justice)

Fisheries Jurisdiction (United Kingdom v. Iceland), *ICJ Rep.* (1974) 3

Fritiofson v. Alexander, 772 F. 2d 1225 (1985) (USA)

Fundepublico v. Mayor of Bugalagrande and Others, described in UN Doc. E/CN.4/Sub.2/1993/7 (Colombia)

Geneva Arbitration (United Kingdom v. United States of America) ["The Alabama Case"] 1 *Moore´s International Arbitration Award* 572 (1872)

Greece v. United Kingdom (1924) *PCIJ*, Series A, No. 2, p. 12

Handelskwekerij G.J. Bier BV, Stichting Reinwater v. Mines de potasse d'Alsace, 21/76, II *ECJ Rep.* (1976) ["Mines de Potasse d'Alsace Case (1976)"]

Handelskwekerij G.J. Bier, et autres v. Mines de Potasse d'Alsace (1983) 15 *NYIL* 1984

Island of Palmas (Netherlands v. United States of America) II *RIAA* (1928), 829

Kings County Farm Bureau v. City of Hanford, 270 Cal. Rptr. 650, *modified*, 222 Cal. App. 3d 516A (Ct. App. 1990), *appeal denied*, No. SO16837, 1990 Cal. LEXIS 4201 (Sept. 17 1990) (USA)

Lac Lanoux (Spain v. France) 24 *ILR* (1957) 101

Legal Consequences for States of the Continual Presence of South Africa in Namibia (Southwest Africa), Advisory Opinion, *ICJ Rep.* (1971) 16

Matter of Canada's Landing Requirement for Pacific Coast Salmon and Herring, 16 October 1989 (FTA Panel)

Mavrommatis Palestine Concessions (Jurisdiction) (Greece v. United Kingdom) (1924) *PCIJ*, Series A, no. 2, p. 11

M.C. Mehta v. State of Orissa, AIR (1992) Ori 225 (India)

Mehta, M.C. v. Union of India (1987), 1 SCC 395; 4 SCC 463 (India)

Mehta, M.C. (Mehta II) v. Union of India (1988), 1 SCC 471 (India)

Minors Oposa, et al. v. The Honorable Secretary Fulgencio S. Factoran, Jr. and the Honorable Judge Eriberto U. Rosario (G.R. No. 101083, 30 July 1993), reprinted in 33 ILM 173 (1994), ["Minors Oposa Case"] (Philippines)

Murali Purushothaman v. Union of India, AIR (1993) Ker 297 (India)

Nationality Decrees issued in Tunis and Morocco (Great Britain v. France) Advisory Opinion, *PCIJ*, Series B, No. 4 (1923)

Natural Resources Defense Council, Inc., v. Nuclear Regulatory Commission (NRC), 647 F.2d 1345 (D.C. Cir. 1981) (USA)

North Sea Continental Shelf (Germany v. Denmark; Germany v. Netherlands) *ICJ Rep.* 4 (1969) 3

Nizam v. Jaipur Development Authority, AIR 1994 Raj 87 (India)

Nuclear Tests (Jurisdiction) (Australia v. France), *ICJ Rep.* (1974) 253

Pacific Fur Seals (United States of America v. United Kingdom) (1893), 1 *Moore's International Arbitration Awards*, 755

Peace Treaties (Bulgaria, Hungary and Rumania), *ICJ Rep.* (1950) 74

People United for a Better Living in Calcutta v. State of West Bengal, AIR 1993 Cal 215 (India)

Powell and Rayner v. United Kingdom, Series A, No. 172 (1990) (Europen Court of Human Rights)

R v. Secretary of State for the Environment, ex Parte Rose Theatre Trust Ltd. [1990] 1 QB 504 (United Kingdom)

Republic of Bosnia-Herzegovina v. Federal Republic of Yugoslavia (Serbia and Montenegro), Application, reprinted in 32 ILM 888 (1993) [ICJ]

Reservations to the Convention on the Prevention and Punishment of the Crime of Genocide Case, Advisory Opinion, *ICJ Rep.* (1951) 15

River Meuse (Netherlands v. Belgium) (1937) *PCIJ*, Series A/B, No. 70, p. 16

Rural Litigation and Entitlement Kendra v. State of Uttar Pradesh, AIR 1985 SC 652; AIR 1987 SC 359; AIR 1988 SC 2187 (India)

Rylands v. Fletcher (1868) LR 3 HL 330 (United Kingdom)

Sierra Club v. Morton, 405 US 727 (1972) (USA)

Southwest Africa (Preliminary Objections) (Liberia v. South Africa) ICJ Rep. (1962) 319

Southwest Africa (Second Phase) (Liberia v. South Africa) *ICJ Rep.* (1966) 6

Thailand - Restrictions of, and Internal Taxes on, Cigarettes, 7 November 1990, BISD/37S/200 (1990) (GATT Panel)

The Case relating to the Territorial Jurisdiction of the International Commission of the River Oder (Czechoslovakia, Denmark, France, Germany, Sweden, United Kingdom v. Poland) 1929 *PCIJ*, Series A, No. 23, p. 5., ["River Oder"]

Trail Smelter (United States of America v. Canada), 33 AJIL (1939) 182; 35 AJIL (1941) 684; 3 UNRIAA 1905

UN Headquarters (Applicability of Obligation to Arbitrate Under Section 21 of United Nations Headquarters Agreement of June 26, 1947), Advisory Opinion, ICJ Rep. (1988) 12

UN HRC Decision No. 67/180 (1990)

US Restrictions on Imports of Tuna, 16 August 1991 (GATT Doc. DS21/R) ["GATT Tuna I Case (1991)"] (GATT Panel)

US Restrictions on the Imports of Tuna, June 1994, GATT Doc. DS29/R, June 1994 ["GATT Tuna II Case (1994)"] (GATT Panel)

Velasquez Rodriguez, 28 July 1988, reprinted in ILM 294 (1989) (Inter-American Court of Human Rights)

Zia, Ms. Shahla v. WAPDA, Pakistan Legal Decisions 1994 Supreme Court 693 (Pakistan)

VI. Literature & Miscellaneous Documents

Adede A. O. (1993). INTERNATIONAL ENVIRONMENTAL LAW DIGEST: INSTRUMENT FOR INTERNATIONAL RESPONSES TO PROBLEMS OF ENVIRONMENT AND DEVELOPMENT 1972-1992, Elsevier Press, Amsterdam/London/New York/Tokyo.

American Law Institute (1987). RESTATEMENT (THIRD) OF THE FOREIGN RELATIONS LAW OF THE UNITED STATES, American Law Institute Publishers, St. Paul, Minnisota.

Attard, J. (1990). THE MEETING OF THE GROUP OF LEGAL EXPERTS TO EXAMINE THE CONCEPT OF THE COMMON CONCERN OF MANKIND IN RELATION TO GLOBAL ENVIRONMENTAL ISSUES, UNEP, Nairobi.

Ba Kader, A., Al Sabbagh, A, Al Glenid, M, Izzidien (1993). BASIC PAPER ON THE ISLAMIC PRINCIPLES FOR THE CONSERVATION OF THE NATURAL ENVIRONMENT, IUCN, Gland.

Birnie, P.W. and Boyle, A. E. (1992). INTERNATIONAL LAW AND THE ENVIRONMENT, Clarendon Press, Oxford.

Boer, B. (ed.) (1993). STRENGTHENING ENVIRONMENTAL LEGISLATION IN THE SOUTH PACIFIC, Workshop Proceedings, South Pacific Region Environmental Programme, Apia, Western Samoa.

Bothe, M., Partsch, K., and Solf, W. (eds) (1982). NEW RULES FOR VICTIMS OF ARMED CONFLICTS: COMMENTARY ON THE TWO 1977 PROTOCOLS ADDITIONAL TO THE GENEVA CONVENTIONS OF 1949, Martinus Nijhoff, Boston/The Hague/London.

Brownlie, I. (1990). PRINCIPLES OF PUBLIC INTERNATIONAL LAW (4th ed), Clarendon Press, Oxford.

Charnovitz, S. (1991). *Exploring the Environmental Exceptions in GATT Article XX*, Journal of World Trade 25, no. 5 (October).

European Communities (1973). *Programme of Action of the Environment*, 15 November 1973 (C 112 (12/20/73),79).

European Communities (1993). *Fifth Environmental Action Programme: Towards Sustainability* (OJ No. C 138 (17/5/93)), ["EC Fifth Environmental Action Plan (1993)"].

European Communities (1993). *Green Paper on the Repair of Environmental Damage*, 14 May 1993 (Com. Doc. (93) 47 (final)).

Fauteux, P. (1991). *L'utilisation de l'environnement comme instrument de guerre au Koweit occupé*, in LES ASPECTS JURIDIQUES DE LAW CRISE ET LA GUERRE DU GOLFE, Proceedings of the Colloquium organized by the Centre de droit international de Nanterre.

Feliciano, M. *et al.* (1992). ENVIRONMENTAL LAW IN THE PHILIPPINES, Institute of International Legal Studies, Manila.

Fleck, D. (1992). *Legal and Policy Perspectives for the Protection of the Environment in Times of Armed Conflict*, in M. Meyer and H. Fox (eds), ARMED CONFLICT AND THE NEW LAW: EFFECTING COMPLIANCE, British Institute for International and Comparative Law, London.

German Federal Ministry of Defence (1990). *The Technical Concept, "Environmental Protection in the Federal Armed Forces"*, Bonn.

Hardin, G. (1968). *Tragedy of the Commons*, Science, No. 162.

Hassan, P. (1993). *Toward an International Covenant on Environment and Development*, ASIL Proceedings, pp. 513-522.

Hassan, P. (1994). *The IUCN Draft International Covenant on Environment and Development: Background and Prospects*, in A. Kiss and F. Burhenne-Guilmin (ed), A LAW FOR THE ENVIRONMENT: ESSAYS IN HONOUR OF WOLFGANG E. BURHENNE, EPLP Special Issue, IUCN, Gland and Cambridge.

Hassan, P. (1995). *The Political and Legal Dynamics of the Implementation of the Convention on Biological Diversity in the Asian-Pacific Region*, Asian Development Bank, Manila.

Herczegh, G. (1984), *La protection de l'environnement naturel et le droit humanitaire*, in Swinarski, C., STUDIES AND ESSAYS ON INTERNATIONAL HUMANITARIAN LAW AND RED CROSS PRINCIPLES, IN HONOUR OF J. PICTET, Martinus Nijhoff, The Hague, for the International Committee for the Red Cross, Geneva.

Higgins, R. (1994). PROBLEMS AND PROCESS: INTERNATIONAL LAW AND HOW WE USE IT, Clarendon Press, Oxford.

International Committee of the Red Cross (1993). *Report to the UN General Assembly on Environment and Armed Conflict* (UN Doc. A/48/269, June 1993) ["ICRC Report (1993)"]

ILC (various). *Reports to the UN General Assembly* (especially UN Docs. A/CN.4/457, A/CN.4/L.497(46th Sess., 4 July 1994, draft only), A/46/687, A/47/584, A/CN.4/L.443)

IUCN/ICEL (1991). *Final Report on Consultation on Armed Conflict*, reprinted in 22 EPL (1992) 63

IUCN/UNEP/WWF (1980). WORLD CONSERVATION STRATEGY: LIVING RESOURCE CONSERVATION FOR SUSTAINABLE DEVELOPMENT; IUCN, UNEP, WWF, Gland.

IUCN/UNEP/WWF (1991). CARING FOR THE EARTH. A STRATEGY FOR SUSTAINABLE LIVING, Gland.

Johnston, D.M. (ed) (1981). THE ENVIRONMENTAL LAW OF THE SEA, IUCN, Gland.

Kalshoven, F. (1991). CONSTRAINTS ON THE WAGING OF WAR (2nd ed.), International Committee of the Red Cross, Geneva.

Kiss, A. and Shelton, D. (1991 and 1994 Supplement). INTERNATIONAL ENVIRONMENTAL LAW, Transnational Publishers, Ardsley-on-Hudson, New York, and Graham and Trotman, London.

de Klemm, C. and Shine, C. (1993). BIOLOGICAL DIVERSITY CONSERVATION AND THE LAW, IUCN, Gland and Cambridge.

McCaffrey, S. (1975). PRIVATE REMEDIES FOR TRANSFRONTIER ENVIRONMENTAL DISTURBANCES, IUCN, Morges.

McCaffrey, S. and Lutz R. (1978). ENVIRONMENTAL POLLUTION AND INDIVIDUAL RIGHTS: AN INTERNATIONAL SYMPOSIUM, Kluwer Law and Taxation Publishers, Deventer, The Netherlands.

McCaffrey, S. (1988). *The Work of the International Law Commission Relating to Transfrontier Environmental Harm*, 20 N.Y.U.J. Int´L L & Pol. 715

Miller, M. (1991). DEBT AND THE ENVIRONMENT: CONVERGING CRISES, United Nations Publications, New York.

O'Riordan, T. (1992). *The Precaution Principle in Environmental Management*, Centre for Social and Economic Research on the Global Environment, Norwich, United Kingdom.

Odidi Okidi, C. (1978). REGIONAL CONTROL OF OCEAN POLLUTION: LEGAL AND INSTITUTIONAL PROBLEMS AND PROSPECTS, Sijthoff Noordhoff, Aphen aan den Rijn.

OECD (1993). *1993 Preamble to Report on Scientific Considerations Pertaining to the Environmental Safety of the Scale-up of Organisms Developed by Biotechnology*, OECD/GD (93)92

Okorodudu-Fubara, M. T. (1991). *Oil in the Persian Gulf War: Legal Appraisal of an Environmental Warfare*, 23 St. Mary's L.J.

Oppenheim, L. (1952). INTERNATIONAL LAW: A TREATISE, Vol. II, DISPUTES, WAR AND NEUTRALITY (7th edn.), H. Lauterpacht (ed.), Longmans Green, London.

Pathak, R. S. (1988). *Human Rights and the Development of the Environmental Law of India*, Commonwealth Law Bulletin, vol. 14, no. 3.

Plant, G. (ed) (1992). ENVIRONMENTAL PROTECTION AND THE LAW OF WAR: A FIFTH GENEVA CONVENTION ON THE PROTECTION OF THE ENVIRONMENT IN TIMES OF ARMED CONFLICT?, Balhaven Press, London.

Price, A. R. G., *et al.* (1994). THE 1991 GULF WAR: ENVIRONMENTAL ASSESSMENT OF IUCN AND COLLABORATORS, IUCN, Gland and Cambridge.

Ramphal, S. (1992). OUR COUNTRY, OUR PLANET: FORGING A PARTNERSHIP FOR SURVIVAL, Lime Tree, London.

Rest, A. (1976). *Convention on Compensation for Transfrontier Environmental Injuries. Draft with Explanatory Notes* (unpublished).

Rest, A. (1991). *New Tendencies in Environmental Responsibility/Liability Law. The Work of the UN/ECE Task Force on Responsibility and Liability Regarding Transboundary Water Pollution*, 21 EPL 135.

Rest, A. (1993). *New Legal Instruments for Environmental Prevention, Control and Restoration in Public International Law*, 23 EPL 260.

Rest, A. (1994). *Need for an International Court for the Environment? Underdeveloped Legal Protection for the Individual in Transnational Litigation*, 24 EPL 173.

Roberts, A., and Guelff, R. (eds) (1989). DOCUMENTS ON THE LAW OF WAR (2nd edn), Clarendon Press, Oxford.

Robinson, N.A., Hassan, P., Burhenne-Guilmin, F. (eds) (1992-1994). AGENDA 21 & THE UNCED PROCEEDINGS, Vols. I-VI.

Sands, P., Tarasofsky, R., Weiss, M. (eds) (1994). DOCUMENTS IN INTERNATIONAL ENVIRONMENTAL LAW, Manchester University Press, Manchester/New York.

Sands, P. (1995). PRINCIPLES OF INTERNATIONAL ENVIRONMENTAL LAW, Manchester University Press, Manchester/New York.

Sierra Club Legal Defence Fund (1994). *Draft Declaration on a Human Right to the Environment* (unpublished).

Supreme Commander of Sweden (1992). *Measures to Improve the Environment* (15 September 1992)

Swedish Environmental Advisory Council (1994), ON THE GENERAL PRINCIPLES OF ENVIRONMENTAL PROTECTION, Stockholm.

Tarasofsky, R.G. (1993). *The Legal Protection of the Environment During International Armed Conflict*, 24 NYIL 17.

UN Commission on Human Rights, Subcommission on Prevention of Discrimination and Protection of Minorities (1992). *Intellectual Property of Indigenous Peoples: Concise Report of the Secretary General* (UN Doc. E/CN.4/Sub.2/ 1992/30).

UN Commission on Human Rights, Subcommission on Prevention of Discrimination and Protection of Minorities (1993). *Study on the Protection of the cultural and intellectual property of indigenous peoples* (UN Doc. E/CN.4/ Sub.2/1993/28).

UN Economic Commission for Europe (1993). *Note by the Secretariat of the UN Economic Commission for Europe for the First session of the Working Group of Senior Governmental Officials, "Environment for Europe"* (UN Doc. ENVWA/WG.6/R.7, 17 December 1993).

UN Secretariat (1984). *Survey of State Practice Relevant to International Liability for Injurious Consequences Arising our of Acts not Prohibited by International Law* (UN Doc. A/CN.4/384, 16 October 1984).

UN Secretariat (1988). *Action in the Field of Human Rights* (UN Doc. ST/HR/2/Rev.3, UN Pub. E.88.XIV.2, 1988).

UN Secretariat (1990). *Global Action on the Right to Development as a Human Right* (UN Doc.E/CN.4/1990/Rev.1, 26 September 1990).

Van-Thinh, T. (1994). *Farewell Speech to the 49th Session of the GATT Contracting Parties*, 26 January 1994.

WRI/IUCN/UNEP (1992). GLOBAL BIODIVERSITY STRATEGY, WRI, Washington D.C., IUCN, Gland. and UNEP, Nairobi.